SHAL

IN A

LANDSCAPE

LLANGYNIDR

THE EVOLUTION OF A COMMUNITY

Printed by Gomer Press, Llandysul

ISBN: 0-9538778-0-9 (Cloth bound edition)
              0-9538778-1-7 (Paper bound edition)

Published by Llangynidr Local History Society, 2000

Contents

Prologue

The vantage point on the road to Beaufort, on the north side of Llangynidr Mountain at Twyn Disgwylfa, is perhaps the place to start.

Choose a fine day, pause awhile and drink in the view. Nestling down in the Usk Valley, directly ahead of you, is the village of Llangynidr with its straggle of farms and houses running down two valleys - the Claisfer directly in front of you and the Dyffryn Crawnon, further west over the other side of Pant Llwyd hill - to the Upper Village. Situated half a mile south of the Usk, the Upper Village runs down to Lower Village, which is comprised of Cwm Crawnon, Coed yr Ynys and Cyffredin along the banks of the Usk and around the fine stone Usk Bridge. You won't be able to see it from here, but the Brecon and Abergavenny Canal snakes through all of them, following the south side of the valley of the Usk.

Away to your left is the handsome mountain of Tor y Foel, outlier of the Brecon Beacons, which Llangynidr residents think of as their very own mountain. North of the Usk, you'll see the fine hill of Allt yr Esgair to your left. From here it looks like a sharply-pointed peak because you're looking at the end of the ridge, rather than at the side as you would see it across the valley from Talybont-on-Usk. In the centre of your view you will perhaps see a glint of sunlight on Llangorse Lake away to the north-north-west. You'll enjoy the wooded slopes of Buckland Hill and the Myarth, north of you just across the Usk, and you'll see the trucks on today's A40, the London to Fishguard road, grinding up a steep section to Bwlch on their way to Brecon, Carmarthen and beyond. A few miles away to the north-east you can see the majesty of the scarp of the Black Mountains, with Pen Cerrig Calch and Pen Allt Mawr looming grey above the rivers Usk and Rhiangoll, and almost due east, but hidden by the shoulder of the hill, is the town of Crickhowell on the north bank of the Usk, below its own Table Mountain.

This must be the finest view in all the Welsh Borders - so no wonder that you'll be fortunate if you are able to have this view to yourself for a while before another visitor arrives to enjoy or photograph it. But no matter, pause for five minutes and let the view caress your soul.

And, since there's no evidence to suggest that our forebears were any less endowed than we in aesthetic appreciation, we can be sure that many others over the centuries have stood where you stand today and relished this view.

Look behind you now and see who else is sharing your pleasure. There's a small group of Mesolithic hunter-gatherers with their flint axes from over 9000 years ago and just near them, some Bronze Age people from 4000 years ago - they've just been to the recently-erected standing stone at Carreg Waun Llech. Along with them there's a Roman legion, glancing nervously south up the slopes of Llangynidr Mountain, fearful of an attack from the troublesome Celts. There's a Norman knight on horseback accompanied by his squire - they look more at home here, more relaxed. Perhaps it's Picard, Lord of the Manor of Ystradyw at Tretower. There's a group of twelfth century clerics - perhaps one of them is Giraldus Cambrensis, who was Archdeacon of Brecon from 1175 to 1203, even though he doesn't record coming this way on his famous journey through Wales in 1188. There are herdsmen and farmers, men toiling back to their homes in Llangynidr after a hard week's work in the coal, iron or limestone works of the hills of iron and fire to the south. There are drinkers and gamblers from the Grouse Inn at Blaen Onneu just half a mile south of here. There are wives returning from selling farm produce in the markets of Beaufort, Brynmawr or Tredegar. There is even a group of Chartists from 1839, dreaming of social change and universal manhood suffrage. Perhaps they've been up to the cave at Ogof Fawr to plan their march on Newport. There are poets and tourists, bureaucrats and children - a vast array of people who are standing behind you - all moved to marvel at this wonderful view.

And, of course, there are animals - because they figure largely in our local history. There are wolves and foxes, sheep and cattle. There are pack mules, pausing briefly in their laborious trek across the mountain, and there are horses and carts. Up above you today there will be skylarks and buzzards: once there would have been red kites, curlews and lapwings - maybe they will be back in numbers before too long.

This army of people and creatures makes up the history of the parish that stretches before you, as you stand here today. Theirs is a story of change and adaptation. It's a local story, but a story that embraces the world in which the village stands. We hope their history will delight and interest you.

The Editor

Editorial and Acknowledgements

The inspiration for this book was Dorothea Watkins. She was a founder member of Llangynidr Local History Society and wrote the small book '*An Introduction to the History of Llangynidr*', recorded the recollections of many of the village's inhabitants and inspired others to go much further than she had in researching aspects of our local history. Today, as a result, we know much more about the history of our village and its environs than she ever did and we have been motivated to capture that increased knowledge in this book.

Figure 1: Dorothea Watkins, author of "An Introduction to the History of Llangynidr" (1986).

But if Dorothea Watkins was our muse, there have been three others who have been driving forces behind the project. Each of them has been a colossus, a power-house of scholarship, research, writing and enthusiasm for the project. They are Michael Scott Archer, Chairman of the Llangynidr Local History Society who has been a tireless enthusiast for Llangynidr and its history; Michael Porter who has researched and originated large parts of this book; Peter Jones from Tredegar, who has forgotten more about the hills and valleys around Llangynidr than most of us will ever know and who, likewise, researched and wrote part of this book. Without these three people, this book would not have been written.

In addition to these three, many others have also contributed to the book - either by careful research, their recording of recent history in the village, their willingness to write drafts for chapters of the book, by raising money that was necessary to fund this project, by contributing to the debate and discussion about what should be in or out, or by giving permission to use illustrations as listed below - in all these ways and many more, the book has been a team effort. I should say thank you particularly to the following members of the Llangynidr Local History Society: Moyra Ball, Eric Brown, Charles Clarke, John Dinsdale, Rosemary Evans, David Filsell, Linda Games, Ann Jessopp, Adele Jones, Janice Meredith and Chris Porter. I am also most grateful for specific guidance and advice from: Gil Chambers, Margaret Davies, Tim Evans, William Gibbs, Ray Haydon, Will Hughes, Sheila Leitch, David Morgan, John Norris, Edward Parry, Peter Powell, Hywel Price, Pamela Redwood, Nancy Thomas, and Pip Woolf.

As well as these individuals who have so generously contributed to the writing of the book, we have been greatly helped by a number of organisations who have co-operated in this work or been invaluable sources of information for us. These include the Brecon Beacons National Park, Clwyd-Powys Archaeological Trust, Cadw: Welsh Historical Monuments, The National Library of Wales, The National Museum of Wales, The Welsh Folk Museum, The Royal Commission on Ancient and Historical Monuments, Brecknock Museum, Brecon Library and the Powys County Archives Office.

Of course a project like this takes money. Researching, accessing sources, drafting, publishing - all of these activities incur cost. We were anxious to produce a book that would look good, that would do justice to our subject, that would grip the imagination of our readers. Fortunately, we were able to attract funding from Trusts, Organisations and individual subscribers who, between them, enabled the production of this book. Without their generosity you would not now be holding the finished product in your hands. Our major sponsors were: The Brecon Beacons National Park, the Morel Trust and Tredegar Town Council. Individual subscribers are listed at the back of the book.

We were also extremely fortunate in finding Peter Owens, from Crickhowell, to work with us in producing our drafts, word-processing and layout. In Peter, we had a rare combination of someone with hi-tech layout skills and a real feel for local history. It was a great pleasure to work with him on this project. The attractive layout of the book owes much to his skills, as well as to the skills of Jonathan Lewis and his staff at our Printers, Gomer Press.

I also owe thanks to the many people in and around Llangynidr whose recollections and observations are included in this book. They are the bright colours in the tapestry that is the history of our village.

It seems appropriate to me that this book is published in the first year of the new millennium - in August 2000, rather than in the last year of the old millennium, as we had thought at first when we embarked on the project in 1997. This publication date gives the book a forward-looking quality - and this forward-looking anticipative quality is just as much part of the history of Llangynidr as is the Bronze Age, the Roman presence, or the building of the Canal. There have been people inhabiting our village and its surrounding hills and valleys for a good few millennia already - and we hope that a new history of Llangynidr will be written by a new generation of local historians, many years from now. Hopefully, we will have provided a useful reference for them and perhaps given them a bit of inspiration.

For now though, the book must stand, with all its limitations and imperfections, for what it is. We have tried to make it accurate, readable, fact-based and sometimes speculative. Finally, though, its limitations are my responsibility. For these I apologise, and sincerely hope that they will not seriously limit your pleasure from this book.

Martin Wibberley, Editor

The Boathouse, Llangynidr, June 2000

Illustrations Acknowledgements

Cover painting of Llangynidr Bridge by Pip Woolf.

The Llangynidr Local History Society thank the following institutions and individuals for permission to reproduce the illustrations which are listed after their names.

Brecknock Museum and Brecknock Society: 103, 134, 136, 171. Brecknock Museum, Smith and Jones Collection: 135, 142, 143. Brecon Library: 3. Case UK (Tractors): 76. National Library of Wales: 24, 25, 30-34, 37-39, 41, 42, 50, 91, 163. Museum of Welsh Life - St Fagans: 48, 72, 73, 75, 77, 78, 90. National Museums and Galleries of Wales (Industrial and Maritime Museum Collection): 60. Powys County Archives Office: 8, 53, 55, 105. John Addis Collection: 86. Michael Scott Archer: 5, 28, 29, 43, 47, 49, 52, 56, 99, 133, 148, 153, 158, 166, 179-186, 190, 192, 193, 196, 197. Carri Carter: 26. Gil Chambers: 35, 36, 89, 138, 139, 145, 146. Charles Clarke: 124, 126, 129, 160, 172. Margaret Davies: 144. Nick Downes: (courtesy of Dr and Mrs J Gibbs): 137. Mrs S P Evans: 96, 109, 110, 188. Tim Evans: 15, 174, 177, 178. April and Gilbert Games (courtesy of Rosemary and Tim Evans): 112, 173. Linda Games: 121, 149, and from the Sparrow Collection: 44, 51, 94, 98, 111, 131, 157. The Gibbs family: 154-156, 175, 176. William Gibbs: 80. Gwyn Briwnant Jones: 164. Peter Jones: 2, 4, 7, 9-13, 16-20. Michael Porter: 6, 14, 21-23, 27, 40, 45, 46, 70, 79, 83, 92, 93, 95, 140, 141, 150-152, 165. Mr and Mrs J Thomas: 125. Dorothea Watkins: 167-170. Molly Wozencraft: 194. The remaining illustrations are taken from the archives of the Llangynidr Local History Society.

Foreword

Although Theophilus Jones's *A History of the County of Brecknock* was published a couple of centuries ago, it would be fair to say that by the time that milestone work appeared, the county had already been well served by a handful of systematic researchers, amongst whom were Hugh Thomas and Henry Vaughan. In the tradition of county histories which had origins in the seventeenth century, Jones's was a confection of essays on chronology, genealogy and topography, transcribed and edited from estate, manorial, county and other archival repositories, diligently assembled and interpreted in the *mores* of the day. Unfortunately, fashion did not then always include acknowledgement of all assistance, and a significant component of the work had been generated by his friend, Archdeacon Henry Thomas Payne. Not surprisingly, therefore, Payne, who was a quite exceptional scholar, seeing proper acknowledgement for his own contribution cleverly substituted by Jones's deferential dedication, righteously protested how his original research had been 'shamefully abused'. Whilst not condoning Theophilus Jones's behaviour, it should be said that without his catalytic driving force, Payne's important observations would probably have remained unread and unappreciated for another one and a half centuries.

Local histories also originated in the seventeenth century. Although lacking significant local or parish histories until well into the nineteenth century, some select Brecknockshire localities were, nevertheless, well-described in the late eighteenth century by many of the outsiders who followed the Usk Valley as part of the contemporary picturesque tourist route through Wales. Local studies were then to be well served: first, by the Cambrian Archaeological Association through contributions to its journal *Archaeologia Cambrensis* then, after 1955, by the Brecknock Society through *Brycheiniog*.

The impetus for a study of Llangynidr originally came from Dorothea Watkins. Her book *An Introduction to the History of Llangynidr* of 1986 provides a foretaste of the present work, and her enthusiasm, and that of the others who helped found the Llangynidr Local History Society, may now be appreciated as the catalyst which ultimately brought to fruition the project which resulted in this new, more comprehensive book. Some of the work's main contributors were originally participants in a WEA class which concerned itself with matters archaeological and historical. The extensive editorial acknowledgement of help from individuals and institutions is testimony to the continuing collaborative and cooperative spirit upon which successful extra-mural learning is still so dependent. Some of the chapters break new ground. Indeed, it is encouraging to see here (*inter alia*) references to Payne's original manuscripts. The presentation of this primary research should attract readers from well beyond Brecknockshire. Most importantly, some of those familiar with the historical problems raised will indubitably be stimulated to further inquiry.

Nowadays, Llangynidr's position within a National Park brings certain pressures from tourism and recreation which ultimately must erode its landscape. Although parts of the locality enjoy environmental and historic landscape designation, legislation alone cannot protect for all time. Education is likely to have more lasting effects. Indeed, an interest in the local history and archaeology of a place should generate commitment and respect for the values both of conservation and community. This book will make a significant contribution to those values.

Dr C. Stephen Briggs

Royal Commission on Ancient and Historical Monuments in Wales

Chapter 1

Prehistory

Archaeology is not an exact science. As old evidence is re-interpreted and new evidence appears, differing opinions may arise. If knowledge of local everyday life but a few centuries ago is limited, that of periods with no written record must be far less clear.

British evolution resulted more from new ideas than new peoples. DNA studies indicate British genes have remained largely unchanged from earliest times. British racial differences result from environment, not blood. English, Scots and Welsh are genetically similar, descended from the same Palaeolithic settlers. Climate moulded landscape and peoples. Local History is merely a record of regional reaction to wider events.

Landscape

The southern moorlands and scarps are formed by Millstone Grit overlying a thick band of Carboniferous Limestone. The Usk Valley lowlands are predominantly Old Red Sandstone and its marls. Ice movement created a rounded landscape and where the ice melted, approximately BC 12000, it exposed a tree-less tundra-like region with marshy valleys. Locally, ice lingered in Cwm Cerrig Gleisiad (around SO 965220, north-west of Storey Arms) until approximately BC 8000. Post-glacial purple saxifrage is found here, just north of its southernmost UK limit at Cwm Oergwm SO 044197 (M Porter, pers. com.). No clear evidence exists for Palaeolithic hunters, although there were probably herds of reindeer, bison and horse in the area.

Figure 2: The Long Wall.

A brief prehistoric outline

Mesolithic Period *About BC 7500*

Hunting and gathering people appear. Woodland clearance with stone tools began which led to the development of heath and moorlands.

Local Evidence: Charcoal, flint flakes and artefacts.

Neolithic Period *About BC 3500*

Food cultivation begins in a warm climate. Woodlands spread and peat bogs develop. Selective burial in large communal tombs.

Local evidence: Stone tools, chambered tombs, and an important ritual site near Talybont.

Bronze Age *About BC 2200*

Copper alloy tools introduced. Good climatic conditions encouraged high upland settlement. About BC 1200, the climate deteriorated and soil erosion accelerated - blanket peat spread. This led to upland depopulation plus abandonment of ritual sites.

Local evidence: stone tools, cairns, standing stones, alignments.

Iron Age *About BC 600 - AD 43*

Continuing wet and cool. Iron implements aided lowland cultivation and tree clearance. Heath and moorlands spread - settlements at lower levels - indications of social pressures and a warring, tribal society. Moves towards urbanisation.

Local evidence: Forts and enclosures.

Roman *First to Fifth Centuries AD*

In a gradually improving climate, Wales was a military frontier region experiencing demands for slaves, timber, iron, lead, leather, grain etc. Road/river transport develops. Urbanised settlements appear. Strong rule discourages tribal warfare.

Local evidence: Forts, roads, signal stations, bath houses.

Dark Ages *6th - 10th Centuries AD*

Roman rule ends. Wales reverts to tribal societies. Some Irish influences. Christianity develops.

Local evidence: 'Ogham' stones, possibly some earthworks.

The Mesolithic Period - Middle Stone Age

Approximately BC 7,500 - 3,500

Woodlands and peat cover had begun spreading about BC 10,000

From BC 8,000 to 5,000

With temperatures at least 3°C higher than today's, valleys and hills became covered by birch, hazel, oak and elm, where red deer, aurochs (early cattle) and wild boar roamed.

About BC 7500

Mesolithic (Middle Stone Age) food-gathering, hunting and fishing peoples appear. Microliths, i.e. small flint/chert flakes, originally mounted onto wooden shafts/handles with birch bark resin glues to form tools, have been found locally.

Woodland was systematically fire-cleared for grazing, thus attracting animals, aiding hunters and producing heavier carcasses. Circa BC 7500 small wolves were being domesticated by Yorkshire Mesolithic hunters. (Sonia Cole, *Neolithic Revolution*).

The Neolithic Period - New Stone Age

Approximately BC 3,500 - 2,000

There is considerable evidence for early agriculture within Wales - the largest UK collection of Neolithic seeds was found at Gogerddan, mid-Wales, in 1985. DNA evidence suggests Mesolithic hunter/gatherers gradually evolved into Neolithic hunter/farmers as need arose and land served. Flint and other artefact stone was not necessarily obtained by 'trading' as it exists in local glacial deposits. (Dr C S Briggs, pers. com.). Polished stone axes felled trees or ring-barked them for burning - grazing restricted re-growth. The Upper Rhiangoll Valley (around SO 185285) and southern slopes of Castell Dinas retain naturally regenerated woodland. Burial Chambers were sited between 175 and 375m above sea level, in areas of considerable tree clearance. Cwm Sorgwm chambered tomb (SO 162284) was sited where sessile oak and alder areas were easy to clear and cultivate with digging sticks. Neolithic society possessed great skill in transporting/positioning large stones and constructing dry walls. Inhumation and cremation was practised; associated grave goods indicate spirit world beliefs. Theories that local tombs were built by peoples migrating from the Severn-Cotswold region are now discounted (RCAHM *Bronze Age Inventory*).

Settlement

Well-drained easy-to-work mid-levels were probably preferred. Little is known of Neolithic housing but they were possibly stakes and wattle. A Neolithic hut-site at Cilsanws, Vaynor, measured 3.5m by 2.2m, constructed of multiple light sticks, probably tied tent-like at a ridge. Diet included corn, sheep, goats, pigs, cattle, and dog. Ty-isaf and Gwernvale tombs produced emmer wheat impressions and hazelnuts.

Tree clearance

Danish experiments with original Neolithic axe heads proved three men could clear 500 square metres of birch forest in four hours. One axe, unsharpened for 4000 years, felled more than 100 trees. (Sonia Cole, *Neolithic Revolution*)

The Bronze Age

About BC 2200, when copper alloys were first used, to BC 600 and the introduction of iron

Early Bronze Age

In a warm dry climate, sessile oak, beech, ash, alder and hazel woodlands, covering uplands to 800m above sea level, were being cleared for pasture, cultivation, huts and fuel. Well-drained lowlands were also settled. Around BC 2200 copper alloys were being worked. There was probably no intervening copper period: bronze existing from the beginning. Established herding, hunting, cultivation and burial patterns continued; flint and stone artefacts were still employed. There was significant social change and landscape impact. Settlement was taking place at surprisingly high levels, creating something akin to the bare uplands of today. Woodlands were being stripped for shelter, pasture, forges, cremation and exploitation of their thick soils. Serious erosion ensued; Llangorse Lake silts revealing this to have been considerable (RCAHM, *Bronze Age Inventory*). The local landscape had now lost its primeval character.

Many burial cairns - the most numerous prehistoric monuments - exist locally, while others may have been removed or eroded away. In limestone districts convenient heaps of stone were utilised by later lime-burners, e.g. 'Clo Cadno' (SO 11611628) where only a cairn curb remains. 'Carn Caws' (*Cheese Cairn*) at SO 12961679 suggests this was also robbed - limestone resembling dried cheese. Burials were often grouped in the same cairn, and satellite burials exist. Even though some cairns indicate high upland settlement, the majority lie between 185m and 300m contours. (RCAHM, *Bronze Age Inventory*)

Burial

Bronze Age cairns had replaced Neolithic chambered tombs, but group burial and grave goods continued with beakers, pigmy cups, urns of pottery and knives of bronze etc., placed with the dead. Although certain cairns are claimed to have been deliberately sited against skylines or on view-points, the great majority have no such relationship.

Cremation burials - another demand upon timber - took place in stone-lined cists under mounds of earth or stone. At Fan y Big (SO 03712057) in the Brecon Beacons, path erosion exposed a single male cremation, two Bronze Age corded urns and a bronze knife/razor. A single emmer wheat grain impression was noted. The covering cairn, visible until post-war years, was destroyed by walkers throwing its stones over the edge. It is possible another on nearby Cribyn suffered the same fate.

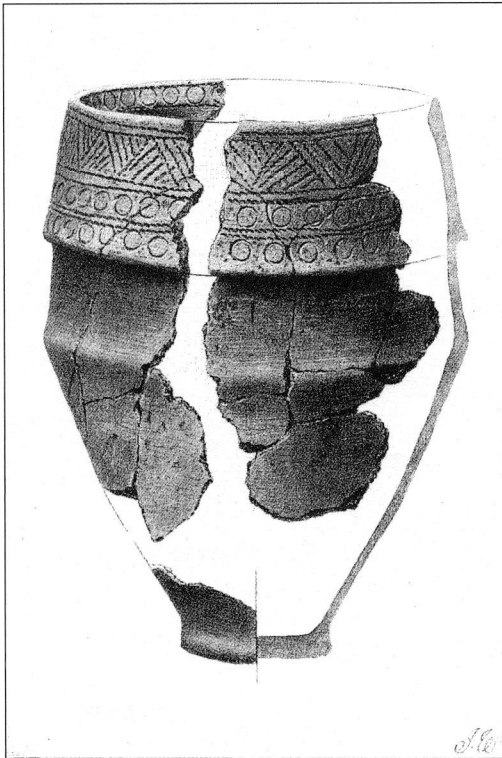

Figure 3: Cinerary Urn. A Bronze Age decorated urn which contained ashes from a cremation, discovered by workmen in a field near Waun-ddu (1909). From Archaeologia Cambrensis, Vol XIX, (1919)

Folklore and legend may provide clues to Bronze Age social and religious practices. Stories of 'bottomless lakes' harbouring strange creatures, or providing gateways to an underworld are common, perhaps indicating human or animal sacrifice, for example Llyn y Fan Fach in the Carmarthen Fans and Llyn Cwm Llwch in the Beacons. Even though it cannot be proved that these tales have a Bronze Age context, it is intriguing how many refer to a 'fear of iron', the superior metal which followed.

Offerings were thrown into lakes (e.g. the Llyn Fawr Hoard at Rhigos, near Hirwaun, where 24 objects, including cauldrons, sickles, swords and knives, were discovered). At Princetown, near Tredegar, a timber-lined structure (offertory well?) was found, containing two bronze spear heads and an enigmatic bronze object, now in the National Museum at Cardiff.

Figure 4: Princetown Hoard. A collection of Bronze Age objects found in a putative offertory well at Princetown near Tredegar.

Monuments

Stone circles, alignments and standing stones are usually ascribed to the Early Bronze Age, but earlier Neolithic peoples had also handled massive stones. Bronze Age monuments were natural progressions of this megalithic culture and some at least might belong to it.

Figure 5: View from Twyn Disgwylfa northwards across the village towards Allt yr Esgair and Llangorse Lake.

Figure 6: Looking east down the Usk valley from the slopes of Tor y Foel.

Late Bronze Age

Approximately BC 1000 - 600 - Upland Disaster

Upland settlement depended upon soil and climate. Volcanic dust was already causing a succession of poor summers which, combined with poor husbandry and serious soil erosion, was making high level settlement less viable. Around BC 1200, the Icelandic Hekla 3 volcano erupted, accelerating this decline which changed upland life. Widespread emissions covered the sun, triggering heavy rainfall and considerably lowering mean temperatures. Winters became colder with upland soils washed into lakes, streams, underlying limestone water-systems, and eventually the Bristol Channel. Acid conditions accelerated blanket peat which would conceal most Bronze Age upland features. Over recent years massive peat erosion has exposed sites and artefacts hidden for millennia. Bronze Age society changed dramatically: high upland occupation became impossible and settlement/ritual sites were abandoned. Uplands would have remained suitable for summer pasturage. Although there is no evidence whatsoever other than later place names, an early form of transhumance, i.e. the summer movement of herds from the 'Hendre' (*Old House*) to the Hafod (*Summer Home*) may have originated then. It is also worth noting that Bronze Age culture had a true hill farming element. Present-day 'hill-farms' are not on hills but Usk Valley flanks and in sheltered upland valleys.

Bronze tools, e.g. sickles, axes and chisels, reveal that Late-Bronze Age Wales had a flourishing metal industry, with cereal production, tree-felling and timber working. Some iron tools clearly evolved from previous bronze examples.

The Iron Age

In cool and damp weather, peat bogs continued spreading. Deforestation was extensive; oak and alder declined but birch and ash, which prefer open conditions, increased.

A Celtic Race?

"The mass of archaeological evidence is primarily of local continuity from the preceding Bronze Age" (Simon James). Iron was used during the Late Bronze Age, (e.g. Llyn Fawr Hoard - Hirwaun). Any arrival of Celtic peoples is now disputed. Caesar clearly differentiated between Iron Age British and other European peoples. In Britain, DNA testing indicates all British races descend from the same Mesolithic stock, little affected by any new blood and their differences a result of nurture, not nature. "Theories of British Celtic civilisation were an eighteenth century invention, based upon an archaeological record distorted to fit political needs." (Professor Collis, Sheffield). This was a movement of ideas, culture and fashion which, by the first century AD, parts of Britain had adopted. Nevertheless this British Celtic culture collapsed quickly, its language surviving only in isolated regions. Very few Celtic words exist in English, although there are many from an unknown earlier tongue.

Hill Forts

Several sites along the Usk Valley, e.g. Crug Hywel (Crickhowell), Twyn y Gaer (Cwmyoy), Myarth (north-east of Llangynidr) and others, are claimed as Iron Age, although walled and banked enclosures existed during the Bronze Age and some, at least, could have originated then - for example, Bronze Age flints appeared during excavations at Twyn y Gaer fort.

The name 'fort' may be misleading. Local examples vary from small, single-banked and ditched enclosures, e.g. Crug Hywel, to the five-ditched complex at Pen-y-crug, Brecon. But complexity could aid attackers, and extensive palisades would have been difficult to oversee and defend. With no apparent viable interior water supply, their suitability as long-term stock protection is questionable. In Wessex early enclosures were lightly defended and seasonally occupied, later examples had bigger ramparts and possible town-sized settlement. (British Archaeology, 1998). Location on tribal boundaries could indicate warfare, although trading of stock, slaves, captives and produce seems more likely. As with Medieval towns and villages attempting to out-do each other in their churches or spires, so too Iron Age defences may have been more for appearance than function (e.g. resembling those at Tretower Court or applied to church towers - purely decorative). Similarly people of later towns grouped for mutual protection while dependent on surrounding agriculture. A non-defensive role is suggested by a lack of evidence that any local site suffered Roman attack. Probably several remained occupied during the Roman period.

Gradually a tribal grouping ('Silures') developed, with major centres at Usk and Caerwent. Many smaller enclosures existed; excavation indicating a mixed economy based on cattle and some grain. (Hand mills and burned grain at Twyn y Gaer, Cwmyoy). Domestic animals probably formed an important dietary element - a hut floor excavated at Twyn Llechfaen enclosure (SO 082291) revealed bones of 3 oxen, 9 sheep and 4 pigs, although these were undated.

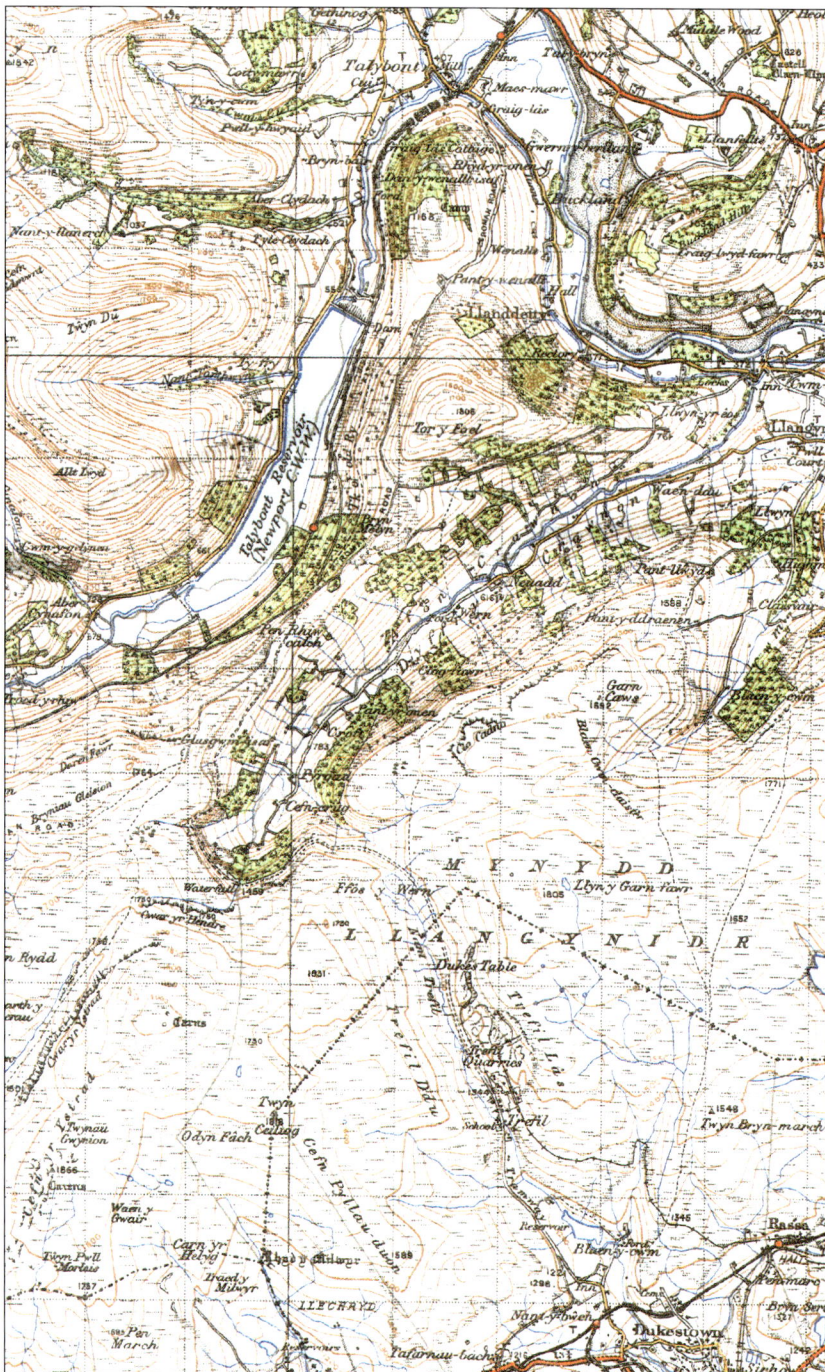

Figure 7: 1947 OS Map showing the topography of the countryside around Llangynidr.

The Roman Period

From AD 43 to the mid fifth century, Britain was part of the Roman Empire, benefiting from strong control. From AD 100 to 400 it seems that the climate improved steadily.

The Landscape

At first, peat bogs and heath continued to spread over local hills 300m above sea level. The polypodium fern which requires damp conditions reached a peak before AD 200. Wales, a military zone, would have faced demands for metals, timber, leather, grain, slaves, etc. with consequent effect upon landscape.

The Roman Conquest

By AD 61 much of lowland Wales was overrun, its tribes contained by Roman forts at Usk, Abergavenny and Cardiff. Large forts such as Clyro and Clifford (60 acres) indicate the scale of operations. By AD 74, Legio 2 Augusta completed the conquest and a new Roman-style tribal capital at Caerwent helped to end resistance. Other than a fine bath-house indicating a large, yet-undiscovered villa at Maesderwen, Llanfrynach (SO 06922585), sites are predominantly military.

By the middle of the second century AD, Wales was only lightly garrisoned, suggesting tribes were pacified and Roman rule accepted, although a late-second-century hoard discovered at Dolaucothi may indicate that some occupation continued. There was extensive Romanization of local tribes and much purchasing of Roman objects and materials. It is difficult to differentiate between Iron Age and Roman-period settlement in Wales and it appears that having evolved out of the Bronze Age, the Iron Age gradually became Romano-British. Crop-marked enclosures are generally trapezoidal. Others are no bigger than half an acre and are surrounded by a slight earthen bank, while some hill forts appear to have been occupied into the sixth century.

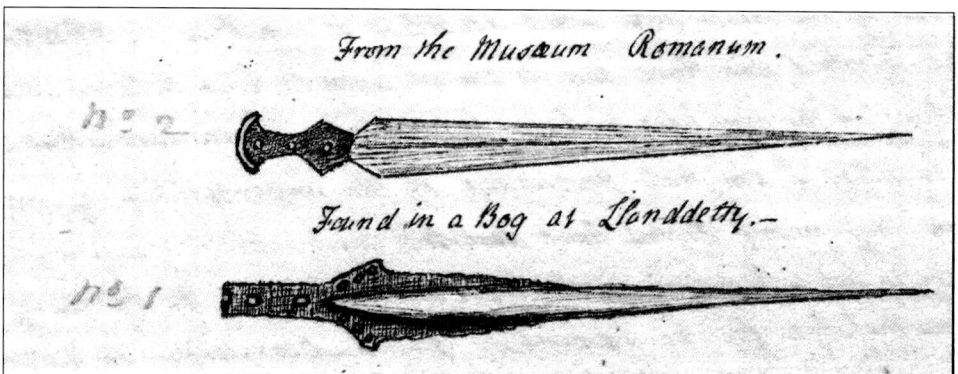

Figure 8: Roman Sword. A Bronze Sword discovered near Glawcoed when the canal was being excavated in 1797. Drawing by Rev H T Payne.

Roads and Rivers

Roman control was maintained by rapid troop movement along a road system defended by forts; it is likely that surveying took place during campaigns. However, any relatively straight track may be claimed 'Roman'. Several local examples remain conjectural, possibly only drover/coach-routes or native trackways. Some postulated roads either never existed, or have completely disappeared, while others altered their line through erosion or local need. For example, the north-south Castell Collen - Cardiff Roman Road is now shown passing through Brecon, a post-AD 1089 settlement, i.e. ignoring Y Gaer fort some 3km west. A complete Roman road system awaits discovery.

A preoccupation with Roman Roads causes river transport to be ignored, even though all local major sites are on, or very near, the Usk or Wye. Locally, from Y Gaer (near Brecon) to Isca (near Newport) the land falls only 142m. Even with today's lower water-tables there are still long stretches suitable for shallow-draught navigation, and more difficult reaches, e.g. near Llangynidr, invite research into possible Roman weirs/ponding. The Anglo-Saxon Chronicle states that, in AD 1049, 36 Scandinavian ships sailed 'up in the Welsh Usk' causing much destruction. Similarly, there are nineteenth century records of commercial boats being hauled over Wye rapids by gangs of men (Hereford Times- 1840).

As Rome disintegrated so did Wales. By the end of the fourth century civilian settlements were collapsing in face of unrest and social disorder. Lacking strong control Wales reverted into internecine tribal areas - the 'Dark Ages' had begun.

The Dark Ages (Early Medieval)

The climate again deteriorated before gradually improving. Apart from heavily wooded valleys, local landscape would have resembled today's. Timber was being felled faster than natural replacement. Coppicing still supplied special needs.

The period following Rome's departure is 'dark' in that knowledge of it relies on sparse monastic records, some carved stones, and a few archaeological sites. Characterised by large estates with ecclesiastical overtones, it was a time of social instability and reliance upon family feuds to settle disputes - Welsh tribes wasted themselves on internecine warring and raids. The Domesday Book records that in Archenfield, a lowland Welsh district of Herefordshire,

"If a Welshman has killed a Welshman, the relatives of the slain gather and despoil the killer and his relatives and burn their houses until the body of the dead man is buried the next day about midday.."

Such customs did little for social harmony.

Figure 9: Ffostyll Chambered Tombs. Two Neolithic chambered tombs on farmland north-east of Talgarth.

Figure 10: Ty Elltud. A Neolithic burial chamber about 1km east of Llanhamlach Church. It has some incised crosses, probably dating from medieval times.

Figure 11: Carreg Waun Llech. A large, shaped, vertical stone standing on Lan Fawr, an area with many signs of Bronze Age activity.

Figure 12: Pant Serthfa Stone. A small, shaped, stone on the south scarp of the Crawnon, an area of intensive prehistoric occupation.

Upland Welsh

There is often confusion over 'upland' and 'hill-dwellers'. After the late Bronze Age these terms no longer refer to those living 'on' the hills, but to occupants of sheltered valleys about 200 m or so above sea level.

Largely self-sufficient in food and clothing, their diet predominantly one of meat, milk and cheese, with drink distilled from wild honey, the upland Welsh had never been 'driven onto the hills' but were there by choice. This was a semi-nomadic people where the warrior-herdsman was supreme. Women, serfs and lower classes worked the soil - one reason why Herefordshire and other lowland Welsh were viewed with contempt, and continually raided. The Domesday Book, AD 1086, records much of Herefordshire, formerly Lowland-Wales, as 'wasta', i.e. 'wasted'.

'Celtic Churches'

A circular churchyard does not indicate antiquity and there are no certain pre-Conquest churches within Wales. Customs and beliefs ascribed to an early Welsh Church arose possibly from post-twelfth century religious and political needs, rather than ancient tradition. Contact with the Irish Church - legend has it that St. Patrick was born in Wales - explains why several local stones bear Irish 'Ogham' script. Locally there are no positive sites of this period although some higher settlements and 'cross-dykes' (banks and ditches) may be so. As with other undeveloped tribal pastoral communities, wealth lay in stock. Raiding continued, particularly against Herefordshire Welsh.

The Norman Period

From circa AD 500 to 1300 an improving climate brought higher temperatures, becoming cooler and wetter during the fourteenth century. Until shortly after the Conquest, the Llangynidr area formed part of Brycheiniog (approximately Brecknockshire), with Gwynllwyg and Morgannwg, two other small tribal areas, lying to the south. All were virtually client states of Deheubarth which covered most of Southern Wales.

The Norman Usk Valley

Norman lordships were lands seized from native chieftains and, although including valley and upland, their grain-based economy generally restricted manors to below the 200m contour. Brecon, whose sheltering hills and rich alluvial soil made possible grain production at higher levels, is an exception. Marked economic differences between higher and lower settlement were emphasised by Norman estates distinguishing between lowland (generally arable) 'Englishries' and upland (generally pastoral) 'Welshries', thereby splitting Wales. 'Englishries' - a cultural, not racial term - were areas populated predominantly by Welsh peoples. Lowland-

Welsh benefited from new methods of cultivation, measurement and coinage. Upland which was incapable of producing wheat was 'desert', i.e. of little value, and due-paying 'Welshries' slowest to gain from new ideas. Wales was now clearly divided into more-prosperous lowland areas and subsistence-level uplands. Lowland towns and an Anglo-Welsh society developed which, although retaining some former customs, generally adopted English ways.

Bibliography and suggestions for further reading.

RCAHM, Wales, *Hillforts and Roman Remains*
RCAHM, Wales, *Later Prehistoric and Settlements*
Holder, C, *Wales - An Archaeological Guide*, Faber
Reed, *The Landscape of Britain*, Routledge
Ordnance Survey, *Field Archaeology in Great Britain*
Guide to Field Archaeology, Collins
Cole, Sonia, *The Neolithic Revolution*, British Museum
Nelson, Lyn, *The Norman Invasion of Breconshire,* University of Texas
Wainright, *Prehistoric Remains in Britain*, Constable
Wilson, *Roman Remains in Britain*, Constable
Emery, *The World's Landscapes - Wales*, Longmans
Council British Archaeology, *Prehistoric and Early Historic Ages* etc
CBA (Wales), *Archaeology in Wales* (Annual Publication)
James, S, *Atlantic Celts, Modern Invention*, British Museum Press
Jones, Theophilus, *A History of the County of Brecknock*
Briggs, C S, *Henry Thomas Payne Letters - transcription*
Rackham, O, *History of the Countryside*
RCAHM, Aberystwyth, *various items of information*

Particular thanks are given to Dr C S Briggs, RCAHM, for his encouragement and assistance over many years.

Many sites/finds in the local area were discovered by amateurs. It is emphasised any new discoveries should be reported to:

RCAHM, Plas Crug, Aberystwyth, SY2 1NJ.

Figure 13:

Maen Llwyd. Over 2m tall, this standing stone is sited in the upper Grwyne Fechan on the south flank of the Black Mountains.

Figure 14:

Llwynyfedwen Stone. This standing stone, on the north side of the River Usk some 400m below the bridge, is one of the tallest in Wales (4.27m). It probably marked a ford.

*Figure19: Fish Stone, Glanusk Park. This tall stone on the north bank of the Usk
also marked a ford.*

Neolithic Sites

Several of the following sites, while not in the Llangynidr area, are included to provide an overall picture.

N 1   Ffostyll Long Cairns   2.5km north-east Talgarth   S0 17893489
Two cairns aligned NNE-SSW with forecourts and false portals between inward-curving dry stone walls. On private land.

N 2   Penyrwrlod Long Cairn   2km south of Talgarth   SO 15053156
Quarrying of a large stone mound exposed human remains in what proved to be a massive burial chamber. No major excavation has yet taken place but three lateral chambers have been noted on the north side. C14 dating - BC 3000. On farm land but access permitted.

N 3   Ty-isaf and Cwmfforest   1km south of Castell Dinas   SO 18192906
Long Cairns
Two wedge-shaped burial cairns, each 30m long, with forecourts and false portals. Burial chambers were on sides. Now filled in but still visible from adjacent lane.

N 4   Blaen Sorgwm   2.5km east of Llangorse   SO 16152843
Long Cairn
A wedge-shaped cairn 25m long and 15m at its widest point with forecourt and false portal plus three burial chambers. Pottery sherds, flint and chert flakes and quantities of charcoal were discovered.

N 5   Gwernvale Long Cairn   At entrance to Manor Hotel SO 21101920
Crickhowell
A large cairn indicated by stone markers. Burial chamber and two entrance-passage slabs are visible.

N 6   Ty Elltud Long Cairn   Manest Court Farm   SO 09842638
Llanhamlach
On low hill, burial chamber, capstone and passageway/forecourt are still intact. Exterior and interior surfaces have incised carvings/crosses which may be medieval. One date - '1510'. St Elltyd was the original dedication of nearby Llanhamlach Church.

Permission to visit must be obtained at the farmhouse.

N 7   Abercynafon   5km south of Talybont   SO 07611731
Remains of posts, split tree trunks and planking were discovered in what had been a small pond. Split tree-trunks, the largest over 3m long, were arranged horizontally NE/SW not necessarily as a walkway but for some other (ritual?) purpose. Tree-ring dating indicated BC 2795/2710.

Bronze Age Sites

BA 1   Black Mountains Area
Although OS maps indicate several upland sites, there may have been others in valleys either destroyed or covered by forestry. Small (Bronze Age?) enclosures, e.g. that on the lower flank of Pen Allt Mawr, suggest much is still to be discovered.

BA 2   Mynydd Llangorse Area
Cairns plus flint and settlement discoveries indicate this region was intensively occupied in Bronze Age times. A very interesting and accessible upland area.

BA 3   Dyffryn Crawnon Area   SO 12961679 and SO 12891700
North Ridge major features are:

SO 12961679 Carn Caws (*Cheese Cairn*). A large stone banked enclosure adjoins south. Other possible enclosures lie immediately north.

SO 12891700 North of Carn Caws - a large cairn of boulders.

BA 4   Blaen Onneu Cairn Field and Settlement   SO 16041738
About 400m east of Blaen Onneu Quarries and car park, near Carreg Waun Llech Standing Stones, are a series of some 40 stone mounds, walls and other features in close proximity. Probably Bronze Age, these indicate extensive cultivation and/or a significant burial area. At least two hut-sites and a walled enclosure lie near the scarp, east of Carreg Waun Llech. Several hut-sites and associated stone walls are visible along the Cwalca outcrop. Other hut-sites of indeterminate age are situated in a small valley immediately west of the Crickhowell road junction. Extensive enclosure-banks are also visible south of here.

BA 5   Trefil Area
The moorlands either side of the quarry road running north from Trefil are especially rich in sites ranging from prehistoric to industrial. These can be hazardous areas, especially in poor weather.

Possible other Bronze Age sites are: about 200m south of Clo Cadno (SO 11611628) two dry valleys running east from SO 117160 towards Blaen Cwmclaisfer containing several hut-sites, enclosures, cairns and field-clearance mounds; others lie between Clo Cadno and the quarry road. The scarp edge running north-east from Clo Cadno provides fine walking, several prehistoric sites and superb views.

BA 6   Cwm Claisfer, Southern flank   Around SO 149167
An elliptical stone-walled enclosure (D Watkins) some 20-30m in diameter with two opposing entrances and containing at least four hut-sites. Externally another hut-circle abuts its south entrance and a second lies 10m west. Another stands in boulder scree 15m south with suggestions of more in the vicinity.

Figure 16: Crug Hywel Fort. A prehistoric hill fort from which Crickhowell takes its name.

Figure 17: Neuadd Reservoir. An ancient landscape is visible during drought conditions. This circular cairn or enclosure is one of several.

SO 149166 Two small hut-circles and at SO 150167 a hut and small enclosure. All are in boulder train running approximately north-south.

SO 147165 Approximately 400m west is a stone banked enclosure, some 20m diameter with an adjoining rectangular enclosure 20m by 20m. There are associated hut sites and probable stone banks in vicinity.

Figure 18: Excavation of a Bronze Age burial cairn, Corn Du.

Corn Du, Brecon Beacons   SO 00752133
The excavation of a boat-shaped Bronze Age burial proved it had been constructed about BC 2000 on what had been a grass-covered surface. Peat had developed over the site (Carn Du, (*Black Cairn?*) but when floor slabs were lifted the grass and plant life of 4000 years ago were revealed beneath. At first yellow-green, within seconds this oxidised and turned black (this also occurred at Pen y Fan, nearby).

Viewing Bronze Age Landscapes

Blanket peat gradually covered most upland sites. When local reservoirs were first flooded, masses of peat were recorded rising to the surface and breaking up, having broken clear of a Bronze Age surface below. (Dr C S Briggs, pers.com.). Dry reservoir floors may thus reveal an ancient landscape. Note: reservoirs are not open to the general public.

Beacons Reservoir   Around SN 989183
When drained in 1987 considerable evidence of early settlement was revealed. Neolithic and Bronze Age flints were discovered together with a number of hut-sites and enclosures. A stone-banked terrace crossing south-west to north-east may have been the Penydarren-Brecon Roman Road or an earlier trackway.

Upper Neuadd Reservoir   Around SO 028190

Evidence of intensive occupation has appeared. On the island are stone-banked enclosures, walling and a cairn. South, under normal water-level, are three cairns. North lie round and ring cairns with another alongside the old track leading up to Bwlch ar y Fan. Numerous Mesolithic, Neolithic and Bronze Age flints have been discovered in this area.

Cairns of the Llangynidr area

Location	Grid reference	Notes
Clo Cadno	SO 11611628	
Garn Fawr	SO 12191518	
Pant Serthfa	SO 12281679	
Carn Caws	SO 12961679	
Carreg Wen Fawr y Rugos	SO 13061750	Possible ring cairn

Iron Age Sites

IA 1   Pendre Enclosure   1km south of Talgarth   SO 15583263
A promontory enclosure of some 1.5ha retaining lengths of double bank and ditch.

IA 2   Castell Dinas Fort   4 km SE of Talgarth   SO 17893008
A large (6.5ha) multivallate enclosure later re-used as a medieval castle-site. An ancient trackway crosses the ridge, passing 'Dinas Well', a pool north of the later castle gate.

IA 3   Allt yr Esgair Fort   2km NE of Talybont   SO 12702430
A very large oval multivallate fort covering more than 6ha at 393m above sea level. A structure at its highest point may have been a Bronze Age burial cairn and/or Roman signal station. Superb views. Footpaths clearly sign-posted.

IA 4   Allt yr Esgair Enclosure   SO 12312420
A small oval univallate enclosure with simple north-west entrance lies west of the fort near the track to Paragon Tower.

IA 5   Crug Hywel Hill Fort   2 km north of Crickhowell   SO 22252065
A flat-topped Old Red Sandstone outlier 451m above sea level with a single scarp and ditch, with ditch spoil employed to create a strong counterscarp. An incurved entrance lies to the east, hut sites are visible within. Other stone banks and structures lie south-west of the site. Accessible by well-signed footpaths and with good views. There is a large stone-banked enclosure plus huts above at SO 220216.

1A 6   Myarth Hill Fort   1.5km SW of Tretower   SO 17302070
A large double-banked enclosure, largely destroyed by quarrying and forestry, at 297m above sea level. Little else remains of one of the largest forts in the region other than an incurved entrance. On private land.

IA 7   Tump Wood Fort   1km south of Talybont   SO 11272149
A small bivallate fort on a hill 357m above sea level approached from south-east by an ancient trackway passing (possibly defensive) outworks. The defences are well-preserved although damaged by forestry. On private farm land although path nearby. A settlement site is 0.5km south of here.

IA 8   Lan Fawr Enclosure   1km SE of Llangynidr   SO 17071838
On Mynydd Llangynidr's northern scarp, the remains of a probably elliptical enclosure measuring some 80m by 50m, with sections of two stone banks and one ditch. Of uncertain date but possibly Iron Age.

IA 9   Coed Pen-twyn Fort   2 km SW of Llangattock   SO 19351622
A large bivallate enclosure with an incurved entrance stands on a naturally defensive site near Darren Cilau quarries. On private land but clearly visible from quarries to south.

IA 10,11 Clydach Enclosures   On promontories either side SO 22311332
**   of the A465 at Cheltenham   and 22821263**
Two possible enclosures (formerly OS-marked 'British Camps') much damaged by quarrying. Both are accessible by road or footpath and provide fine views.

Roman Sites

ROM1,2 Allt yr Esgair Signal   near Llansantffraed   SO 12702430
**   Station and Road (?)**
A suggested Roman Road crosses this ridge (Fort IA 3) from Bwlch to Pennorth. Being a parish boundary suggests antiquity. It may have served a Roman signal station. There are possible remains of a stone structure at the highest point of the ridge. Being half way between Gobannium (Abergavenny) and Y Gaer (Brecon), and on line-of-sight, makes this possible.

ROM 3 Pen-y-gaer Fort   2 km east of Bwlch   SO 16862195
Largely destroyed by eighteenth century turnip farming, but still visible near Pen-y-gaer farm - the present lane tracing approximately its Via Decumana. Built by Legio 2 Augusta, two of their inscribed stones are built into Tretower domestic walls. A bathhouse may have stood at Maesllechau (SO 168221) north of the fort (Dr C S Briggs). A stone-lined underground conduit running downhill towards it has been traced. A small carved contemporary (?) figure is built into the west wall of Middle Gaer farm house.

"An urn filled with bones" was discovered, circa 1801, immediately west of the fort. A probable burial vault was also found to the east in an area (burial ground?) rich in brick and tile. Pots uncovered here were "begged by the poor for their milk".

ROM 4 Roman Road from Abergavenny to Brecon
A conjectural route passes close to Tretower Castle before crossing fields to Lower Gaer farm. In 1801 a paved way near Pen-y-gaer Fort was removed by the Upper Gaer farmer, and an inscribed stone "thrown into rubbish" (perhaps that recorded by Theophilus Jones as one inscribed 'Catacus' about a mile from Tretower "now thrown down"). Its route is then represented by the lane to Ty-mawr farm where it ascends a well-engineered incline to cross the A40 at SO 218150. West of Bwlch its line probably approximated with that of the present A40.

ROM 5 Roman Road (?) from Dolygaer to Talybont and Brecon
A Roman coin, undated before being defaced by amateur cleaning, was found near the highest point of a postulated Roman road between Dolygaer (SO 060145) and Talybont, from where it crossed the Usk to Llansantffraed. Earthworks here are suggested as its agger, but could be remains of post-medieval gardens.

ROM 6 Roman Road from Dolygaer to Abergavenny (?)
It has been suggested the Pen Rhiw Calch road was not primarily to Y Gaer (Brecon) but to Abergavenny. Lane and hedgerow suggest that this could have passed east of Tor y Foel to Bwlch-y-waun, Penybailey, Cwm Crawnon, Llangynidr and Bwlch.

Other Important Local Roman Sites

Y Gaer   near Aberyscir, west of Brecon   **SO 00332966**
An important fort where several roads met north of the Usk, built AD 80 to house Vettones, a Spanish auxiliary cavalry regiment. First timber and then stone-rebuilt about AD 140 - largely abandoned some 60 years later. Some 'caretaker' visits after this are suggested by a few coins of later date. Three gateways and sections of wall remain. It is on farm land but access is permitted. Nearby the 'Maidens' Stone', a Roman tombstone (Brecknock Museum), and an early cavalry burial were discovered.

Romano-British Villa   **Llanfrynach**   **SO 06922585**
In 1783 a large bathhouse, comprising a complete set of baths, two furnaces, a corridor and four mosaic pavements, was uncovered. Part of one pavement is now in the National Museum of Wales. Nearby another ruinous structure contained two human skulls (villa mausoleum?). The villa itself has not been traced and may lie beneath the present Maesderwen House. Eighteenth century antiquarian Henry Thomas Payne recorded quantities of iron working slag nearby as well as large deer antlers. Nothing is now visible. The site is private with no public access.

Dark Age and Sites of Uncertain Period

D 1   Nennius Victorinus Stone   Originally at SO 12511121
A sixth century memorial stone to 'Victorinus' discovered built into a granary south-east of Scethrog - now in Brecknock Museum.

D 2   Llanhamlach 'Moridic' Stone, Llanhamlach Church   SO 08922642
Within the church is a tenth/eleventh century inscribed stone bearing a male and female figure plus inscription "JOHANNIS MORIDIC SUREXIT HUNC LAPIDEM" (*Johannis set up this stone for Moridic*).

D 3   Llangorse Lake Crannog   SO 12822681
Archaeological investigation of a small island near the northern slipway proved it to have been a man-made ninth/tenth century lake settlement.

D 4   Cwmdu Stone   Cwmdu Church   SO 18102381
A sixth or seventh century stone found in the locality is incorporated into a south buttress.   It bears a Latin inscription (transl.) "*Here lies Catacus, son of Tergenacus*" as well as some Ogham.

D 5   'Turpilius Stone'   originally 1km north-east   SO 22511942
**   of Crickhowell**
A 3m thin slab of stone said to have stood at Ty-yn-y-wlad farm and bearing the inscription '*Turpilius, son of Dunocati lies here*' (transl.).   Theophilus Jones recorded it had been thrown down by treasure seekers.   Now in Brecknock Museum.

Figure 19: Burial stone with Ogham inscription, Cwm Criban.

D 6   Llanddetty Stone   Llanddetty Church   SO 12752025

Within Llanddetty Church, a ninth century pillar stone 1.2m tall inscribed *"Guadan the Priest made this cross for his friends Ninid and Gurhi"* (transl.)

D 7   Cwm Criban Ogham Stone   SO 07311325

A sixth century burial stone bearing an Irish 'Ogham' inscription whereby Latin is represented by groups of horizontal, parallel lines. Erected alongside an ancient (?) track.

Sites of Uncertain Period

Many upland sites cannot be accurately dated without excavation. It is possible that higher level sites are Bronze Age. The following is a small selection of those found on local hills:

Figure 20: Carn y Bugail. A Bronze Age burial cairn at 600m on moorland south of Dyffryn Crawnon waterfall.

Mill Stones   Around SO 089137

There are two Bronze Age burial cairns in this area: Carn y Bugail (*Cairn of the Shepherd*) and Garn Felen.

South-east of Garn Felen, millstones were manufactured. Two broken or unfinished stones remain. Rough-outs are also to be found here. It was probably a post-medieval operation - stones being taken away by sled.

Cwar yr Ystrad   Around SO 088138

Two hut sites and enclosures of indeterminate date lie immediately north of Garn Felen (*Cairn of the mill*). The more westerly contains a swallow hole below which auroch and other bones were discovered in a cave passage (K Martin).

Buarth y Caerau Enclosures   Around SO 074137

West of the Ogham stone is an extensive complex of hut-sites and enclosures of uncertain, but possibly Dark Age, date. Another single (Bronze Age?) cairn lies immediately east in the Ystrad scarp - a second lies 150m north. At SO 074125, south of the Ogham Stone, a shallow valley contains a group of 5 huts and enclosures.

Gwaun Nant Ddu   Around SO 086152

A large dried lake bed where peat core investigation (K Martin) revealed pollens spanning Ice Age to present. Flint flakes and cores have been discovered; hut-sites, stone banks and enclosures are in its vicinity. At SO 087153 is a large burial cairn with central cist exposed while at SO 084153 is a 30m alignment of 8 small stones. There are other possible Mesolithic or Bronze Age features nearby.

Dyffryn Crawnon, South   SO 128 158

A stone-banked enclosure some 30m in diameter.

SO 109 155

Close to the junction of Cwm Pyrgad track at 420-460m above sea level is a settlement area consisting of enclosures, walling and a hut circle, between the two streams. Other significant stone banked enclosures lie near the southern and western Clo Cadno scarps.

'The Long Wall' See Figure 2.   Around SO 118169

An extensive stone bank runs approximately 1km SSE-NNW from near Clo Cadno to north of Carn Caws. An important site of uncertain date and purpose, although possibly Bronze Age because of close association with Bronze Age enclosures/cairns at its northern and southern extremities. At either end the wall seems to disappear beneath peat cover.

This walls drops frequently into swallow-holes and other depressions, perhaps the result of rain-water caught along its length causing dissolution and collapse of limestone strata beneath. Many upland swallow holes may have been formed in the same way, i.e. by limestone dissolving under heavy, rain-gathering, structures such as cairns or stone banks (RCAHM, *Bronze Age Inventory*).

Pillow Mounds - Glasgwm-uchaf, near the Brinore Tramroad   SO 093162

This was sometimes referred to as Maesybeddau (*Field of Graves*) because 14 long mounds were visible before afforestation. Formerly considered prehistoric, Roman or medieval, the mounds were perhaps nineteenth century rabbit warrens supplying pelts for hat making and fresh meat to the nearby coalfield. There is also a local tradition that they were the graves of a Roman expeditionary party ambushed by natives (see page 255)

Brinore Tramroad (AD 1815) (Included as a route connecting prehistoric and industrial areas). The tramroad linking Benjamin Hall's Rhymney and Brinore Works with Talybont is clearly visible running around the head of Dyffryn Crawnon although sections have been extensively damaged by recent timber extraction. Although almost exactly 8 miles long, Hall contravened the 1793 Canal Act's 'eight mile clause' by linking it with another built from Trefil to Rhymney.

Cwm Claisfer   SO 132162
Remains of a hut and associated enclosure stand under limestone outcrop. Two other enclosures lie north-east.

Between Cwm Claisfer and the Chartist Cave   SO 127165
Remains of a hut with two small enclosures associated. Several hut-sites and enclosures lie between Cwm Claisfer head and the 'Chartist Cave' around SO 126153.

Blaen Onneu   Around SO 156173
Hafod Sites: Hafods were upland dwellings occupied when stock was moved to higher pastures in summer (transhumance). About 250m north of Blaen Onneu car park are at least three hafod platforms cut into the slope.

Hut sites/settlements: Around SO 154173 an area of boulder scatter has some cleared areas, hut sites and possible enclosure walling.

Cwm Claisfer   At SO 138163
A large rectangular hut base (D Watkins)

Cwm Claisfer   Around SO 135162
A stone bank and ditch forming part of an enclosure together with associated hut-sites.

Blaen Onneu   Around SO 165162
A low stone-banked wall of uncertain date but probably Bronze Age cuts diagonally for some 300m across hillside on a bearing 30° magnetic from the upper end, where there is a deeply sunk circular hut 2.5m diameter. At its lower end is a rectangular hut 3m by 2m, with another hut site situated between the two. Some 30m away, on the same alignment, a large pointed stone marks what appears to be its north-east extremity. On a shelf of land, immediately above the upper end, is other occupation evidence. Several other hut sites and features of indeterminate age have been noted along this scarp.

Standing Stones

Standing stones or 'Menhirs' (*Long Stones*) are enigmatic monuments of indeterminate age, standing either alone or in alignments. Variously dated from Neolithic to Late-Medieval, they have been traditionally attributed to the Bronze Age, circa BC 2200 - 600. Locally, several appear on medieval estate maps as boundary markers - none have been proved to be prehistoric- (RCAHM, *Bronze Age Inventory*). Most stand at lower levels, and there may have been others since destroyed.

Stone rows are sited mainly at higher altitudes in passes or saddles although some ritual link with solitary menhirs may have existed. If genuinely prehistoric, few appear to have funerary significance and their true purpose remains a mystery.

Some stones possess 'cup and ring' markings, i.e. enigmatic hollows and circles incised into their surface, e.g. Llanfeugan, Pencelli (SO 08362447), while several are thought to hint at crude human outline, e.g. Avebury's Avenue has opposing pillars and trapezoids suggested as representing male/female genitalia. There may be some astronomical significance, e.g. Carreg Waun Llech (SO 16381738, 2.5km south of Llangynidr) happens to have flat-axis alignment with the Polaris ecliptic.

Standing stones inspire many theories. Alfred Watkins, of *'Old Straight Track'* fame, considered them track markers in alignment with other prehistoric monuments. Water-diviners claim to sense emanating bands of force, while Professor Alexander Thom suggested they evidenced astronomical observation and mathematical comprehension.

Whatever their true purpose, such monoliths required great effort to move them and place them vertically in a rock-cut pit. Even though adopted by advocates of 'Earth Forces' and the rest, vertical stones remain strangely evocative. Associated myths hint at ritual and ceremonial - they "move", or "bleed", "foretell the future", even "bestow fertility", perhaps faint folk-memories of practices once carried on in their shadow.

Not all monoliths are prehistoric. Vertical stones were also used as gate-pillars, scratching posts or grave markers. Solitary examples are almost impossible to date, although some excavated in other areas have revealed associated Bronze Age burial.

Stones of various sizes were certainly employed as medieval boundary or estate markers, but perhaps because already in situ. Similarly, upright stones in hedge-banks and field walls might be older than the enclosures themselves e.g. the Llanfeugan stone stands in a field-boundary. Old Radnor Church font is recorded as made from a large vertical stone found nearby and that at Partrishow bears a tenth century inscription including 'Menhir', i.e. a mutated 'Maen Hir' (*Long Stone*). However there is little conclusive information about the age or purpose of standing stones - solitary examples are particularly enigmatic.

Local Standing Stones

S 1   **Maen Llwyd,**   **Black Mountains**   SO 22602762
Maen Llwyd (*Grey Stone*) is possibly the highest-sited in Wales, 590m above sea level. A tall shaped stone. On the opposing western ridge (SO 213267) is a deep rock-cut ditch aligned upon it.

S 2   **Peterstone, Llanhamlach**   SO 08942675
Immediately north of A40 roadside. A rectangular pillar 1.45m tall.

S 3   **Bwlch Stone**   SO 15122190
A small stone stands in a field west of the A40. Another vertical stone stands alongside Llygadwy, 0.5km south.

S 4   **Tretower Stone**   SO 18092191
In a hedge line 0.5km north-west of village, a large stone 2.25m tall.

S 5   **Crickhowell Stone**   SO 22221842
0.75km south of Great Oak. A large vertical stone now assumed to be a boundary marker.

S 6   **Llangenny Stones**

Four stones stand in this area:

SO 22181846   A large slab SSW of Coed Cefn
SO 23961784   Two stones stand in steeply sloping woodland 800m north of village
SO 24051787   'The Druid's Altar' on west bank of river, 0.1km south of bridge.

S 7   **Cwrtygollen Stone**   **Cwrtygollen**   SO 21251686
A large stone 4.15m tall at the entrance to Cwrtygollen camp.

S 8   **Gilestone**   **Gilestone Farm, Talybont**   SO 117237
A massive stone 2.6m tall stands in a floodplain hedge-line. On private land.

S 9   **Llwynyfedwen Stone**   **0.5km east of**   SO 15822038
                                            Llangynidr bridge
On private land north of the Usk, at 4.27m it is one of the tallest in Wales and may have marked an Usk ford.

S 10   **The Fish Stone**   **Glanusk Park**   SO 18281985
On private land. A large monolith some 4.2m tall and of fish-like outline.

S 11   **Llangynidr Stone**   **Hedge near Aberyail Farm**   SO 15861995
An upright rectangular-section stone some 1m tall.

S 12   **Pencelli Stone**   **0.2km west of**   SO 08942675
                                               Llanfeugan Church

In hedge line, a pointed stone 1.83m tall incised with two cup marks.

S 13   **Pant Serthfa Stone**   SO 11791675

A shaped stone some 1.5m tall, its longer, western, edge shaped into a series of steps, and possessing flat-side alignment with a deep notch cut through the Crawnon's northern ridge at SO 107183. A short distance west lies what appears to be either an alignment or section of a cairn-kerb. Several other enclosures and circular 'shadow-marks' plus post-medieval lime-burning kilns are near.

S 14   **Pant Serthfa Stone Row**   **3.5km SW of Llangynidr**   SO 11861673

Five stones, the largest fallen, align on another small stone about 100m distant. South-west lie two stone-banked enclosures, possibly ring barrows. Other deep-set and possibly related stones nearby.

S 15   **Carreg Waun Llech,**   **Near B4560 Llangynidr**   SO 16381738
                                               - Beaufort road

The name means *Stone of the slaty moor,* a possible mutation of the more fitting 'Maen Llech' *(Slaty Stone).* A large, shaped, orthostat about 2.5m tall, its flat side orientated approximately north-south, stands in the middle of a flat, almost amphitheatre-like area. Nearby are stone banks and hut-sites plus 40 stone field clearance/burial mounds. The stone's slaty appearance is caused by erosion along its bedding planes.

S 16   **'The Lonely Shepherd'**   **1.25 km west of**   SO 21911432
                                               Llanelly Church

(Not Prehistoric) On Darren Disgwylfa. Otherwise 'Old Man' or 'Peaky (Pica or *pointed*) Stone'. A monolith left attached to bedrock by early nineteenth century quarrymen - included here because of associated ritual. Until the twentieth century early years this stone was whitewashed and robed every Mid-Summer's Eve by local people who ate, drank and danced nearby. That night it would "walk to the river to drink" and "look for a wife" - "death came to any who witnessed it".

Local Discoveries

Location	Grid reference	Object(s)	Map and artefact number
Aberhoywe	SO 16801955	Flint scraper	Map 3, 7
Llwynyfedwen	SO 15612046	Flint flakes	Map 2, 6
Buckland Old Mill	SO 128210	Perforated mace head	Map 1, 3
Pantywenallt	SO 115208	Bronze looped socketed axe	Map 1, 1
Waun-ddu	SO 136189	Urn containing cremation	Map 4, 6
Cwm Claisfer	SO 152189	Socketed axe now in Brecknock Museum	Map 5, 8
Llangenny	SO 241178	1 flint axe, 2 of grey stone	
Crickhowell	SO 176244	Stone axe and bronze sword..	
Pen y Gadair, Black Mountains.	SO 231286	At 750m above sea level - a polished axe of Wiltshire chert	
Trefil Las	SO 12.13.	Palstave axe	
Pen Gloch y Pibwyr	SO 202232	Beakers discovered	
Ty-isaf Burial Chamber	SO 18192906	Beakers discovered	
Gilwern	SO 24.14.	Stone axe discovered - no other details	
Bronllys	SO 14.34.	Mace head discovered - no other details	
Black Mountains	SO 247252	Bronze axe	
600m west of B4560 Beaufort - Llangynidr road highest point	SO 154159	A group of 4 rectangular enclosures/hut bases formed of deep-set stones. Many other sites of indeterminate age exist east and west on this high moorland.	
Canal near Glawcoed	SO 13971985	Roman bronze secespita sword	Map 1, 2
Cwm Crawnon	SO 14501980	Stone mortar, 13th - 15th century	Map 2, 4
Boathouse	SO 14521995	Incised double circle medieval cross	Map 2, 5

Chapter 2

The Manor of Ystradyw

After the Norman conquest of Brycheiniog, Roger le Picard, one of the supporters of Bernard de Neufmarche, was rewarded with a tract of land called Ystradyw uchaf in the Usk valley in the south-east corner of the old kingdom. Ystradyw, usually called Straddewy by the Normans, was probably already a lordship or commote (cymwd) within the cantref[1] of Talgarth and included what subsequently became the two parishes of Llanfihangel Cwmdu and Llangynidr. Picard held this land from the Lord of Brecon in return for such service as providing two armed knights to fight for his overlord in times of war.

For his protection and as a symbol of his dominion over this region, Picard built a castle at Tretower, in a strategic position near the point where the road running west from Abergavenny to Brecon divides to send a branch up the Rhiangoll valley towards Talgarth. The first castle was of the motte and bailey form, with a defensive timber building on an earthern mound within an area protected by a palisade. These wooden defences were replaced by stone fortifications, including a stone shell keep, by about 1150 and successive generations of Picards periodically enlarged and strengthened the castle. The great tower, which is still such an impressive landmark, (see Figure 25) was built in the first half of the thirteenth century.

From their stronghold and administrative headquarters at Tretower the Normans imposed a feudal system of government on the native Welsh population. The regime was based on land tenure in return for services and exploited the existing Welsh custom of obligatory gifts for the maintenance of the local ruler and his court. Picard, as Lord of the Manor, would have retained an area of fertile ground known as the demesne land, which was cultivated by his servants and tenants to supply food for his household. An area near the castle would have been settled by Anglo-Normans and was usually referred to as the Englishry (see Figure 30), while the lands within the Manor populated by the native Welsh, in this case the uplands of Llangynidr and Cwmdu, were referred to by the Normans as the Welshry.

Before the conquest there were both free men and villeins (taegion) in the kingdom of Brycheiniog, who rendered dues and services to their local leader. Under the Laws of Wales traditionally associated with Hywel Dda, the ruler of most of Wales in the first half of the tenth century, various obligatory gifts (cymortha) such as levies for food and drink (gwestfa) and a payment on the death of a tenant (ebediw) were claimed by the lord, and men were liable for short periods of military service. The feudal regime imposed by the Normans exploited these Welsh customs and in many respects probably was little different from the previous form of government, except that payments and services became more closely linked with land tenure than

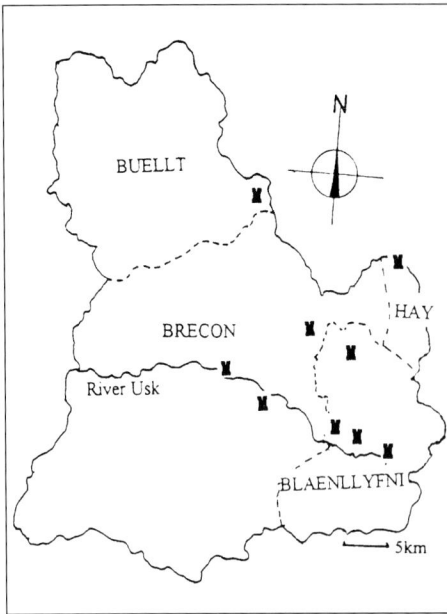

Figure 21: Lordships in the former kingdom of Brycheiniog in the fourteenth century.

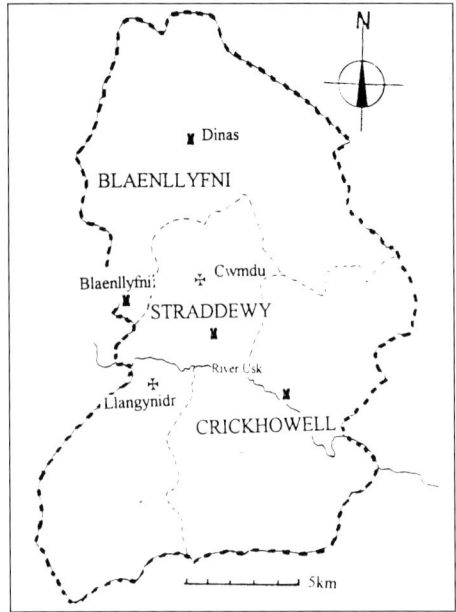

Figure 22: The sub-lordships of Blaenllyfni in the fourteenth century.

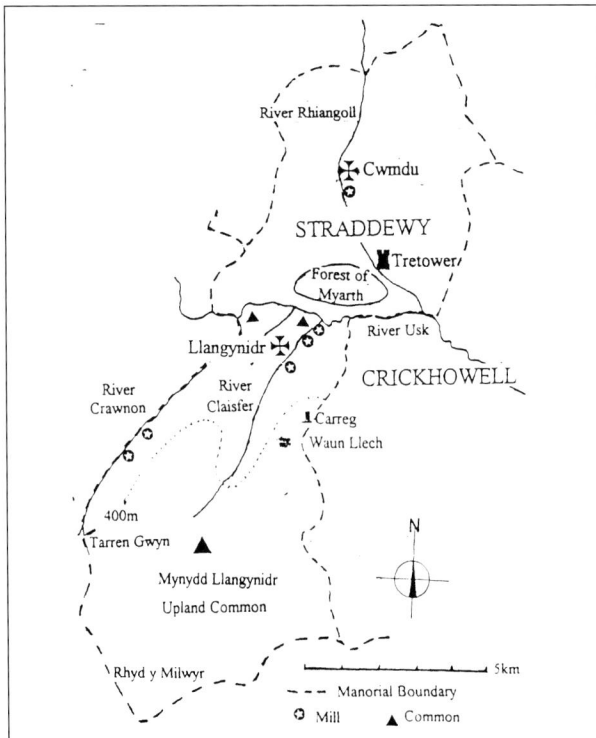

Figure 23: Straddewy (Ystradyw) Lordship, which became the Manor of Tretower in the sixteenth century.

Figure 24: Tretower Castle from the south. Line engraving by S and N Buck, 1741.

with family or community loyalties. No doubt the conquerors imposed a harsher regime and added considerably to the range of services, to meet the labour requirements for the cultivation of arable crops, but in the Brecon lordship, where men worked on the lord's demesne for up to ten days each year, labour services were much less onerous than in many other marcher lordships. Another aspect of Welsh law exploited by the Normans was that of land inheritance. In some lordships women were not allowed to inherit family (gwely) land[2] and, in the absence of a male heir, this land was claimed by the lord in the name of escheat.

The Normans placed a premium on growing arable crops, particularly cereals, on the fertile soil in the valleys. Their policy may well have strengthened the agricultural economy of the area, supplementing the Welsh pastoral system, based largely on the rearing of cattle and sheep, which continued to hold sway in the uplands. A charter[3] (probably c.1175) from John Picard, grandson of Picard who built the first castle at Tretower, granting a portion of the tithe on his lordship to the Priory Church in Brecon, lists the various products of his demesne. The crops - corn, peas, beans, flax and apples and livestock products, horses, cows, sheep, pigs, cheese and wool, indicate a type of mixed farming which survived for a long time in these parts. A very similar economy is indicated by inventories accompanying the earliest local wills some four hundred years later. Curiously both poultry and honey are omitted from Picard's Charter. In early medieval times only a small fraction of the area of the lordship was cultivated. Large tracts, mainly on the higher ground, were used for common grazing as on Lan Fawr, part of Llangynidr Mountain (*Mynydd Llangynidr*), or set aside as hunting areas such as the Forest of Myarth.

Each lordship was an independent territory with its own courts and officials. Although comparatively little is known about the organisation of Straddewy Manor in medieval times, information has survived from the neighbouring manor of Crickhowell and from Llanddew manor near Brecon. Copies of a Crickhowell custumal[4] of c.1295 set out the duties and privileges of both the lord and his tenants.

Those relating to Straddewy would probably have been very similar, as at this period both manors were sub-lordships of Blaenllyfni (established early in the thirteenth century) and at a later date under the Earl of Worcester, the same steward supervised both Crickhowell and Straddewy, holding courts at each on consecutive days. In 1300 the Lord of Straddewy, then John Picard, was obliged to provide in times of war, three armed knights with horses at Blaenllyfni Castle (Bwlch) for forty days each year. He was expected to attend the court there each month. By this date the king had granted him the right to hold a market at Tretower every Wednesday, and a fair lasting four days once a year[5]. At first the fair was held in November but that was later replaced, or supplemented, by a fair on St. Margaret's Day (July 20th[6]). The markets and fairs, which took place in a square outside the west gate of the castle, were very profitable occasions because the lord could charge a toll on all produce brought for sale. Much of the administration of the manor took place at the manorial courts which were held about once a month at Tretower. The tenants were obliged to attend these courts regularly and pay their rents and dues to the bailiff. Taxes known as heriots - usually a sheep - were paid when a tenant died or land changed hands (alienation). The bailiff selected one of three sheep set before him; if he had doubts about their quality he could go to the flock to choose the best beast. Law and order offences were also dealt with in these courts.

Figure 25: Tretower Castle. The Great Tower from the east. Line engraving by MW Bond after H Gastineau, about 1830.

Figure 26: Tretower Castle, Court and Barn viewed from the south. Today the buildings are cared for by CADW.

Figure 27: Forest of Myarth seen from Lan Fawr. After the Norman Conquest it was hunting ground for the Lord of Straddewy.

All the labour on the lord's demesne was carried out by the Welsh or customary tenants. They brought their oxen to plough and harrow his land, sowed seed, weeded and later harvested crops. Sometimes the lord provided food or drink. At Llanddew, near Brecon, for instance, the customary tenants had to mow the lord's meadow, providing their own food, and then make and harvest the hay with the lord providing 18d worth of food between them for three days. In addition the tenants did all the haulage of timber, lime and building materials. They were obliged to have their own corn ground at the lord's mill (for which there was a charge) and they had to keep the mill and weirs in repair and scour the leats and mill pond.

Customary tenants had to accompany the lord to war if they were chosen. The Marcher lordships, like the Welsh kingdoms they replaced, were fiercely independent. Although the Norman lords paid homage to the King of England, English law was not observed in the Marches. During medieval times there was frequently fighting either among the remaining independent Welsh princes or between the Welsh and the Normans. During the thirteenth century Llywelyn ab Iorwerth and later his grandson Llywelyn ap Gruffudd campaigned vigorously to unite the Welsh kingdoms and drive out the Normans. There was also war in England between the King and the barons in the early years of the century so no doubt there were many occasions when the local tenants were summoned for military service. About 1262 Roger Picard, involved in Llywelyn ap Gruffudd's campaign, forfeited Straddewy to his overlord at Blaenllyfni, but recovered his lordship in 1277. In 1297 he was ordered by King Edward I to raise 50 men from the lordship and take them to fight in France. There is no record of his return and the following year his son John Picard was Lord of Straddewy. In 1355 Ralph Bluet, then Lord of Straddewy, was commissioned to raise troops to serve in the Poitiers campaign in France.

An inquisition[7] following the death of John Picard in 1305 stated that the Manor of Straddewy consisted of 300 acres of land worth 2d an acre, 200 acres of woodland, and a grist mill and fulling mill together worth 40d. The manorial income from the rents of the 99 tenants was recorded as £4 16s 5d, only slightly larger than the income of Llangynidr Church from tithes, which was £4 6s 8d in 1291 according to the Taxatio[8]. However the manorial revenue would have been augmented by an array of taxes, tolls, fines and other extortions. Perquisites or dues in kind valued at 40s, noted in the inquisition, suggest that the Welsh tenants were still rendering their dues of cattle, mead and ale in kind. The castle was recorded as "worth nothing per annum beyond reprisals", so presumably, by this time, the lord had built more comfortable living accommodation within the castle precincts. In 1308, following the failure of the male line of Picard, the manor passed into the hands of Ralph Bluet who had married Amicia Picard. From this date the lords lived at Raglan Castle and there was no resident Lord of Straddewy at Tretower. From this time the demesne lands around the castle were probably leased to increase revenue. Towards the end of the thirteenth century there was a deterioration in the climate, which led to poor harvests and famine in the early years of the fourteenth century. Outbreaks of plague, known as the Black Death, from 1349 onwards resulted in depopulation and a period of economic decline. Possibly the abandonment of the medieval village site on Persondy field in the centre of Upper Llangynidr dates from that period, but at present there is no firm evidence though it may be significant that the field just across the River Claisfer is named Cae Cowyn (plague field) on the parish tithe map.

Shards of medieval pottery c.fourteenth - fifteenth century have been collected from Persondy field. Attempts to map the site (see page 62) using resistance and magnetic measurement techniques have proved inconclusive due to interference from the earthing systems of electricity pylons. A flat stone crudely incised with a cross in two concentric circles, and a stone mortar, both from the medieval period, have recently been found in Cwm Crawnon. Apart from these items the only other medieval remains in Llangynidr are the stoup (twelfth century) on the south wall of the nave of Llangynidr Church and the damaged thirteenth century font outside the west door. The Black Death led to untenanted holdings, a shortage of labour and a fall in the income of the manor. There was a general trend to commute labour services into money payments. Marcher lords turned from cereal cultivation to sheep farming which was less labour-intensive. It is recorded that 3,000 fleeces were exported from the Brecon lordship in 1370[9]. Although this move no doubt bolstered the incomes of the lords, it was one of several factors which contributed to the discontent and disorder in the countryside which was brought to a head with the

Figure 28: Double circle medieval cross recently discovered at The Boathouse, Cwmcrawnon.

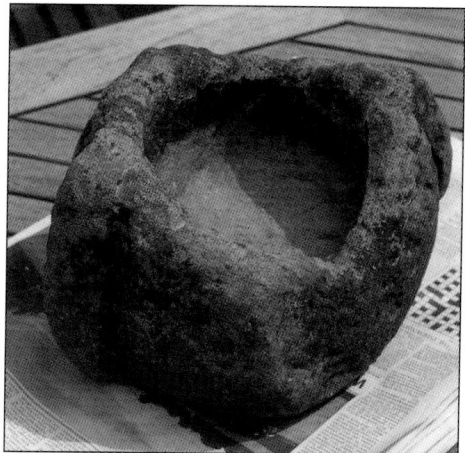

Figure 29: Medieval mortar discovered in Cwmcrawnon by Mr & Mrs V Hill-Male.

Figure 30: Part of the plan of Tretower from the 1587 Manorial Survey. The dwellings which made up the Englishry are clustered around the Castle. An orchard is marked (perllan) on the west side of the Castle.

Figure 31: This plan is fairly typical of those in the 1587 Manorial Survey. It shows Pantypaerau and three neighbouring holdings rented from the Manor.

uprising of Owain Glyn Dwr in 1400. Sir James Berkeley, who had inherited Straddewy through his marriage to Elizabeth Bluet, was commanded to fortify Tretower Castle, but in spite of his efforts it was extensively damaged by Glyn Dwr.

Unrest and warfare continued through most of the fifteenth century with the struggle between the dynasties of York and Lancaster for the English throne. These Wars of the Roses saw the rise of Sir William Herbert, created Earl of Pembroke in 1468, probably the most powerful figure in Wales at that time and a strong supporter of the House of York. In 1429 his father, Sir William ap Thomas, had bought the lordships of Tretower and Crickhowell from Lord Berkeley, his stepson, for £300[10]. The fine fortified house known as Tretower Court probably replaced the castle as a dwelling place early in the fourteenth century. It was given to Roger Vaughan by his half-brother Sir William Herbert about 1450 and was home to the Vaughans for almost three hundred years. In 1463 the lordship of Tretower was separated from Blaenllyfni and granted directly from the king. Through the marriage of Sir William Herbert's grand-daughter the manor passed to the Earls of Worcester, (later created Dukes of Beaufort). From this period in the sixteenth century there is much more information about life in Llangynidr available from documents in the Badminton Archives, now at the National Library of Wales.

The powerful and wealthy Earls of Worcester could afford to employ very able stewards to manage their estates. As the leading representative of the lord, the steward was in charge of the manorial courts which supervised not only the financial transactions but also the enforcement of law and order. The steward needed considerable legal knowledge; Sir David Williams of Gwernyfed, Recorder for Brecon, Queen's Attorney for South Wales and, eventually, Justice of the Court of King's Bench, was steward at Tretower in 1592. He owned land in Llangynidr in addition to his large estates in several parts of England. In the indenture of Llewellin John Thomas[11], who leased a farm in Dyffryn Crawnon, Sir David Williams is described as a "Caricante at Law". His tomb can be seen in Brecon Cathedral. Sir Henry Williams, his son, was High Steward from 1609 until about 1636.

The day to day running of the manor was the responsibility of the bailiff, helped by the Welsh beadle who collected rents from Welsh or customary tenants and the English beadle who collected rents of English tenants and burgesses at Tretower. Gwalter Thomas of Llangynidr, who leased land called Llanerch Gwythell, on the south side of Nant Claisfer near present Llwyn-yr-ynn, was the Tretower bailiff around 1615-1625. In earlier times there had been a reeve in charge of the demesne farm, a forester managing the Forest of Myarth, and various other minor officials. Sometimes one person undertook two offices; Watkin ap Llewellyn was both reeve and Welsh beadle in 1526, and in 1553 Philip ap Howell was bailiff and reeve. The court was held at Tretower, originally on the Castle Green and later in the Court Room in the north range of Tretower Court (see Figure 32). Representatives of each community, later a jury of tenants, reported on events such as misdemeanours, alienations and heriots. When William Vaughan of Tretower Court sold land near Cyffredin Mill to Thomas Price in 1609 he had to pay a heriot of one sheep or the money equivalent of two shillings[12]. When Jevan Thomas Price died in 1639 the family had to pay a heriot of their best beast, valued at sixty shillings[13]. New tenants paid a fine when they took over a holding.

Figure 32: Tretower Court Room. A door, now blocked, led from the road into the Court Room in the north range. Drawn by C Eyre about 1820.

Relatively settled conditions in the second half of the sixteenth century witnessed an improvement in the farming economy. More land was brought into cultivation and farmers bought or rented extra land to increase the size of their farms. The enclosure of fields allowed the breeding of better quality livestock, though shortage of winter fodder still necessitated the autumnal slaughter of many animals. Earlier in the century John Herbert the Rector had assembled a considerable holding by adding to his forty acres of glebe some seventy acres leased from the manor, including much of present-day Aberyail, Pant-teg and Glanyrafon (then known as Tyr Carne Bobre). His extra acres cost £2 8s 8d per annum. (In 1536 the income of the parish church from tithes was recorded, in Valor Ecclesiasticus[14], as £13 4s 7d). Many farmers were building substantial homes on their lands and some of the oldest farmhouses in the parish of Llangynidr, such as Aberyail and Aberhoywe, date from this period. In 1556 when William Vaughan, son of Christopher Vaughan of Tretower Court, married Kateryn Havard of Brecon, money for the marriage settlement was raised on the houses of Rice Thomas ap Rice, Philip John Williams, William John Williams and Meredith ap Jevan in Llangynidr[15]. The first three named had holdings near the Vaughan's land, south of the River Claisfer in the east of the parish.

Figure 33: A plan of the Cyffredin area from the 1587 Manorial Survey. Cyffredin Mill is shown (top left), together with the Maes Cabalva holding occupied by Rice Thomas ap Rice, and the holdings which later became Aberyail and Pant-teg.

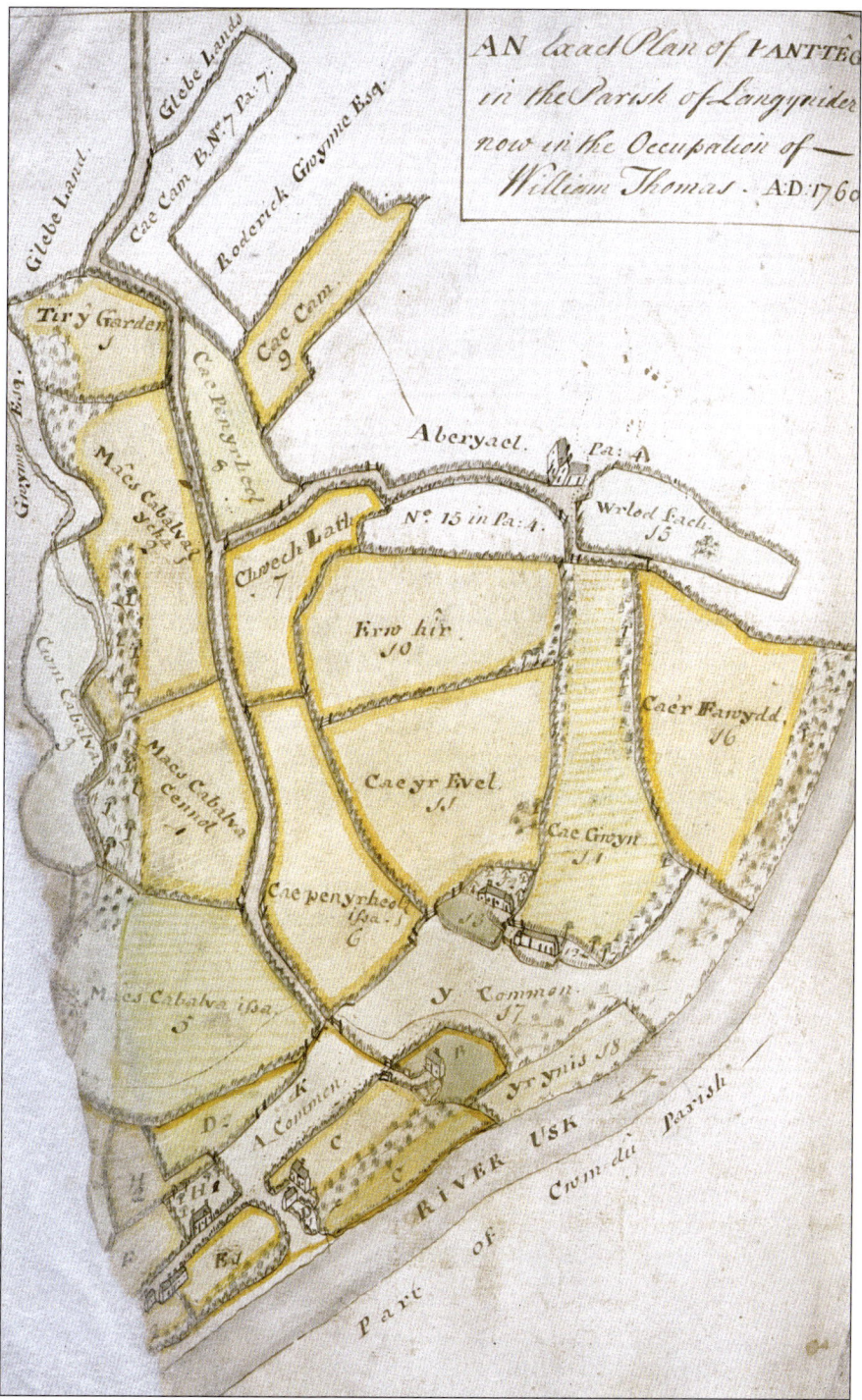

Figure 34: A plan from the 1760 Manorial Survey showing part of Cyffredin Common, which by that date had been largely enclosed.

By the end of the sixteenth century the local population was increasing. The scanty evidence available from rentals, surveys and tax returns is shown in the table below. It refers only to numbers of men.

Population of Llangynidr Parish[16]

Date	Source	Population (men)
1561	Rental (NLW Badminton 406)	69
1587	Rental & Survey (NLW Badminton 3)	74
1608	Court Roll (NLW Badminton 58)	103
1664	Hearth Tax (PRO E179/263/28)[17]	124

A duty called Toll Cense which was levied in the parish also gives an indication of the population size. Possibly this was a money payment to replace the due of mead or ale, sometimes called 'Tolsestre', which dated back to pre-Norman times. In 1587 twopence was paid by households with man and wife, but a widow only paid a penny. The annual yield was ten shillings, unchanged since 1561, indicating a population of about 60 men at that time. Rising prices posed problems for the administrators of the manor because much of their revenue came from low fixed rents related to ancient customs. Annotated comments in the margin of a rental[18] (c. 1561) indicate that the authorities considered that rents should be increased steeply - from ten shillings to forty shillings in the case of David ap Jevan alias Taillour, who leased a house, barn and seven acres where Ty Petr now stands.

Figure 35: Drawing of Llangynidr Church as it appears in the Tretower Manorial Survey of 1587.

Figure 36: Coat of Arms of the Price family of Aberhoywe, first recorded on the wall memorial of Jevan Thomas Price, 1639.

To address the problem of inflation, the Earl of Worcester commissioned a survey[19] to record all his assets in the Manors of Crickhowell and Tretower (as Straddewy was known from this time). This handsome volume, dated 1587, rather like a local Domesday Book, gives details of the lord's sources of revenue, records the boundaries of the upland commons and maps the parcels of land leased to tenants who had indentures. These maps were probably the first to be produced to a consistent and accurate scale. In Llangynidr they show only the property formerly held by David Jevan ap Hoell hyer (probably hir meaning tall) which had reverted to the manor by escheat as a result of his conviction for some serious offence prior to 1456. His lands were extensive, and, as adjacent landscape features or buildings are shown on the plans, a rare portrait of a Welsh village in Tudor times is provided. Llangynidr Church is shown with a buttressed tower of two storeys surmounted by a pitched roof. (see Figure 35) Comparison of the details on these maps with surviving buildings indicates that they were accurately depicted. It has been possible to trace all the 1587 holdings as sufficient hedgerows had survived until 1845 to be able to locate the fields on the parish tithe map.

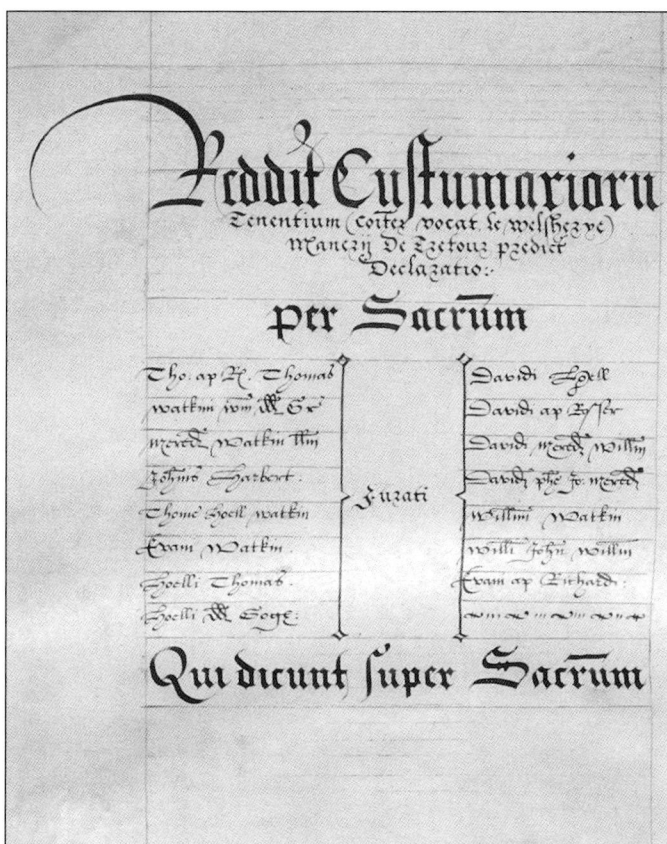

Figure 37: Welsh Jury for the 1587 Manorial Survey. Thomas Rice ap Thomas, father of Jevan Thomas Price, is at the top of the list. Number 8 is Howell David (Gogh) Blacksmith.

Figure 38: Plan of Coed yr Ynys from the 1587 Manorial Survey. At that time the common extended to some 80 acres. The old wooden Usk bridge is shown about 200m upstream of the present stone bridge.

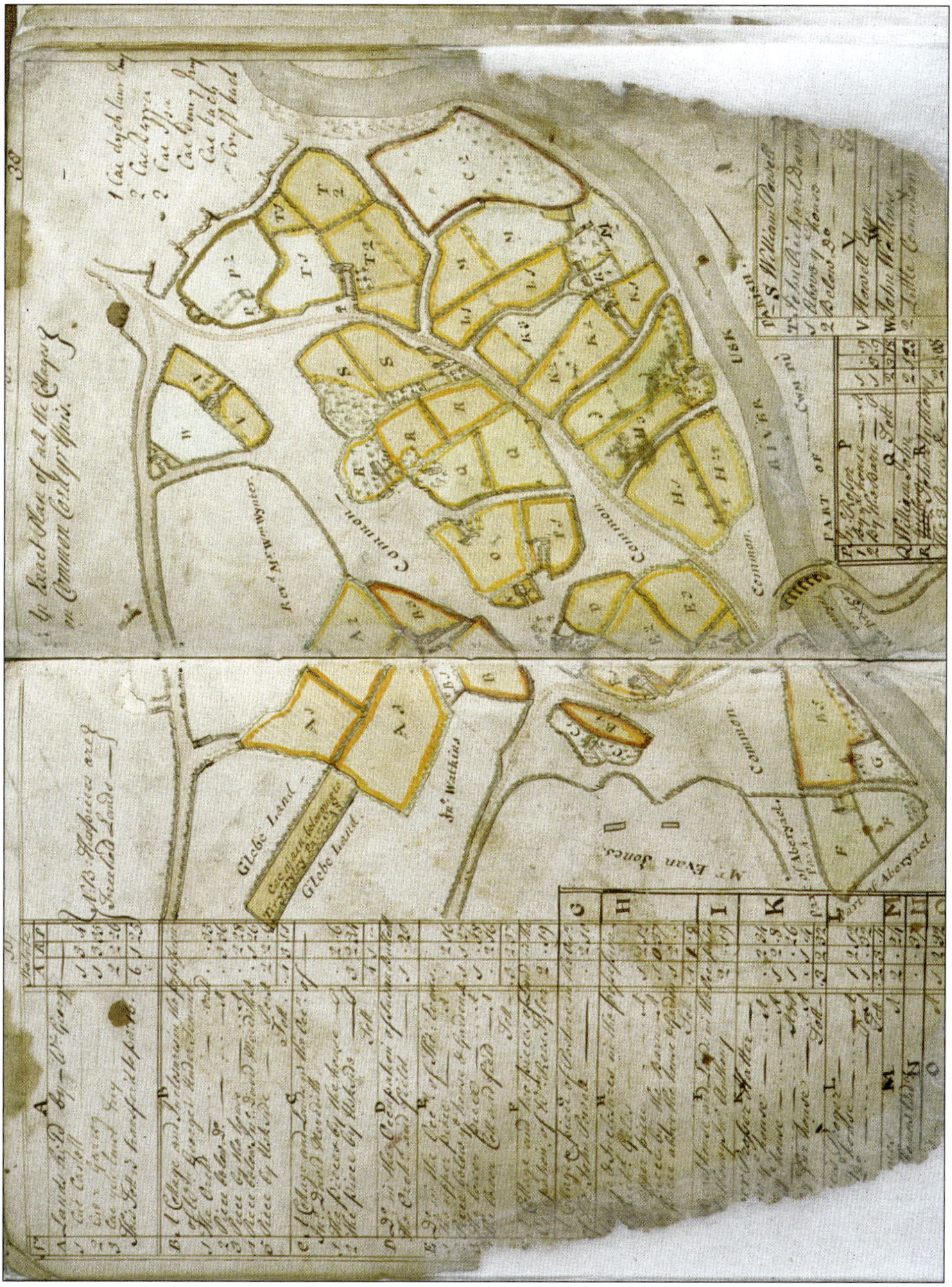

Figure 39: Coed yr Ynys from the 1760 Manorial Survey. By that date the common had disappeared under encroachments. A stone bridge with six arches is shown.

The Manor of Ystradyw

The survey lists both the free and the customary tenants in the parish, names their holdings and notes the annual rent and the cymorth which was paid on May 1st every third year. A jury of respected local farmers verified the information (see Figure 37). The cymorth, under Welsh law an obligatory gift, had been transformed by the Normans into a cattle due, which by this time had been commuted to a money payment. Although sheep-farming increased after the Black Death, cattle continued to be the mainstay of the Welsh agricultural economy. In the fourteenth century the cymorth payable by Welsh tenants in the lordship of Brecon amounted to 120 cows with calves. It is reported that 400 cattle were driven from Brecon to the de Bohun estates in Essex in 1349[20]. Originally levied on family groups, the cymorth seems to have survived in an older form in the neighbouring parish of Llangattock in the Manor of Crickhowell where, about 1560, groups of between 3 and 18 tenants combined to raise a 10s tax for the 'family' cow[21]. In Llangynidr the rate was much lower and only nineteen shillings and sixpence three farthings in total was levied in 1587. The cymorth, a long-established form of extortion, had been illegal since the Act of Union 1536-42, but seems to have continued long afterwards and was still being paid by local Welsh tenants as late as 1675. According to a rental survey of 1561, leirwyte, a payment made when a daughter was married, was still being imposed on customary tenants at that time.

Annual rents of Welsh (customary) tenants ranged from three farthings to fourteen pence, but the size of the farms is not given. Most holdings are named after previous tenants e.g. Tire Ryce Thomas ap Jevan Meyricke and are difficult to locate without other clues. A few, such as Tir Lloyn Kellwyn, farmed by Philip John William with annual rent of twopence, and Keven Krige held by David Meredith with a rent of twopence halfpenny, have names which have lasted to present times. Rents were payable in three instalments, at the feasts of St Michael, St Andrew and the Annunciation of the Blessed Virgin Mary. By 1587 most of the customary tenants held their land by copyhold and the distinction between free and customary tenants had become blurred. Many of the customary tenants had freehold land and some leased additional land from the manor. Only three men in Llangynidr were officially listed as free tenants. The numbers of free and customary tenants in Llangynidr and some neighbouring parishes is shown in the table below.

Tenants in local parishes

Parish	Customary tenants	Free tenants
Llangynidr	68	3
Llanfihangel Cwmdu	42	41
Crickhowell[22]	3	42
Llangattock	38	31

The high proportion of customary tenants in Llangynidr is probably a reflection of its topography, comparative remoteness from the castle and being part of the Welshry; all but two of the local people had Welsh names. The escheat of David Jevan's land had allowed the manor to lease it on more profitable terms. Twenty five customary tenants now held parcels of this land by indentures, mostly for periods of twenty one years, allowing more frequent increases in rent. Earlier leases had usually been for periods of forty years or even longer. Until 1584 one holding at the top of Cwm Claisfer, including a meadow called 'Gworlod y come' had been rented by Thomas ap Thomas and William John Williams, who had inherited an indenture dating from the first year of the reign of King Richard III (1484)[23]. All these holdings are shown on coloured plans which indicate the fields of each tenant using symbols (see Figures 31, 33 and 41).

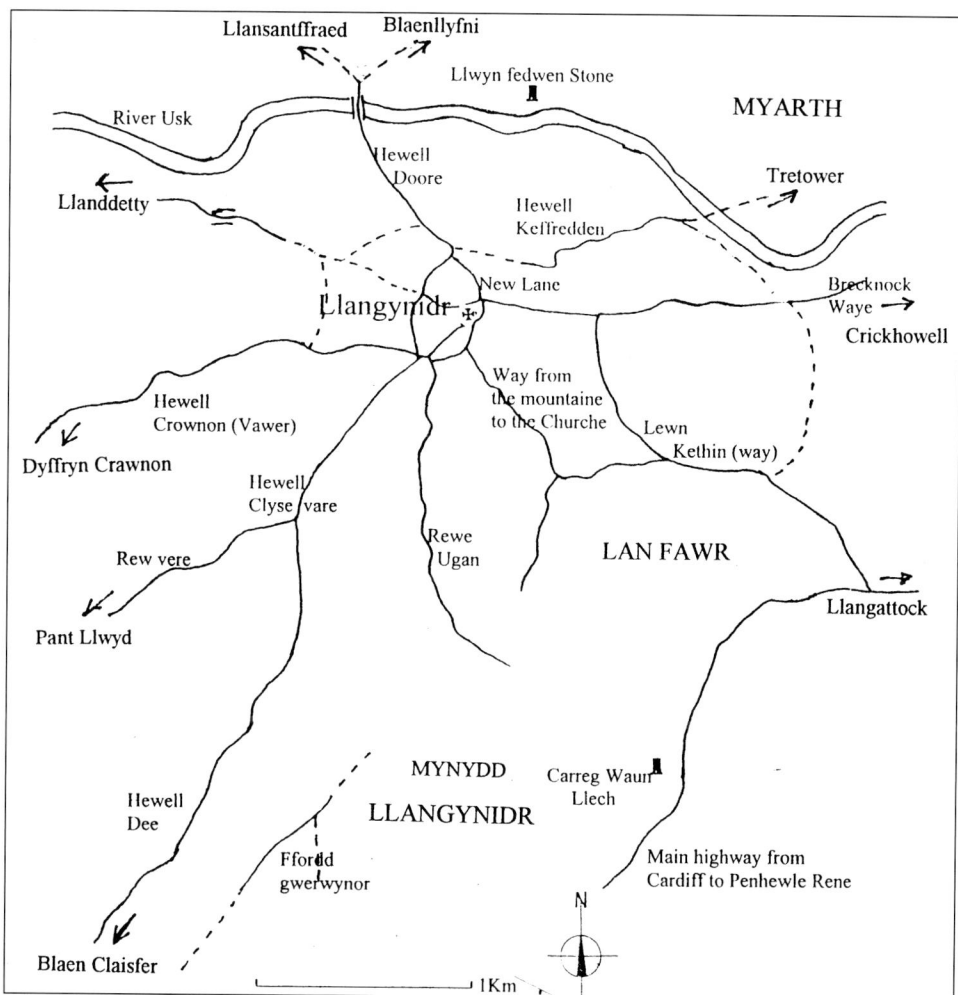

Figure 40: Sketch map of Llangynidr showing the roads named in the 1587 Manorial Survey. Hewell Olenith and Pen Rhiw Gedecke which led from Hewell Crawnon to the open hill, are omitted.

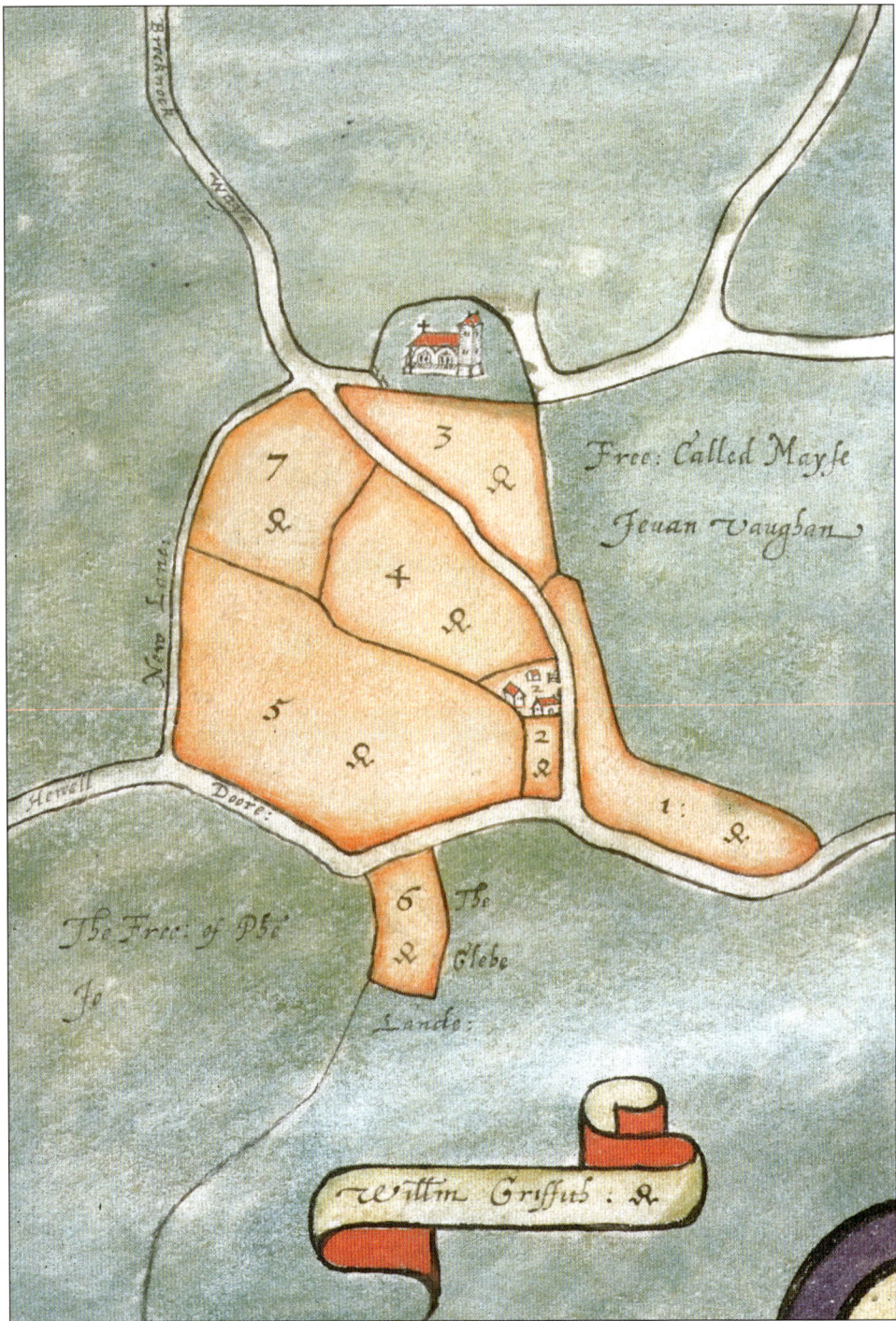

Figure 41: The church and a holding called Ter Carn Bobre, based on the present-day Glanyrafon ground, are shown in this plan from the 1587 Manorial Survey.

On these maps there are names which survive to the present day, such as 'Bryn Becky' fields near Pentwyn Farm and 'Ter y Gloge vawre' in Dyffryn Crawnon. Fields were generally much smaller than they are today: Thomas David Maddock had twelve fields in his fifteen acre holding near Waun-ddu, and there were eight fields on the thirteen acres of Ter Carne Bobre (see Figure 41) on the site of the present Glanyrafon. Fields of over ten acres were exceptional and usually known as coed caeau (*wood-pastures*). Indenture details are set out in tables. All the tenants had to provide two capons (fat hens) each year. These presumably finished up on the dining table at Raglan Castle where, in 1630, it is said 150 people were fed each day. A heriot (best beast or implement) was demanded if a tenant sold his lease or died. Significantly, the column allocated for labour services has been left blank, so probably these had been commuted to money payments. In a column marked 'surplussage' the difference between the new accurate measures of land and the amount recorded in the indenture is noted. Rice Thomas ap Rice was actually leasing 22 acres at Ter Maes Cabalva instead of the 10 noted in his indenture. Holdings ranged in size from 3-46 acres and 75% had houses on them. Rents were considerably higher than those of the other customary tenants, ranging from 5d to 3s 9d per acre. Where comparisons are possible, the annual rents appear to have doubled between 1561 and 1587, e.g. that for Ter Maes Cabalva had risen from 10d to 1s 8d per acre. This holding was situated beside Cyffredin Lane which led to a ford across the River Usk and on via common land over the Myarth to Tretower. As this was the most direct route to the manorial court the lane was probably very busy in medieval times. Ter Maes Cabalva (see Figure 33) was leased by the Price family of Aberhoywe from 1533 until about 1650. The 1583 indenture of Rice Thomas ap Rice[24] required him to do suit of mill and to take his horses or oxen to plough the lord's land; failure to comply could result in a fine of 10 shillings for the former and 20 shillings for the latter offence. The suit of mill dispute[25] in 1675 (see page 60), focused on the former service. Was the labour service still enforced, or is this merely a vestigial legal phrase? The practice fell into abeyance during the Civil War, but the lord was still trying to reinstate the custom in 1766.

The total income from rents in Tretower Manor in 1587 was £86 10s 6¼d; a rise of 79% compared with 1561, which was largely due to increases in the annual rents of the tenants with indentures. Manorial income was furthered bolstered from 1622 when a coal rent was introduced. In 1628 this amounted to £15 12s 0d. Jevan Thomas Price (grandson of Rice Thomas ap Rice), had to pay 6 loads of coal or 4s depending on the wishes of the lord. Each load was of 2 bushels and the coal had to be delivered to Raglan Castle each summer[26]. Livestock prices, as shown in local inventories, also provide a measure of inflation in the late sixteenth and early seventeenth century, and help to put rents and fines into perspective. Between 1575 and 1640 the average price of oxen increased from £1 to £1 6s 8d, the price of cows rose from 15s to £1 8s 0d. and sheep from 1s to 2s 6d.

Additional income came from the heriots and fines imposed in the court. This had been an important source of income for the manor for centuries; it is recorded that more than half the revenue of the Brecon lordship in 1398 came from court issues and 'occasional' penalties. Four sessions of the Tretower court between Michaelmas 1572 and April 1573 produced a total of £7 17s 3½d according to the bailiff's account[27]. The courts dealt with a wide range of matters from tax collection to the imposition of fines for offences such as assault, trespass, or encroachment. The fines recorded were not necessarily those actually levied, as Affeerers appointed from each parish had the task of adjusting the fines. In October 1572, William Thomas was fined 6d for carrying a knife in court. Howell Llewelin was fined 2/- for insulting and assaulting Philip ap Jevan; the following court saw dishonours even as Philip was fined the same amount for 'getting his own back' on Howell. At the same court, thirty villagers were fined 6d each for playing illegal games - possibly gambling or playing games on Sundays. Four of them appear to have been engaged in an early form of 'Fives', often played against church walls with consequent risk of damage to the church fabric. Eleven Llangynidr villagers, including David John Tailor (Ty Petr), Evan ap Watkin (Aberyail) and James Higgins (Tyle-bach) had been involved in an unspecified ball game, 'lusit ad globos', in the churchyard. The game might have been skittles, stool-ball (a fore-runner of cricket) or football, which at this time was a ferocious game which had few rules but could involve an unlimited number of players and last all day. In 1572 eleven people, including John Gunter and Thomas Philip from Llangynidr, were presented in court for keeping taverns and selling beer illegally 'quia custodit taberna et vendit cerevisium illic contra forma statuti'. Seven were fined 3d each but four, including John Williams clerk, were not, presumably because they had the licences required under the Alehouse Act of 1552. Immediately afterwards another thirty eight people were fined for playing illegal games - in this case probably gambling games in the tavern. In 1609 four Llangynidr alehouse keepers were presented for 'unlawful measures and unlawful games'; Rosser David had the additional charge of playing cards[28]. Top of the list on this and other occasions was Watkin William alias Smith. Watkin William the Blacksmith lived somewhere between the playing field and the old village school. 'Ero Gove', Smith's Acre, which probably belonged to his father, is shown on a plan in the 1587 Badminton Estate Survey (see Figure 33) near Aberyail and two fields away there is ' Kayr Oden' (Kiln Field) which may have been the site of an ancient smithy. In 1630 the Blacksmith sold his house and 9 acres of land to Thomas Vaughan of Llansantffraed (father of Henry Vaughan the Silurist) and Jevan Thomas Price (Aberhoywe). The sale deeds[29] contain the first reference so far discovered to the 'New bridge upon the Uske', built sometime between 1587 and 1630 to replace the wooden bridge shown on the 1587 Survey about 200m upstream of the present Llangynidr Bridge (see Figure 51). Further wrongdoers reported to the courts in 1609-10 included Jonet verch Rees of Llangynidr for breaking the hedge of Nest verch John Meredeth, Howell John Howell of Llansantffraed for digging up and carrying away gorse from Cefn Moel and 17 Cwmdu parishioners, including William William, clerk, 'for bowlling being an unllawfull game viz bowles'.

The Forest of Myarth (see Figure 27) was the scene of many incidents recorded in the court rolls. In early medieval times the forest was probably reserved by the lord for hunting. It was protected for long afterwards, though it does not seem to have been managed primarily for timber production like Benny Wood near Brecon, which was maintained, properly fenced against stock, as a 'standards with coppice' wood in the sixteenth century[30]. There was a resident forester at Myarth in the fourteenth century. Evidence was produced at an inquiry in 1561[31] that from the time of King Richard II (1386-7) tenants had been fined for allowing their cattle and goats to trespass in the Forest of Myarth and that a forester had been employed to manage the wood. 'In the midst thereof doth yet remain the foster's house called Castle bagh and the remains of a great enclosure walled about it'. But even at this time the winter grazing was leased at 6s 8d per annum. In 1543 an indenture was granted to Meredeth ap Meredeth for 'the waste land called Myarth' allowing him all woods, timber and growing trees for 21 years at 40s yearly and a pair of capons at 'Neweyeres tyde'[32]. Others contributed to the clearance; in 1572 Edward Morgan was fined 6d "quia habuit capras in Miarthe", for keeping goats in Myarth, and Lewis Miller was fined 12d for cutting wood[33]. In the 1587 Survey the extent of the forest is recorded as 584 acres and it is noted that the tenants of Tretower paid 19s a year for the winter grazing. In 1588 the Earl of Worcester brought a suit against the Vaughans of Tretower in the Court of Star Chamber claiming rent for the grazing of Myarth Wood[34]. The Vaughans argued that it was common land and, as tenants, they had grazing and estover rights there. Although the outcome of this case is not known, it appears that by this time the forest was being treated like a common by the local people. A rearguard action was fought by the manorial authorities, as in 1609 widow Genett verch Bevan of Cwmdu was prosecuted for 'cutting five burdens of young okes in Myarth to the spoyle of the lord's wood'[35]. Encroachments of common or waste land seems to have become widespread practice by that time; in 1610 more than twenty people were presented in court for encroachments on the Myarth[36]. These took the form of small primitive houses erected overnight (Tai un nos), surrounded by enclosed plots of one or two acres of land. This type of development seems to have been condoned by the manorial authorities, presumably because the rents were a welcome source of revenue. From 1600 enclosure of common land gathered momentum. The 1760 Beaufort Estate map shows more than fifty smallholdings on the Myarth[37]. In 1587 only 13 houses (without gardens) are shown on Coed yr Ynys common, which extended over 80 acres between Cwm Crawnon and the western boundary of Aberyail (see Figure 38). There were no dwellings on the other small lowland common of thirteen acres at Cyffredin (see Figure 34). By 1760, when the next set of manorial maps was produced, both commons had been obliterated by enclosures, which must have caused hardship to the poorer smallholders who depended on common grazing to support their livestock. In 1299, John fitz Reginald, lord of Blaenllyfni, had conceded the right of common pasture, together with hunting and fishing rights, to his tenants in return for a payment of 100 marks (about £66)[38]. For centuries local farmers have depended on the summer pasturage afforded by the large upland commons.

The Manor of Ystradyw

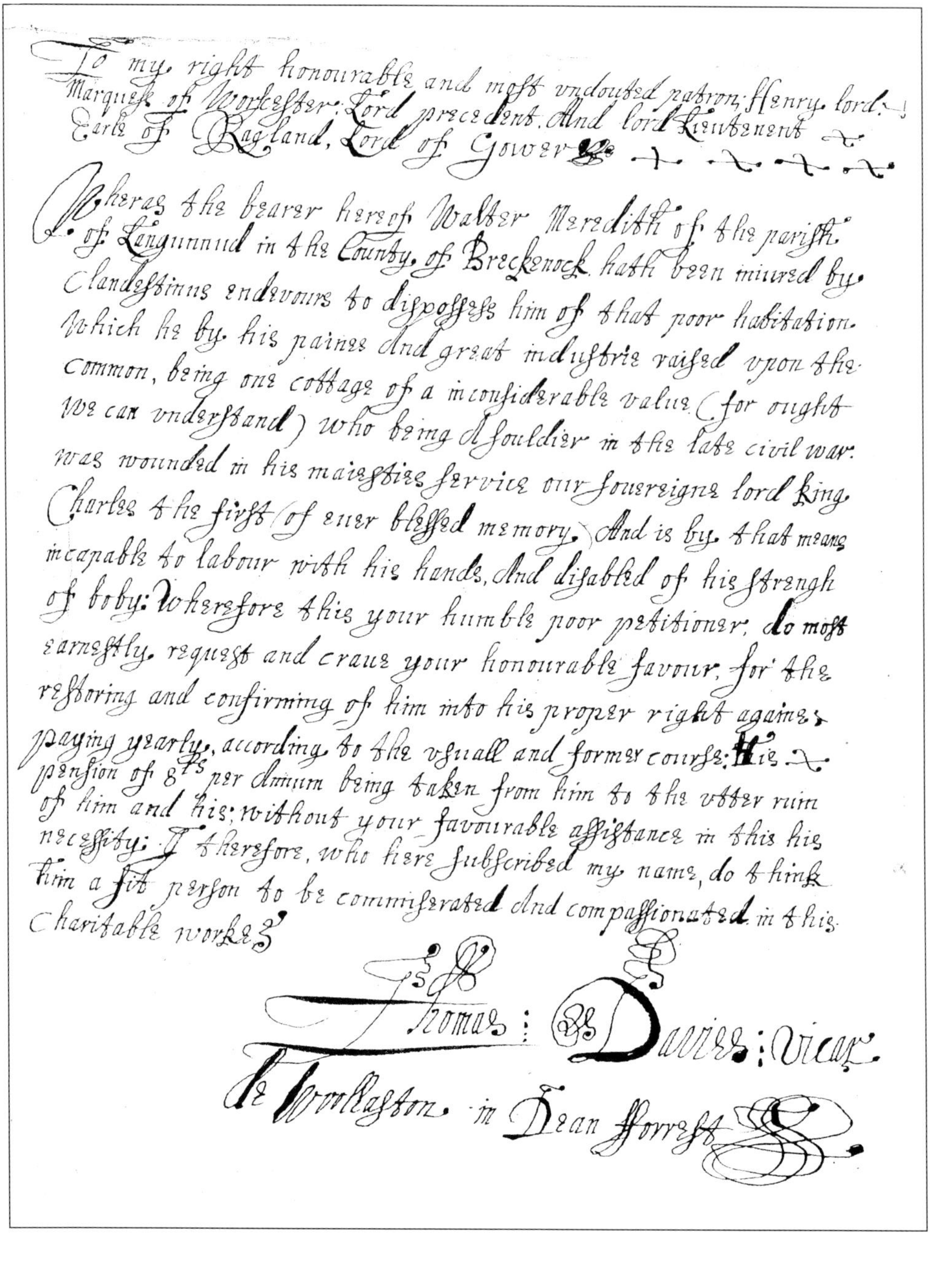

To my right honourable and most vndoubted patron, Henry, lord Marquess of Worcester, Lord president, And lord Lieutenant Earle of Ragland, Lord of Gower &c.

Wheras the bearer hereof Walter Meredith of the parish of Langunnud in the County of Breckenock hath been iniured by Clandestinus endevours to dispossess him of that poor habitation Which he by his paines And great industrie raised vpon the Common, being one cottage of a inconsiderable value (for ought We can vnderstand) who being a souldier in the late civil war was wounded in his maiesties service our soueraigne lord king Charles the first (of euer blessed memory) And is by that meanes incapable to labour with his hands, And disabled of his strength of boby: Wherefore this your humble poor petitioner, do most earnestly request and craue your honourable fauour, for the restoring and confirming of him into his proper right against paying yearly, according to the vsuall and former course: His pension of 8s per annum being taken from him to the vtter ruin of him and his, without your favourable assistance in this his necessity: I therefore, who here subscribed my name, do think him a fit person to be commiserated And compassionated in this Charitable workes

Thomas : Davies : Vicar.

de Woollaston in Dean fforrest

Figure 42: Petition of Llangynidr soldier injured in the Civil War.

It is clear from the detailed description of the bounds of the common on Mynydd Llangynidr in the Manorial Survey of 1587 that, even at this date, parts of the common near Penyrheol-rhyn had already been enclosed. By the early seventeenth century the livelihoods of many farmers were threatened by the gathering pace of encroachment. In the Tredegar collection of manuscripts at the National Library of Wales there is a petition drawn up for presentation to Parliament on behalf of farmers in fifteen parishes, including Llangynidr, in the region of the Black Mountains. The petitioners called for a halt to the encroachments and restoration of the land previously enclosed. Sir David Williams of Gwernyfed, formerly steward of the Manors of Crickhowell and Tretower, had bought over forty thousand acres of upland common from the Crown and allowed its piecemeal enclosure. According to the petitioners his estate was collecting £500 per year in rents. "By reason whereof your petitioners are greatly impoverished in their stock and estates and rendered unable to pay and discharge the great taxes and impositions imposed upon them and private cottages are daily raised on the same commons whereby your petitioners are greatly endamaged by the great numbers of vagrant beggars and other lewd persons residing thereupon".

It is apparent, from a study of contemporary wills and inventories, that by the end of the sixteenth century a wide gulf had opened up between the living standard of the smallholders and that of yeoman farmers like Jenet verch John and Jevan Thomas Price. The earliest local will to have survived is that of Meredith ap Higgin who died in 1574. Like many parishioners of that period, he had scraped a precarious living from the land. Meredith, like his father before him, had leased Tyle-bach, a holding of 8 acres in the Dyffryn Crawnon, for 13s 8d a year[39]. In his will he left £1 6s 8d and a hive of bees to his brother James Higgins and 4s 7d and the rest of his chattels to three other relatives. When James Higgins died in 1579 he left a cow, a heifer, three sheep and his 'household stuff', valued at 10 shillings, which consisted of a little brass pot, a pan, a shirt, a 'flyge' of bacon and two and three quarter yards of 'russet cloth'. The cloth suggests that he may have been a weaver or tailor. Even these meagre belongings might have seemed worth a fortune to the encroachers living in hovels on the Myarth. A petition drawn up by the Vicar of Woollaston in the Forest of Dean on behalf of Walter Meredith, a soldier from Llangynidr wounded in the Civil War, who had been evicted from his dwelling on the common is illustrated[40] (see Figure 42). At the opposite end of the scale was widow Jenet verch John who lived in the vicinity of Rhiwgarn. Nine local worthies, including Gwalter Thomas, were witnesses to her will, dated 1626, in which she bequeathed farms to three of her grandchildren. She also left 20 shillings a year to be distributed among the poor people of Llangynidr and Llanddetty. Jevan Thomas Price, whose coat of arms (see Figure 36) can be seen on the south wall of the nave in Llangynidr Church and above the front door at Aberhoywe, left 37 cattle, 240 sheep and 4 horses, as well as the 'swyne, geese and poultrie about the house' to be divided among his young family of four sons and four daughters. The daughters took turns to receive the rent from a smallholding called Tir Kay Allson in Dyffryn Crawnon for 14 years. Jevan Thomas Price died on 29th July 1639 just before harvest time, so the standing crops on the farm were noted. Although by this period sheep rearing had become an important part of the agricultural economy, substantial amounts of arable crops were still grown; 30 acres of wheat and rye valued at £15 and 50 acres of 'Barlie, oates and peasen' valued at £13 13s 4d were recorded in his informative inventory. Thomas, the eldest son, inherited the family farm and two other holdings, while the third son John was left Tir Kay Allson.

The Act of Union incorporated the Marcher lordships into the administrative Welsh counties, including the new shire of Brecon, and this, together with other legislative measures, reduced the dominance of the Marcher Lords. The Civil War further loosened their oppressive grasp. As the farmers became more prosperous there were signs of their growing impatience with the restrictions imposed by the manorial regime. Locally this frustration surfaced in 1675 in a dispute regarding suit of mill between the Lord of Tretower, then Henry, Marquis of Worcester, and three substantial farmers and owners of mills, Giles Nicholas, Rector of Llangynidr, Henry Williams and Rice Price[41]. The lord complained that the tenants were not bringing their corn to be ground at his mill, as he claimed they should, and so he was losing the toll charged on the process. He had lost all his evidence of the manorial customs in 'ye late troubles', as he called the Civil War. The farmers claimed that their land was held not by customary or Welsh tenure but by soccage and so they paid rents but were not required to do services such as suit of mill. Unless tenants had been forced to take their grain to Cwmdu for grinding, it would appear that suit of mill had been in abeyance for several years, for, as Henry Williams pointed out, there had not been a manorial mill operating in Llangynidr for a long time. In fact, the whole affair seems to have been a cunning scheme devised by Edmond Jones of Buckland, who had bought Felin-genol, the mill in this dispute, from William Phillip Powell, who lived at what is now Tyr William Richard. Because trade was poor, there followed a game of 'pass the parcel' between Edmond Jones and the lord in which the mill changed hands three times in three days, finishing with Edmond having leased Felin-genol from the lord for 99 years at 1d a year. Meantime the lord instituted proceedings to enforce suit of mill by the tenants. The skullduggery was not all on one side. During the case it emerged that, in the past, it had been the practice of local millers to rent the lord's mill and let it fall into decay while they carried on normal business at their own mill. As two witnesses on behalf of the lord expressed it 'the plaintiff's mills within the manor were always frowardly farmed by those that had mills of their own'.

The changes initiated by the legislation of the Tudors brought greater independence to local people, although strong links with the manor survived. Llangynidr remained essentially a farming community and the pattern of agriculture and way of life which had evolved changed only slowly during the next two hundred years.

References

Carr, A D, *Medieval Wales*
Cooke, M, *The Family of Picard*
Davies, J, *A History of Wales*
Davies, R R, *Lordship and Society in the Marches of Wales (1282-1400)*
Davies, R R, *Conquest, Coexistence and Change in Wales (1063-1415)*
Jones, Theophilus, *A History of the County of Brecknock*
Ralegh Radford, C A, Tretower Court: The Castle and the Court, in *Brycheiniog VI*
Redwood, P, Crickhowell Manor in 1587, in *Brycheiniog XXIX*
Rees, W, The Medieval Lordship of Brecon, in *Transactions of the Honourable Society of Cymmrodorion*
Rees, W, *A Historical Atlas of Wales*

Notes

1   A cantref was an administrative area, subdivided into commotes (cymydau). Before the conquest the kingdom of Brycheiniog contained three cantrefs, of which Talgarth was the easternmost.
2   Davies, J, *A History of Wales*
3   *Arch Camb IV*, xiv p 168
4   NLW Badminton 379, 380
5   Cal. Charter Rolls (1294, 1298) noted in Rees, W, *The Medieval Lordship of Brecon*. See also Ralegh Radford, Tretower Court: The Castle and Court, *Brycheiniog VI*, p 12
6   Ibid
7   Cal. Inquisitions Edward I, iv 352, quoted in Cooke, M, *The Family of Picard*
8   The Taxatio was an assessment of annual church income, made between 1288-1291. Pope Nicholas IV had granted a tithe of this to Edward I for six years to help finance an expedition to the Holy Land. Jones, T, *History of the County of Brecknock*
9   Carr, A D, *Medieval Wales*
10 NLW Badminton 2287
11 NLW Badminton 7295
12 NLW Badminton 58
13 NLW Badminton 72
14 The Valor Ecclesiasticus of Henry VIII at British Museum recorded the value of the ecclesiastical establishment in England and Wales in 1536. A translation of the section relating to parishes in Breconshire and Radnorshire parishes in the diocese of St. Davids is given in Lloyd, J, *Historical Memoranda of Breconshire*, Vol II, pp 21-37
15 NLW Penpont 711
16 For further details on population, see page 193

...continued

Notes continued

17 This unpopular tax was introduced by Act of Parliament in 1662. Every householder owning property worth 20s a year or more was liable for a payment of 2s for each fireplace or stove in the house. The statute was repealed in 1689.

18 NLW Badminton 394

19 NLW Badminton 3

20 Rees, W, Calendar of Ancient Petitions quoted in Carr, A D, *Medieval Wales*, p 97

21 NLW Badminton 392

22 Redwood, P, Crickhowell Manor in 1587, *Brycheiniog XXIX*, p 29, gives figures for the parishes in Crickhowell Manor, and further discussion

23 NLW Badminton 405

24 NLW Badminton 6633

25 NLW Badminton 7722

26 NLW Badminton 411, 412

27 NLW Badminton 25

28 NLW Badminton 58

29 NLW Maybery 6987

30 Lloyd, J, *Historical Memoranda of Breconshire*, Vol 1, p 156

31 NLW Badminton 402

32 NLW Badminton 408

33 NLW Badminton 25

34 NLW Badminton 163,164

35 NLW Badminton 58

36 NLW Badminton 58

37 NLW Badminton 7

38 Davies, R R, *Lordship and Society in the Marches of Wales*, p 105

39 NLW Badminton 405; for his father's lease see Badminton 408

40 NLW Badminton 12850

41 NLW Badminton 6715-6724 (inc), 7713

Persondy Field - recent research

Dorothea Watkins first noted irregularities in the field surface in the 1970s and reported a visual survey to CADW in 1984, along with pottery fragments from the field dating from the thirteenth century.

Helen Burnham has interpreted the surface topography in her *Guide to Ancient and Historic Wales, Clwyd Powys* (HMSO) as a group of house platforms with associated gardens.

Members of the Llangynidr Local History Society carried out a careful topographic survey under the guidance of Glyn Smith and magnetic and resistance surveys using specialist equipment provided and supervised by David Jordan of Terra Nova (see

Figure 43). This work was carried out in August 1997 under the supervision of Mr Peter Dorling of the Brecon Beacons National Park and funded by a grant from them.

Figure 43: The Persondy Field investigation unit, 1998.

Part of the ground surveyed has two substantial lengths of earthing cable buried in connection with two power supply poles and transformer; their effect on the magnetic survey was considerable.

The summarised results of the surveys is shown in Figure 185. The topographical study matches Helen Burnham's conclusions but the combined resistivity and magnetic surveys suggest that there may have been as many as five platforms on the site. It is hoped that these other two sets of observations will help in the choice of the best locations for archaeological excavation at some future date.

Figure 44: Tarren Gwyn. A limestone cliff at the head of the Dyffryn Crawnon - a landmark in the sixteenth century.

Figure 45: The entrance to the sixteenth century cider cellar at Tretower Court.

Chapter 3

Place names of Llangynidr

Names of fields, farms and topographical features can provide clues about the history of a place and its people, but the interpretation of old names is a hazardous process. Nowadays fields are generally only referred to as numbers on Ordnance Survey maps, but less than a hundred years ago nearly all the fields in our parish had Welsh names which were sometimes several centuries old. Many of those referred to here were first recorded in Tretower manorial documents of the sixteenth century, but the parish tithe map (1842) has been another useful source. Most of the earliest recorded names were written down by English clerks who did not speak Welsh, at a time when spelling was inconsistent, and it can be difficult to work out their meaning. A field marked **Erw siog** on the tithe map is seen on a Church terrier (1720) to be **Erw Drissoge** (probably **dyrysiog**) (*difficult or intricate acre*), perhaps because it was overgrown with brambles. **Chwech Llath** (*Six yard field*) on an estate map (1760) became **Church Llath** on the tithe map! The lane from the upper village to the mountain near Blaen Onneu was called **Rewe Ugan,** probably from **Rhiw y garn** *(Cairn Lane)*, in the sixteenth century. At that time the mountain above was called **Pen y Garn**. The lane became **Rewe Owgan** in the next century and **Heol Wogan** by 1760.

River names are usually very old and their meanings obscure; that of the River Usk (*Afon Wysg*) dates back at least to the twelfth century and probably means *'River abounding in fish'*.[1] Both the Claisfer and its tributary the Hoywy probably derive their names from obsolete Welsh words for stream. In the sixteenth century the former was written as **Clyse Vayr** (spelt in various ways), possibly derived from Clais Fair (*St Mary's stream*). It is thought that St Mary was introduced by the Normans as an additional patron saint, to accompany the native St Cynidr, to confer greater respectability on the parish church. The Ail or Yail may be derived from the old Welsh 'iail' (*choked with reeds*). The earliest reference which has come to light for the name of the church is **Egluseyll**, a corruption of **Eglwys Yail** (*The church by the Yail*), in the 'Taxatio Ecclesiastica' of Pope Nicholas IV (1291). The name is curious as the church is actually closer to the River Claisfer. It is possible that there was an earlier church nearer the Yail, or perhaps the stream was diverted away from the church along a section of the old road **Heol Dwr** (*Watery Lane*), which is now part of the course of the Yail. Both **Eglwys Yail** and Llangynidr (spelt in many ways), either separately or in combination, e.g. **Llangynydr Egloyesyoll** (1561), were used in the sixteenth century. In later times Llangynidr became established as the parish name, which, as Theophilus Jones commented in 1809, "the inhabitants pronounce Llangynid (sounding the y like the English u in gun)".

The river which for centuries formed the boundary between the parishes of Llanddetty and Llangynidr was written as **Crawnon** or **Crownon** in sixteenth century documents. Its derivation is uncertain; both Garwnant (*rocky stream*) and Crafnant (*wild garlic stream*) have been suggested, and both would be appropriate. The Dyfnant (*deep stream or ravine*) provides the boundary with Llangattock parish to the east. At the end of the nineteenth century it was written **Dunvant**, which is what some local people call it nowadays. Dunvant, near Swansea, has undergone the same transformation of its name.

Some old names have become distorted and meaningless, like **Origey** a field in the east of the parish, but if a name is traced back to an earlier form its meaning can sometimes be discovered. A small holding, now part of Pentwyn Farm, has been known as **Bryn Becky** since 1587. However, in Watkin Meredeth's lease of 1527 it is called **Bryn Bage**, perhaps a corruption of Bryn Bach (*Little Hill*). Alternatively, the significance of a name may have been lost. The event commemorated by **Reyd y Millwr** (*Soldiers' Ford*) at the head of the River Rhymney, where the lordships of Tretower, Penkelly and Senghenydd met, has been long forgotten. Likewise names may have been lost. The limestone cliff at the head of Dyffryn Crawnon, damaged by irresponsible rock-blasting c.1941, was known as **Tarwen Gwin** (Tarren Gwyn) (*White Cliff*) in the sixteenth century (see Figure 44).

Enough old landmarks have survived to trace the extent of the large upland common on Llangynidr Mountain recorded in detail in 'The Bounder of the Common of Langenider', part of the manorial survey of 1587. Some boundary marks are still obvious, like the standing stone then called **Mayen Gwayne y Lleth** (now Carreg Waun Llech) (*The Stone of the Moorland of Flat Stones*), which still stands on moorland south of Twyn Disgwylfa (*Look-out Hill*) (see Figure 11).

Another ancient boundary mark, formerly situated about one km to the south of Carreg Waen Llech, was **Crosse Jevan Husman**. This was a pile of rocks about a foot high in the form of a cross at a place where the boundary between Llangynidr and Llangattock met the 'hyghway leading from Cardiff to Penhewle Rene' - Pen Heol Rhyn (*The Top of the Hill Road*). Archdeacon Payne (1759-1832), who provided Theophilus Jones with much local information for his 'History of the County of Brecknock', recorded that in 1759 there had been a dispute between the two parishes about the sheepwalks and the exact line of the boundary. A riotous gathering of Llangynidr men had destroyed Jevan Husman's Cross, swearing that it marked only the burial place of a red cow![2]

More than a thousand field names have been recorded from the parish, covering the period from 1500 to 1845. About a hundred names refer to field sizes, such as **Cae Bach** (*Small Field*) or **Wrlod Mawr** (*Large Meadow*), or rarely more precisely **Cae Pymp Llath** (*Five 'Yard' Field*). (In earlier times llath was a measuring stick about 14 feet in length). Some names describe the shape of the field; **Cae Main** (*Narrow Field*) or **Cae Cam** (*Crooked Field*). Many note some feature in the field such as

Wrlod Ffynnon (*Spring Meadow*), **Erw bant** (*Acre with the hollow*), **Cae Quarrel (Chwarel)** (*Quarry Field*) or **Cae Llewyber (Llwybr)** (*Field with footpath*). Certain names reflect the quality of the fields, such as **Cae Gwyn** (*Fair or Sunny Field*) and **Cae Poeth** (*Warm Field*); **Erw Ddu** (*Black Acre*) might refer to a shady field or one with dark, peaty soil. The disparaging **Cae Pwdwr** (*Rotten Field*) was applied to three fields which were probably of a boggy nature. In more than a hundred names the position of the field in relation to the house or other feature such as a barn is indicated e.g. **Wrlod dan Scybour Isaf** (*Meadow below the lower barn*). Uchaf (*higher/highest*), isaf (*lower/lowest*) and cenol (*middle*) are included in about seventy names to locate fields with reference to others with a similar name or function.

The frequency of names containing the elements **gorof** (*wooded bank*), **coed cae** (*wood pasture*) or **wern** (*alder swamp or marshy ground*) suggests that the local landscape was more wooded in former times. Nearly all our native trees figure in local place names, though oak is most commonly encountered; **Llwynderi** (*Oak Grove*), **Coed Llwyfin** (*Elm Wood*), **Llwyncelyn** (*Holly Grove*), **Cae'r Helig** (*Willow Field*), **Ffynnon Ddraenen** (*Spring by the hawthorns*) , **Cae Collwng Gunter Issa** (*Lower hazel field of Gunter*) and **Cae Bedw** (*Birch Field*) are examples. **Caerhisgl** (*Bark Field*) indicates that this former smallholding in Dyffryn Crawnon was involved in the harvesting of oak bark, used in tanning leather. In his diary (24th April 1872) Rev Francis Kilvert recorded the harvesting of oak bark in Clyro Woods. Later (4th July 1872) he noted that a Scotsman had accumulated an enormous stack of oak bark, said to be worth £6,000, at Hay Station. **Caer Ffawydd** (*Beech Field*) near Pant-teg suggests that the natural range of Beech extended to our area and this is confirmed by other 'beech' place names in the south-east of Breconshire. Smaller plants only made an impression when in quantity, such as on **Twyn y Rhicos** (*Heathery Hill*), **Ero Heske** (*Rushy Acre*) and **Cae Ysgallog** (*Thistle Field*) - the latter no doubt enjoyed by earlier generations of goldfinches in Dyffryn Crawnon. A field near Aberyail called **Cae y Reden** in 1532 might be translated as *Ferny Field*, but the presence in the same area of **Kayr Oden** (*Kiln Field*) in 1587 illustrates one of the problems involved in the interpretation of old names.

Colours in names may also be a guide to vegetation; **Bryn Melyn** (*Yellow Hill*) was probably inspired by tracts of gorse and **Wyrlod Goch** (*Red Meadow*) may have been prompted by the soil colour or a profusion of sorrel in the hay. **Wrlod** (various spellings) (*meadow*), often signifying rich, low-lying land, is in eighty local field names but is absent from field names in south-west Breconshire, according to Mr R F P Powell. In contrast, gwaun (waun), usually spelt 'wain' locally, described a mountain pasture or moorland. These were often on black, peaty soils, hence **Wain Ddu**. Arable crops, because of their transitory nature, are not recorded in field names. Several farms had small orchards, indicated by such names as **Cae'r Berllan** or **Coed Cae Perllan**, and a large orchard of about eight acres **Tire y Berllan** formed part of the church glebe in 1720. Probably these were mainly cider orchards, following the example of Tretower Court where there was a large orchard in 1587 and a cider cellar was built in the sixteenth century[3]. A cider cellar at Aberhoywe dates from about 1640 (see illustration on page 64).

Wild animals are rarely recorded in local place names. The track from Claisfer Lane past Pantllwyd-isaf to the mountain is marked on the manorial survey of 1587 as **Rew Vere (Rhiw Veri)** (*Kite Lane*). Kites were common birds-of-prey in medieval times. After a long period of persecution in Britain, they were close to extinction until thirty years ago. On rare occasions in recent years single birds have been seen near Llangynidr. Perhaps soon the red kite may return to breed and its effortless flight grace the skies above the village as it did four hundred years ago. **Gwirlod Vadrynge** (*Fox Meadow*) existed in 1587, but has not been pinpointed. **Nant y Wenynen** (*Stream of the Bees*) is a tributary of the River Crawnon. Bees were important in the domestic economy before sugar was readily available and wall recesses(boles) for housing straw bee-skeps can still be seen at Neuadd, Pantllwyd-isaf and Glaisfer-uchaf.

Figure 46: Bee boles in the wall of a barn at Y Neuadd. Each bole held a straw skep with a colony of bees.

Llwynyreos (*Nightingale Grove*) is a farm at the foot of Tor y Foel. Nightingales no longer breed in Breconshire and have been recorded only occasionally during the past century. According to 'The Birds of Breconshire' the last record of nesting birds was at Glangrwyney in 1926[4].

Livestock is well-represented in field names. The importance of cattle in the local economy in earlier times is demonstrated by the abundance of names like **Cae Dych**

Lawr Ty (*Oxfield below the house*). Fifty six field names incorporating the corrupt element **'dych lawr'** have been noted in parish records. **Llanerchybeudy** (*Glade of the Cowhouse*) is a farm in Dyffryn Crawnon; on the other side of the valley is **Nant y Llaethdy** (*Stream of the Dairy*) which gave its name to two sixteenth century farmhouses, **Nantyllaethdy-issa** and **Nantyllaethdy-ycha**. They illustrate one of the problems involved in tracing the history of old dwellings. On the manorial surveys of 1587 and 1760 both houses are shown, the former on the east bank of the stream two fields above **Heol Crawnon**, and the latter high on the hillside near the mountain wall. Nant y Llaethdy Ycha was deserted before 1840, although the site is marked on later maps as Tyle-uchaf. Nant y Llaethdy Issa continued as Nant y Llaethdy, but later in the nineteenth century exchanged names with **Tir Howell Sais** *(The land of Howell the Englishman)*, on the west bank of the stream. (see Figure 141)

From about 1890 the original Nantyllaethdy-issa has been known as **Penwaun** (*Top of the Meadow*). All three farms are now in ruins. Referring to the upper regions of Dyffryn Crawnon there is a comment on a manorial survey of 1760 "The coedgaes are on the upperside so steep that it is impossible for any Beasts except sheep and goats to climb them". Several field names such as **Coed Gae Gavir (Gafr)** (*Wood Pasture of Goats*) support that claim. **Llwyn y March** (*Horse Grove*) at the head of Cwm Claisfer is a rare example of horses appearing in a place name, and surprisingly, no names featuring sheep have been noticed. Evidence of the former practice of transhumance, when a farmer's household and livestock moved up to the hills for the summer, survives in field names from the sixteenth century such as **Kay Havod Vawre** (*Field of the large summer dwelling*). The hill called **Havott**, marked east of Clog-fawr on the 1587 manorial survey, might indicate the site of earlier summer homes. Usually the main homestead or winter home (*hendre*) would have been in a more sheltered site at a lower altitude, which makes the name **Hendre Crawnon**, for the area on the hill above the Crawnon waterfall, a puzzle. **Carn y Bugail** (*Shepherd's Cairn*), on moorland nearby, (see Figure 20) recalls the days when flocks of sheep were closely guarded. In former times most of the people were involved in agriculture or ancillary occupations. **Erw Gof** (*Smith's Acre*), near Aberyail, and **Cae dan yr Evel** (Field below the Smithy), now Groesffordd, record the activities of blacksmiths, once important figures in the community. **Tir y Odyn** (*Kiln Land*) and **Kay'r Oden** (*Kiln Field*) were probably associated with blacksmiths rather than lime production. "The great limekiln", another sixteenth century parish boundary mark, which was situated on Mynydd Llangynidr, just over 2km (412 perches in 1587) south of the source of the River Crawnon, indicates that lime was being produced at this remote place over four hundred years ago.

Another important figure at that time was the miller. **Wrlod Velen** (*Mill Meadow*) and **Wern Velen** (*Mill Swamp*) belonged to Llangynidr Mill which had operated from medieval times but closed down in the nineteen thirties. Below the mill on the east bank of the River Claisfer was a field called **Cae Cawen** on the tithe map. This is possibly a corruption of **Cae Cowyn** (*Plague Field*) and linked with the desertion of the medieval village site on Persondy field on the other side of the river. **Wrlod Pound** (*Pound Meadow*), near Pont Ganol, was the field where stray animals were penned. There was an older pound beside **Heol Rhiwgarn** where 'The Garth' now stands and, at the end of the nineteenth century, there was a pound near the church, in what is now the garden of Cynidr House. The manorial regime is recalled by **Tyr yr Arlwydd** (*Lord's Land*), a smallholding which preceded Pen y Garn, and **Kay Mayle** (*Lord's Field*) at the bottom of Pant Llwyd track. In the sixteenth century three fields on the east side of Cyffredin Lane formed a holding called **Tyre Mase Cabalva** (*Land of the field by the ford or ferry*), referring to the crossing of the River Usk below the islands near Worcester Cottage.

Figure 47: Cyffredin Lane, near the Usk ford which led across to the Myarth - common land before its enclosure in 1856.

With a few notable exceptions, present farm names appear to be no older than the eighteenth century. Before that most holdings were named after previous tenants and names changed frequently. Some villagers became 'fossilised' in farm names; Dafydd Peter and William Richard were the tenant farmers of **Ty Petr** and **Tyr William Richard** in the eighteenth century. Several field names also recall former parishioners. **Erw Gunvin** (*Kynfin's Acre*) is probably associated with Daniel Kynfin who had a cottage in Mardy Lane and land on the Myarth in the eighteenth century. Even less is known about other former parishioners commemorated in field names, such as Maddock Llewellyn, Treherne, Howell Sayse *(the Englishman)* or Gwilliam Dee (*Black William*), farmer of the land around Pencommin prior to 1587.

Plenty of questions have arisen from this brief study of Llangynidr names. What was the significance of **Ter y Castell** (*Castle Land*), near the present Castle Farm? Does the name indicate the site of an early castle, or was the land previously retained by the lord of the manor at Tretower or his overlord at Blaenllyfni Castle? Traces of a large univallate enclosure, and the flattened hilltop at the centre of this, would support the suggestion of an earlier castle. Ter y Castell was the freehold of Rice Thomas ap Rice in 1587. Several events connect his family with the Vaughans at Tretower Court and a daughter of Rice Thomas married Edward Vaughan of Tretower. Another holding of Rice Thomas illustrates the mutability of farm names. **Tir Penrwgan** (*Land at the top of the cairn lane*) was bequeathed, six generations later, by his descendant William Price to his son-in-law William Prydderch, who was High Sheriff of Breconshire in 1756, the year William Price died. **Tir Penrwgan**, which became **Ty Sheriff**, was also known as **Rhywgan** and **Ty Fry** (*Upper House*) during the nineteenth century. Penrhiw-garn is now the name of another farm, known as **Tyr Gwenllian** (*Gwenllian's Land*) in the nineteenth century. Was there ever a fulling mill at Twyn Pandy? On old maps this area is called **Pentwyn Pandy** (*Top of the hill with the fulling mill*). The origin of the name of a smallholding formerly on the site of Glanyrafon is another puzzle. It was called **Kay yr Kay Bobre** when it was leased to the Rector, John Herbert, in 1531, and **Ter Carne Bobre** in 1587 (see Figure 41). Could it have been connected with the "bobers" who were employed to prevent churchgoers from dozing during the sermon by tickling them with a long feathered wand- as related by Rev Jenkyn Edwards in his 'History of the Dyffryn Crawnon'? Some names have a more recent origin. On a moonlit night, 15th of January, 1876, Dyfnant Wood was the scene of the murder of George King, head gamekeeper on the Glanusk Estate, shot at close range by poachers[5]. Since that time the plantation has been known as **King's Wood**.

Figure 48: Dyfnant Barn, photographed about 1960. The plantation nearby was the scene of the murder of George King, the Glanusk gamekeeper, in 1876.

Place names of Llangynidr

We are grateful to Mr RFP Powell for looking through the draft of this chapter, and helping to interpret some of the more puzzling names.

References

NLW Badminton Manorial Records: Leases of holdings from 1486-1800
NLW Badminton 3 Estate Survey 1587
NLW Badminton 7 Estate Survey 1760
NLW Badminton 408 Rentals (1527-1544)
NLW Maybery III 4176 Church Terrier
Llangynidr Tithe Map, 1842
Llanddetty Tithe Map, 1839
OS Maps: various editions
Davies, D, *Welsh Place-Names of Breconshire*
Jones, T, *A History of the County of Brecknock*
Morgan, R & Powell, RFP, *A Study of Breconshire Place-Names*

Notes

1   Morgan, R & Powell, R F P, *A Study of Breconshire Place-Names*
2   NLW MS 4278C, Payne, H T, *A Parochial Visitation of the Deanery of the Third Part of Brecon*
3   Radford, C A R, Tretower: The Castle and the Court, *Brycheiniog VI*
4   Massey, M E, *Birds of Breconshire*
5   The Brecon County Times, 22/1/1876, 12/2/1876 available on microfiche at Brecon Library

Note: The archaic names quoted in this chapter in bold type are not included in the index.

Chapter 4

Transport and Communications

The Development of Roads and Tracks in Llangynidr

In this chapter, we will explore how transport and communications developed in and around Llangynidr from prehistoric times to the present day. We look in detail at the Brecon and Abergavenny Canal, because it is a transport feature of our village which has contributed significantly to the development of the community, and we also look at the development of wheeled road transport and the influence of the internal combustion engine. But our exploration down the paths, roads, canal and rivers of our Usk Valley starts in the Mesolithic period almost 10,000 years ago.

The life-style of people living here at that time was based on family groups. As hunter-gatherers, they would have needed an intimate knowledge of their locality - and paths which avoided dense forest and bogs might have become well-established. In time the domestication of livestock and the growing of crops stabilised the population who made use of both lowland and upland areas in a benign climate, using pathways which would skirt cultivated land and link upland and lowland. The Mount Hekla volcanic eruption about 3200 years ago triggered a dramatic fall in temperature of some 3°C in a relatively short time and the uplands were no longer usable except for summer grazing. However, lowland paths would probably survive unaltered as there would have to be some good reason to re-route from well established tracks

Figure 49: The old track on the east side of Tor y Foel.

When the Romans came, they found this established pattern of routes, but their need for rapid communication by foot and by cart called for wider, better surfaces and gentler gradients, as in main routes like Abergavenny to Y Gaer, the Roman fort west of Brecon. Richard Colyer's account of Roman roads in West Wales identifies their impact on the nature of established tracks and, on page 269, we describe local routes such as the route which links the Roman fort at Gelligaer, by way of the Iron Age Dolygaer to Bwlch-y-waun on the shoulder of Tor y Foel, before descending a path which has been deeply worn by human and animal feet, taking its level down 1m to 2m, coming down the ridge to Penybailey and thence via a deep lane to the River Crawnon (see illustration on the previous page).

Three possible late Bronze Age or Iron Age forts have been identified in the area - Tump Wood, Lan Fawr and a similar D-shaped site above Bwlch. Tracks leading up to these from the valley may well have become lanes that exist today, such as the lane from Llwyncelyn to Lan Fawr and Twmp Lane to Pantywenallt. We know from the 1587 survey that several other lanes have been in use for over 400 years.

The origin of 'Castle' - Ter y Castell on the sixteenth century plan - is uncertain. There is a slightly elevated area of land measuring approximately 200m by 200m centred on Castle Farm and there are distinct 'kinks' in the lanes where they meet the boundaries of this area, which could have been a protected enclosure, but we cannot be sure.

As the churches of Llangynidr, Llanddetty and Llangattock were all possibly founded in the sixth century, there might have been tracks linking them during the Dark Ages. The route from Llanddetty might have followed today's B4558 to the River Crawnon and then Castle Road. The medieval village of Llangynidr was sited at the hub of roads leading to the uplands to the south and the lanes following the Claisfer and Crawnon valleys. After the Norman Conquest the community was administered from Tretower, and the Cyffredin route became more significant.

The 1587 plan shows the earliest-recorded bridge over this stretch of the River Usk (see Figure 50). A wooden structure, it stood some 200m upstream of the present bridge and below Pen-y-bont on the north bank of the Usk. The road from this bridge up to the village of Llangynidr was called Hewell Doore, i.e. Heol Dwr (*Watery Road*). By 1630, a 'New Bridge' across the Usk was in existence, on the site of today's structure. By 1700, this bridge was reported as 'ruinous' - it was probably also built of wood because in November 1700 William Powell of Llangattock had contracted to replace it with a bridge with 'pillars and arcs of stone'. It cost £350 to build and is still in use, albeit frequently repaired. In 1716 Anthony Prees repaired the bridge for £9 10s and maintained it for the next 5 years. The approach roads for the New Bridge were also new - the one coming down from Bwlch cut across old field boundaries, while the road up from the south bank ran across Coed yr Ynys Common.

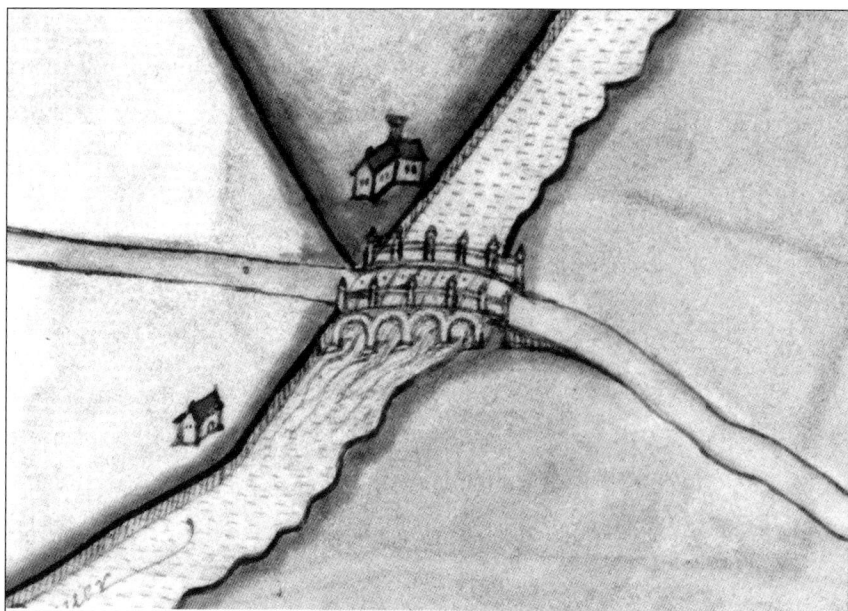

Figure 50: The Usk bridge of 1587 - an enlargement of part of Figure 38, showing the old wooden bridge.

Figure 51: The present Usk bridge, photographed by Mr Sparrow about 1890.

The Badminton Estate was re-surveyed in 1760 - by which time Coed yr Ynys Common had been largely enclosed. The lanes on this survey have survived except for minor lanes to dwellings now gone and deviations when the canal was built. These changes include the top of Orchard Lane which once joined Pen-yr-ale Lane by Gwynfa, the west end of Coed-yr-ynys Road and Castle Road, which used to run down a steep bank to Pont Crawnon, but was later re-routed over a canal bridge by the Coach and Horses.

In the mid-eighteenth century, turnpike trusts were improving the roads of England and Wales, coaches were able to travel more widely and many carried fare-paying passengers. In 1784, Palmer introduced mail coaches, also carrying passengers, which gradually built up a nation-wide network. The first local mail coach, from Monmouth through Bwlch to Brecon, ran in 1797 (see page 91). Parallel developments in transport were the use of canals and plate-ways or rail-ways which allowed horses to pull substantial loads.

Figure 52: The Gloucester, Hereford, Brecon to Aberystwyth Mail Coach from a lithograph by J Harris, after CC Henderson 1843.

The proximity of iron ore, coal and limestone in the heads of the valleys of Monmouthshire and Glamorganshire resulted in a rapidly-growing iron industry extending from Merthyr Tydfil to Brynmawr and Blaenavon. The quarrying of limestone expanded; apart from its use for mortar and for neutralising acid soils, it was also used in iron making. At the same time there was a growing local demand for coal for domestic use in Brecon, Crickhowell and beyond.

The earliest surviving minute book of the Turnpike Trustees for Brecknockshire in Llandrindod Wells Record Office starts in 1789 by stating that the new road from Llangattock to the Blaen Onneu limestone quarries was now complete and was to be improved over the mountain to Beaufort, where coal was being extracted. On 17th November 1789, the trustees authorised their surveyor, John Jones of Denbigh, to contract for a new road from Llangynidr through the 'Glaisfer' to the 'lime kilns' at

76

a price not exceeding £100 a mile. On 11th May 1791 the contract for this new road from 'Watery Lane' (remember Hewell Doore?) to Blaen Onneu was let to John Williams of Llangattock, labourer and David Jones of Llangynidr, farmer. In June 1792 the contract for a stone bridge near the glebe was let for £13 to William Morgan of Bwlch - this survives today as the old Pontganol Bridge over the Claisfer. In the Autumn of 1792 the new Llangynidr Toll-gate by the Red Lion cross-roads was let for £96. The present occupant of Turnpike Cottage, Mr Bill Parry, is a direct descendant of William Parry who had the turnpike contract in 1808.

A year later it was agreed that a turnpike gate be set up on the Bwlch side of the Usk Bridge - in March 1794 a new house and gate were under construction (cost £27/15/9d) with an additional stepladder and boarding for a room above for £2. The contractor was Thomas Jones of Llangynidr, who also had the contract to clean and paint all the milestones between Brecon and Abergavenny at 2/6d a time - he was paid 15/- if a new one had to be provided. The Tollgate House was completed in August 1794 and both village tolls were let for £121 to Roger Wynter in the security of David Price. Gwyn Briwnant Jones has painted the Usk Bridge site as it would have appeared two hundred years ago (see Figure 164). In times of flood, the ground floor could well have been under water!

The 1809 Turnpike Act listed charges:

Each horse or beast not drawing a vehicle	1½d
Any animal drawing a vehicle	4d
Carts carrying lime - wheels less than 6"	3d
- wheels broader than 6"	1½d
Every score of oxen	15d
Scores of calves, swine, goats, sheeps or lambs	7½d

Entries in Breconshire Quarter Sessions Rolls for 1822 note that both village bridges over the Claisfer were in need of repair; they were 'Pont y Ffrwdd' (Pont Claisfer) and 'Pont Rheolrhucan'. Benjamin James, who had built locks and canal bridges twenty years earlier, rebuilt both bridges for £10 and £4/4/- was spent on road resurfacing. In the same year Thomas Madocks was paid £6/12/- for resurfacing the approaches to Llangynidr Bridge.

In the 1830s the road from Porthmawr (Crickhowell) by way of Llangattock and Llangynidr to Derwen y Groes (*Cross Oak*) was improved. In Llangynidr this involved new stretches of road from Pontganol Bridge to the Yail Brook and from the school (Hen Ysgol) to the Coach and Horses. The Turnpike Trustees also sought tenders for the repair of the road from Glawcoed to Ashford in 1833 - these ranged from 1/10d to 15/6d a yard! John Thomas won the contract and promptly went bankrupt - he was replaced by Charles Williams at 2/6d a yard. From 1835 a new Highways Act relieved parishes of the old compulsory labour scheme for road maintenance that had burdened them for 300 years - Llangynidr Parish was allowed to levy a road rate yielding £22/10/-.

Breconſhire Turnpikes.

NOTICE IS HEREBY GIVEN,

THAT the TOLLS ariſing at the ſeveral Turnpike Gates, called Pontcumbeth, Penpedair-Heol, and Crickhowell Bridge Gates: And alſo the TOLLS of the Gates, called Llangunider Gate, and Llangunider Bridge Gate, will be LET to the Beſt Bidders at the Shire-Hall, in the Town of *Brecon*, on *Wedneſday* the Tenth Day of *September* next, between the Hours of Eleven and Twelve in the Forenoon, for *One* Year, to commence from the Twenty-ninth Day of *September* aforeſaid, in Manner directed by the late Act of Parliament in that Behalf.

The TOLLS of Pontcumbeth, Penpedair-Heol, and Crickhowell Bridge Gates, are let for the preſent Year at the clear yearly Rent of 260*l.* and thoſe of Llangunider and Llangunider Bridge Gates, at 244*l.* but will be put up at ſuch Sums reſpectively, as the Truſtees ſhall think fit.

The Bidders muſt be prepared at the ſame Time with ſufficient Sureties for Payment of the Money monthly.

JOHN POWELL,
Clerk to the Truſtees.

Brecon, AUGUST 13th, 1800.

W. AND G. NORTH, PRINTERS, BRECKNOCK.

Figure 53: Notice advertising an auction for the collection of tolls at local tollgates, including Llangynidr, 1800.

The road alongside Yail Brook from Glanyrafon - the line of the sixteenth century route - was little used after 1830 and Dorothea Watkins recorded that in 1853 the lane was sold to the Duke of Beaufort for £10 by the Parish Overseers.

Minutes of the Village Highways Committee note the lack of a bridge over the Claisfer between High Meadow and Glaisfer-isaf in 1859: it was probably built, or rebuilt, soon afterwards.

A new section of the mountain road (B4560) was built in the late nineteenth century. The original road can still be traced - it turns left some 50m before the first hairpin bend and continues for some distance below the present road climbing to join the old Rhiwgarn track. Today it is a pleasant walk with fine views.

Dyffryn Road in the upper village was commented on by Dorothea Watkins:

"The road was made into hard stone (not Macadam) in the nineteenth century. Miss Mabel Watkins said that she could remember the road being altered in the early 1870s when she was six. Mr Tom Thomas recalled his father saying that it was made up from a grass track in the 1840s."

By 1587 the main route through the upper village probably followed the churchyard wall on the south side and then Mardy Lane - on eighteenth century house deeds referred to as 'the street of Llangynidr'.

The District Highways Board had the use of a steam roller from 1901, driven by Mr Farr from the Boatman's Arms at one time, but it was the 1920s before the rural roads were metalled.

Figure 54: Steamroller resurfacing the road, accompanied by a water tender.

Railways never came to Llangynidr, but an Usk Valley Railway was seriously considered in 1858 on a line closely paralleling the line of the canal but the plan fell at the first hurdle. Eight years later an Act of Parliament for a railway from Abergavenny to Brecon was passed but the scheme was abandoned in 1867.

The Railway reached Abergavenny in January 1854, linking Newport, Hereford and Shrewsbury. The line to Brynmawr from Abergavenny, built in 1862, crossed the canal at Govilon and goods for Llangynidr were trans-shipped there (see Figure 60). The nearest railway link for Llangynidr was the Brecon and Merthyr line through Talybont - opened on 1st May 1863, it brought Brecon and the Valleys towns within easier reach. In 1900, the building contractors who were at that time modernising the Three Salmons Inn travelled to work from Brynmawr by this route.

References

Archer, M S, and Porter, M, *Archaeology in Wales*, Vol 38, pp 43-50

Colyer, Richard, (1984) *Roads and Trackways of Wales,* Moorland Publishing

Clwyd Powys Archaeological Trust, Printout of Sites and Monuments has been invaluable in correlating past and present dwellings and other structures both in the text and on the maps

Makepeace, (1998) *Archaeology in Wales,* Vol 38, p 103

RCAHM Inventory (1997): *Ancient Monuments in Brecknock, Part 1*, pp 275, 276

Powys CRO, BQS/T/M 1792 et seq, Minutes of Turnpike Trustees

Powys CRO, Quarter Sessions Rolls

The Brecon and Abergavenny Canal

Introduction

Thanks to coal, limestone and the need to transport heavy cargoes more efficiently than ever before, the 1790s saw a great surge in canal construction - the first five canals built in South Wales were all largely completed in this decade and they all involved a dynasty that dominated canal building - the Dadford family - Thomas Dadford and his sons John and Thomas. The Monmouthshire Canal and the Brecon and Abergavenny Canal received Acts of Parliament in 1792 and 1793 respectively - they were to meet at Pontymoile, near Pontypool. Shareholders of the Brecon & Abergavenny Canal Company included the Duke of Beaufort, Thynne Howe Gwynne of Buckland, Walter Jeffries of Brecon and Walter Wilkins, who was appointed treasurer.

Figure 55: Part of the plan of the Brecon and Abergavenny Canal surveyed by Thomas Dadford Junior in 1792.

The route of the Brecon & Abergavenny had been surveyed by Thomas Dadford Junior in 1792. The section from Dyfnant to Ashford is shown in Figure 55. The organisation of the Canal Companies involved a General Assembly which met twice yearly from April 1793, and two committees - one for the Brecon & Abergavenny and one for the Monmouthshire, although in practice, the two committees met simultaneously.

Construction of the Brecon & Abergavenny Canal

The October 1793 General Assembly of the Brecon & Abergavenny Canal Company ordered that a re-survey of the proposed canal be undertaken and this was completed by Hugh Henshall who reported back to the committee on 23 May 1794. Then, in March 1796, tenders were sought for cutting several 'lotts' between Clydach and Llangattock. The length of the lot would vary according to the nature of the ground, but they averaged 700 metres. The rates paid also varied according to the work involved:

> **Cutting the canal** was paid at 3¼ pence to 5 pence per cubic yard;
> **Cutting the puddle gutters** was paid at 2 pence to 4 pence;
> **Puddle banking and forming** was paid at 6 pence to 8 pence per yard;
> **Forming road and backing at a bridge** was paid at 1½ to 4 guineas.

In August 1796, two more lots were let, in September a further three, and in December of that year, a further two. Three of these lots may well have been for the stretch from Dyfnant to the Claisfer.

Contracts were usually completed in four months, approximately 100 working days, with the digging advancing seven yards a day. Digging to a depth of two yards over a width of fifteen to twenty yards meant that between 200 and 300 cubic yards were shifted every day. According to Coleman in 'The Railway Navvies', a labourer could shift some fourteen cubic yards in a day so a contractor would need a team of fifteen to twenty strong men. With as many as 200 workers employed at any time, the impact on a community like Llangynidr, with a population of just 600 in the 1790s, would have been considerable. This must have been a boom time for Llangynidr's alehouses! Some local labour would have been employed and accommodation would have been needed for skilled labour during the building of the wharves, the aqueduct over the Crawnon and the series of locks, from 1796 to the end of the century. It is likely that the Boatman's Arms was built in the late 1790s, quite probably to house such key workers. Five more lots were let in Spring 1797, taking the canal to the Usk Bridge road and in April that year the Engineer was instructed to survey from Llangynidr to Brecon and also from Clydach to the junction with the Monmouthshire Canal at Pontymoile.

Figure 56: Stone stile near bridge 126. These are a feature of the canal towpath.

Masonry work was successfully tendered for by Benjamin James of Blaenavon - records show that he completed all the stonework from Clydach to Ashford, probably including the Crawnon Aqueduct, which was completed some time before 1800 at a cost approaching £1000, about the same cost as the works at Clydach and Caerfanell. Bridges cost about £30 each. Benjamin James also built all the locks; Thomas Wells of Newport did all the carpentry work at bridges, gates and locks; Thomas Jones of Merthyr was given the contract to construct Ashford Tunnel in January 1798. It would seem that the Ashford section caused considerable problems - with bank slippage and water seepage from Wenallt Farm. Minutes of meetings from 1799 to 1809 all bear witness to these continuing difficulties.

Water Supply

To say that a canal depends on a water supply is perhaps a blinding glimpse of the obvious - but just as important as a level construction is the head of water to keep the canal topped up. The Engineer's report of 26 April 1798 is the first to draw attention to the water supply, "Feeders are cut from the rivers Clydach, Onny, Claisfer and other small brooks to supply the Canal with water", in preparation for the opening of the canal from Clydach to "near Llangynidr". This report was shortly after letting the lots from Llangynidr to Talybont but no mention is made of the leat at Cwm Crawnon. However, at a committee meeting at the Golden Lion in Brecon in March 1799, a minute "resolved that the Company will purchase of Mr Thomas, Attorney, the parcels of land below the Canal Feeder at Cwm Crawnon" and this purchase was duly effected on 17 May 1799 for the sum of twenty pounds, seventeen and ninepence, paid to Thomas Williams, the vendor. We also know, from archive plans, that a leat ran from the original Pontganol bridge over the Claisfer to the canal and the remains of this leat can be seen in a field to the north of the junction of the B4558 and the B4560 below Tyr William Richard to this day.

Figure 57: Limekilns at Llangynidr Wharf, about 1930.

Commercial Operation of the Brecon & Abergavenny Canal

The 26 April 1798 report from Engineer Thomas Dadford, Junior, tells us that the length from Clydach to near Llangynidr was now navigable. At Llangynidr Wharf there was a coalyard to house 2000 tons of coal, an Agent's house and a weighing machine. Two lime kilns were under construction. The Act of Parliament had laid down maximum tolls for the carriage of goods and by August 1794, the Company reflected these - although at that time these tolls were just for "Railways and Stone Roads", not yet for the canal itself. There were four levels of charges:

At one penny per ton per mile   for agricultural products and building materials such as lime, limestone, slate, bricks and hay;

At two pence per ton per mile   for industrial cargoes such as iron ore, coal and charcoal;

At three pence per ton per mile   for finished products such as iron and lead;

At four pence per ton per mile   for other loads such as timber goods, livestock or merchandise.

It is clear that these tolls could vary over the years, upwards as well as downwards. By 1862, for example, coal was three farthings, lime and limestone a halfpenny, pit props, cordwood and sleepers were one penny, iron and building materials were a halfpenny, while other goods were 1½ pence, all per ton per mile.

In 1798, it seems that five boats were working the canal from Llangynidr Wharf, built by the Brecknock Boat Company there. By April of the following year, the Canal Company had leased the houses at the Wharf for eleven years at £21 per annum and had granted use of the Wharf, kilns and stabling rent-free, provided they did not let any of these for profit. The buildings rented included the Agent's house and weighing machine (in today's Braeside), four labourers houses built in 1798 for a cost of £50 each and all roofed for £39. At the same time, the Canal Company also required the building of two more limekilns, running repairs to the two kilns built the year before and the construction of railings and gates to prevent boats being 'pillaged'. Clearly Llangynidr Wharf was becoming a thriving concern.

By the end of 1799, £1557-worth of coal and £555-worth of limestone had been carried on the canal in its first eighteen months of operation - which suggests that around 18,000 tons of coal and 52,000 tons of limestone were moved by the company, either by barge along the 8¼ miles of the canal or the 5 miles of railroad wagon transport from pit or quarry - not a bad start for the fledgling operation. By early 1801, the canal was in use all the way to Brecon - thereby providing the opportunity for a viable business, as was reflected in the Canal Company's own reports.

The 1806 report of the Brecon & Abergavenny Company declares an income of nearly £3500 in the preceding 12 months. The report doesn't give us a breakdown between the categories of goods transported, but with the bulk being coal and limestone, much of it taken as far as Brecon, the total volume carried would have been more than twice the amount carried in 1799, just 6 years earlier. To carry this volume of approximately 1,500,000 tons would, we have estimated, have required a fleet of at least 15 boats, with an average carrying capacity of 21 tons. John Lloyd's 'Early History of the Old South Wales Iron Works' published in 1906 tells us that the Boat Company had 16 boats of this capacity at that time. But as well as the boats of the Brecknock Boat Company, there were other traders using the Canal. Their volumes would have been included in the totals recorded by the Canal Company, even though they were generally treated on a less-favourable basis than the Brecknock Boat Company by the Canal Company. For example, when the Llangynidr locks were out of action for a while in 1808, they were the only trader offered a rebate amounting to half of the cost of transporting their cargoes from the bottom lock to the top.

Figure 58: Empty barges at the Cwmcrawnon depot about 1930.

Severe frost was a common winter problem for the canal operation. A Canal Company minute of 11th December 1812 ordered that two ice-breaker boats be built immediately, in order to break the ice on the canal and keep the barges moving, and the income from them flowing in.

In 1822 Benjamin Hall applied to the Canal Company for a tramroad to be built from Brinore Coalpit and Trefil Quarry to Talybont. The Canal Company saw this as a commercial threat because by bringing the coal down the Brinore Tramroad to Talybont rather than down to Gilwern, they would lose 11 miles-worth of tonnage, from Gilwern to Talybont. In the event, the tramroad was built and opened in 1815 and the Canal Company reported a revenue drop of £392 2s 6d as a result in the following financial year. The route of the Brinore Tramroad makes a splendid walk - in a number of places the original stone slates which supported the iron track survive. On the route up to Trevil and Brinore, there were several passing places and three inns - Rock Inn, Pen Rhiw Calch and Glasgwm-uchaf.

The Brecon to Hay tramroad opened in 1816 - with coal at Brecon costing 12 shillings a ton, whereas by the time it had reached Glasbury and Hay its price was 18 shillings a ton. No doubt much of this coal was from Brinore via the tramroad to Talybont and thence by barge to Brecon. Meanwhile, other shipments of coal were being unloaded at Llangynidr Wharf and then carted over the Usk Bridge (paying a toll there of course) to Hay. Coal which travelled this way could undercut coal sent via Brecon. Certainly in 1831, Benjamin Trusted, who traded in Hay, complained that coal via Llangynidr and Llangattock sold there as low as 21 shillings per ton, while coal via Brecon cost 23 shillings per ton. Clearly there was a lot of competition between the various routes to get coal and lime to Hay and beyond to Hereford. A proposal was put forward in 1831 to build another tramroad from just above the fifth Llangynidr lock, near Llanddetty. It's possible, from what was reported in the Hereford Journal on 7th November 1831, that the proposer, Harfords of Penmark Iron Mines and Colliery, intended the tramroad to pass Trefil and come down the Dyffryn Crawnon. Harfords had wanted to link up with the Brinore, which was rejected by Hall's Company, and after the Canal Company hedged for some years, Harfords went bankrupt in 1843, so no tramroad was ever built.

As well as receiving water from streams such as the Claisfer and the Crawnon, the Canal Company also provided water along its route. A minute of 18th October 1821 reads, "Agent to get a 2" bore pipe down 6 inches under top water in the towing path at Personage House, Llanddetty to supply with water". One hundred years later, the water supply which operated the chaff-cutting machine and the grind-stone in the stables opposite the Oaklands saw-mills also came from the canal.

Commercial directories of the time listed canal carriers - mostly for goods, but passengers were carried as well. Before, or in the absence of railroads, canal journeys were certainly cheaper and probably more agreeable for passengers than travel by coach. In the family history of the David Morgan department store in Cardiff, for example, there is a mention of travelling by boat from Newport to Brecon in the early 1800s.

Pigott's Monmouthshire Directory of 1844 details:

By Canal to Brecon etc	
Every Monday	Ann Prosser's boat from the Moderator Wharf
Every Wednesday	North & Co's boats from the Tredegar Boat Company's Wharf, William Wild, Agent

Slater's Directory of 1858 lists carriers on the canal under:

Newport, Crickhowell and Brecon, passing through Llangynidr en route:	
Between Brecon and Pontymoile	daily, agent Tom Pratt
Between Brecon and Newport	twice weekly, (Bristol Packet Wharf), agent Wm Thomas
Between Brecon and Newport,	once or twice weekly, (Moderator Boat Co), agent James Morris
Between Brecon and Llanelly (Clydach)	occasionally, (Brecknock Boat Company), agent Mordecai Jones

Figure 59: The Canal Inspector's boat, towed by a horse, about 1930.

The years from 1799 to the 1840s were busy and successful for the Brecon & Abergavenny Canal Company, but success was relatively short-lived. With Victorian Britain entering the railway age, many canal companies found it hard to compete. By 1845, the General Assembly of the Brecon & Abergavenny Canal Company was seeking to sell the canal - it was offered unsuccessfully to the Welsh Midlands Railway Company for £182,500; in 1851 the Breconshire Railway Company turned it down, even though the price-tag had declined to £105,750. Later, it was refused by the London and North Western only to be eventually bought by the Monmouthshire Railway and Canal Company in 1865 for £24,750. This company was, in turn, absorbed into the Great Western Railway Company in 1880.

Figure 60: Govilon Wharf, late 1930s. The dock and sidings for the trans-shipment of goods between canal and rail can be seen.

Of course, the railway companies did not buy up canal companies in order to run them, but rather to remove them as serious competitors and thereby to move more freight onto the railways. By the early 1890s, only one or two boats a week served Llangynidr Wharf - 80 years earlier, the number calling in or passing was about 50 times that number. By this time the most common outgoing cargoes were railway sleepers, pit-props and other timber products. The senders were either Wm Parry or Davies & Co and the journey was usually to Govilon, where there was a link with rail at Govilon Station. Incoming cargoes were mostly coal, but others included manure, gravel, sand, stone and even livestock, with maximum loads still around 20 tons. Pleasure boats still ran occasionally at about 1¼ pence per mile for a full boat - Mrs Jane Davies recalls childhood Sunday School trips to Gilwern and a photograph of the Baptist Chapel Sunday School trip in the early 1900s is shown in Figure 106.

After 1900, the use of the canal was spasmodic - the last recorded entry in the Abstract of tonnages was 1911 - pit props sent by E J Goddin from Llangynidr Wharf to Govilon. 16 tons travelled 9.9 miles at a price of 11 shillings and 4 pence. There had been a grain store on the south bank of the canal just west of the King's Arms, Aberhoywe. Grain had been brought here from Newport by barge and then transported by horse and cart to Llangynidr Mill. In the 1920s, the grain store had gone and the canal was transforming from a transportation artery to a neglected, disused waterway, which was becoming a haven for wildlife. As Mrs Delphine Ford recalls:

"... the canal was used for sheep washing near the aqueduct over the Claisfer and at the Dyfnant, opposite King's Wood, below Aberhoywe. Just beyond that, in the wood above the river, was a heronry for many years. ...the canal in those days was alive with wildlife - coots, moorhens, kingfishers, tadpoles and various kinds of fish. In the late 1920s, men would come from the industrial areas and fill barrels with canal water and dace, and take them to restock their local ponds"

John Prothero, of Waterloo House, was the last person in the village to hold a licence to carry goods on the canal. His barges were tied up between Lower Pencommin and the Forge Road bridge, slowly rotting and disintegrating. His sisters, Hannah and Sarah, went down in the evenings to bale them out - but to no avail. According to Company records, the last commercial load on the Brecon & Abergavenny Canal was at Llangynidr in 1933, but Mr Dewi Parry's reminiscences extend to commercial cargoes as late as 1939 - he recalled Bill Morgan at The Grove operating his own barge and selling coal from it at 1 shilling per barrowload. According to Dewi Parry, he was the last commercial barge operator left on the canal in 1939.

Today, once again, the Brecon & Abergavenny Canal is thriving, but now the cargoes are not coal or limestone or pit-props, but holiday-makers and leisure boatmen. The canal is now a tremendous asset to residents and visitors alike. Its charm and elegance win national awards for British Waterways. But it wasn't always so - in the period between the demise of commercial traffic and the arrival of recreational boating, it was badly neglected. Dewi Parry started working on the canal in 1939 as a Mason's Mate. At that time there were just six local staff on the canal in charge of the locks and bridges between Brecon and Goytre. Dewi tells an amusing story of a time when the canal had been drained so that they could work on the tunnel walls at Ashford. Arriving at work in the morning, the foreman went into the tunnel while Dewi started to unload the truck. With a loud shout, the foreman fled from the tunnel entrance, pursued by an angry badger who was not well-pleased at the fact that what he had decided would be an ideal sett had been so impolitely entered by the canal foreman!

References

Powys CRO, Dadford's 1792 Canal Plan
British Waterways Archives, Gloucester, BW 36.87 (1888) F-Plan Box - Pontganol leat
Public Record Office (PRO), Rail 253, Piece 133, - GWR records, canal cargoes
Norris, John, Transcript of the Brecon and Abergavenny Canal Company Minutes, deposited with the Monmouthshire, Brecon and Abergavenny Canals Trust
Lloyd, John, (1906) *Early History of the South Wales Ironworks*
Rattenbury, Gordon, (1980) *Tramroads of the Brecknock and Abergavenny Canal*, RCHS, Penzance
Rattenbury, Gordon, *The Brecknock Boat Company*, Penzance
Stevens, R Alan, (1974) *Towpath Guide to the Brecon, Abergavenny and Monmouth Canals*, Goose & Sons

Figure 61: GWR Milnes-Daimler bus in Crickhowell, 1920s.

Wheeled Transport

Wheeled transport in the district was uncommon before the nineteenth century. Few farmers owned carts - most relied on pack ponies, but the opening of the canal in 1798 quickly led to an expanded road system in the village, enabling larger carts to be used for transporting heavy goods to and from the wharves.

By 1791 there was a twice-weekly stage coach service from London, terminating at Abergavenny. A carrier service (North & Co.), using wagons, was available through Crickhowell to Brecon, by-passing Llangynidr. Special arrangements had to be made for heavy goods to be brought into the parish - but the amount of goods so transported was very small, farmhouse furniture, for example, usually being made on the premises by visiting craftsmen. Most farming families (see page 111) relied on the horse alone until the 1930s; traps and light carts remained the province of the gentry and the tradesmen (such as the 'huckster' recalled by Mr Brinley Nicholls, who collected the whinberries he picked as a child and took them over the mountain to sell in the Valleys towns).

During the nineteenth century, Llangynidr folk only had to get as far as Bwlch to pick up a daily service to London - in the first half of the century, this might be the Nimrod or the Fusilier operating from Brecon, or the Paul Pry from Carmarthen - whilst the Royal Mail ran a service direct from Milford Haven or Pembroke. Services also ran regularly from Brecon to Hereford and Cheltenham, Merthyr, Neath and Swansea, providing a better public transport network than at almost any time since. Despite the various carriers operating on the canal, the road hauliers also prospered, North of Abergavenny being superseded by several generations of the Battey family on the Brecon run, up to at least 1884, augmented by Haines & Co. and also by the GWR. Llangynidr was not served direct from either Brecon or Abergavenny - other than for canal goods, people were expected to make their own arrangements to get to Bwlch or Crickhowell.

It is on record that the first country motor bus service in Britain was that run from Helston to Penzance by the GWR, using crude open-top buses with chain drive and solid rubber tyres. These were based on a German Daimler chassis and were assembled by Milnes & Co of Shropshire. When registration was first introduced in 1904, these vehicles were allocated numbers in the Cornish AF series, such as AF 101. The Helston service was not successful and in 1905 these buses were transferred to the Brecon-Abergavenny route. As the 1906 'Kelly's' stated, "A motor omnibus runs from the Great Western Railway station at intervals during the day to Crickhowell and Brecon for passengers and luggage." This service was taken over by the Red and White Omnibus Company in 1930 but, for some reason, the ancient Milnes-Daimlers, rebuilt several times, but by now in a desperate condition both bodily and mechanically, continued in slow and noisy use up to about 1935. The last of these vehicles was broken up in a Brynmawr scrapyard about 1970. The Milnes-Daimlers would have been too heavy for the canal bridges and the first buses to divert through Llangynidr were probably the much lighter GWR Thornycrofts of the late 1920s

Figure 62: GWR Thornycroft bus crossing Pont Crawnon, late 1920s.

Private motor transport came late to Llangynidr. Primitive veteran cars visited the village from Crickhowell and even from Newport in the early years of the century but the first car based in the village appears to have been the 12/16 Sunbeam of 1911 owned by Captain Sparkes of Pwll Court. "Everyone knew when Captain Sparkes was coming because he sounded his klaxon". The Sunbeam lasted until 1932, when it was superseded by a more mundane Morris Major, though the engine of the old Sunbeam survived until 1945, powering a workshop lathe in Crickhowell.

After the 1914-18 War there was a sudden upsurge in the ownership of private cars, with greater public awareness of the advantages of motors for private mobility, helped along by the mass-production of the Ford Model 'T' (see Figure 63), by the cost-cutting of William Morris and by the increased availability of cars with low running costs such as the Austin Seven. These years saw a gradual increase in the number of cars in Llangynidr but the majority were second-hand, except for those owned by the gentry. Breconshire tax records for the early years are sparse but between 1923 and 1930 the newspaper-owning Berry family across the river at Buckland registered no less than nine new vehicles; two Rolls-Royces, two Hillmans, two Rovers, one unspecified, an Overland van for the estate and a 49.4hp Daimler enclosed landaulette in ultramarine, registered EU 3334 in 1927. This was the sort of car used by Royalty and was generally rated a cut above a mere Rolls-Royce!

Figure 63: Ford Model T, about 1922. Was there a legal age-limit at that time?

Enterprisingly, William Bevan, the builder bought his daughter Nancy (Thomas) a brand new car on her 21st birthday in 1931. In her Jowett 'Black Prince', registration number EU 4389, with black spoke wheels and a red steering wheel, Nancy drove to outlying farmhouses to give piano lessons. Later on she used the car to ferry sick folk and expectant mothers to the doctor in Crickhowell.

Up to 1930 there were as many motorcycles registered in Breconshire as all other vehicles put together. This was not untypical - two wheeled transport was very popular in those days. It is noteworthy that a 'Neracar' was registered to Lady Glanusk, although the family more typically also had their Daimlers. The Neracar was a fully enclosed motorcycle especially suited to lady riders, felicitously designed by a Mr Neracher. Prior to the 1914-1918 War there were several motorcycles in the village, the first probably being owned by John Hodgkiss, the electrical engineer, who favoured particularly the flat-twin Douglas made in Kingswood, Bristol (see overleaf). After the War he set up an agency and repair workshop and one of his early customers was William Morgan. Billy Morgan made a typical progression from solo motorcycles through a 'combination' to an Austin Seven saloon, meeting family needs.

Commercial vehicles were even later on the scene. Probably because of the limitations of the local bridges, draught horses rather than steam traction engines or road locomotives were retained by local firms involved in heavy haulage. The first locally owned truck is thought to have been the Ford Model 'TT' used by the builders Watkins and Bevan in the mid-20s. A 1929 model Manchester tipping wagon succeeded this (see overleaf). By this date, road deliveries by motor van from Crickhowell and Brecon were the norm and this development perhaps kept down the number of vehicles based in the village. The Second World War saw a further change in the rural economy, with a reduction in the number of services provided by vehicles from outside the village and an ever-growing dependency on the private car to meet personal transport needs.

Figure 64: John Hodgkiss with his flat-twin Douglas.

Figure 65: Manchester Tipping Wagon, 1929.

Chapter 5

Hedges

With help from the teachers and children of Llangynidr School we have investigated the age of local hedges. Pioneering studies in measuring the age of hedges by counting the number of shrub species present were carried out by Dr M D Hooper et al, in the East Midlands and Devon, about 1970. From studies of more than 200 hedges, which had been dated by documentary evidence, it was found that the number of shrub species present was directly proportional to the age of the hedge. Dr Hooper calculated that new species invaded at about the rate of one species every hundred years. As a rough guide:

Age of hedge = 100 x n (where n is the number of shrub species recorded in a 30 yd/m length of hedge). This assumes the hedge was planted with one species. Although such was often the case, later research indicated that in some areas, notably parts of Shropshire, it was customary to plant mixed hedges. Variation in such factors as soil, climate, and distribution of native shrubs might also alter the equation.

During our project the number of shrub species in 750 samples (30m lengths of hedge) were recorded. 30 species of trees and shrubs were found. The percentage of samples in which the more common sorts occurred is noted below.

Species	%	Species	%	Species	%
Hawthorn	93	Elder	39	Dogwood	4
Hazel	86	Holly	28	Willow	3
Rose	81	Oak	14	Beech	2
Blackthorn	59	Sycamore	13	Alder	2
Ash	43	Wych Elm	11		
Maple	41	Bird Cherry	5		

Another 14 species including Rowan, Crab-apple, Downy Birch, Guelder Rose, Gooseberry, Cherry and Yew, were recorded in less than 2% of the samples.

It was difficult to find documentary evidence of dates of local hedges. Our study concentrated on those along boundaries shown on the 1587 Beaufort Estate Survey, and sections of the B4560 which was established as a turnpike road in 1792. This is the only hedge we can date precisely, as the turnpike accounts record payments to farmers for the planting of hedges, e.g. Rees Griffiths was paid £11 4s 0d for planting 106 perches (530m) of hedge in the Ffrwd region, on 13/2/1793. For this road the exercise was confined to sections, from the A40 to the Usk Bridge, and Llwyncelyn lane to Penrhiw-garn, which are known to have been built as a new road, unlike the route through the village which followed existing roads. The average number of shrub species from over 90 samples was 4.7; if only one type of shrub had been used to make the original hedge, the rate of invasion is twice that expected. Although half the samples had 4 or fewer species, there were a few with 8 and one with 9. Sometimes the sections with 4 or less species extended over more than 150m.. Almost every sample contained hawthorn, hazel and rose; possibly the first two were planted as the original hedge. Perhaps the samples containing a large number of species can be explained by the new road having been constructed alongside ancient field hedges in some parts. Comparison of the turnpike route with earlier estate surveys offers limited support for this theory. Counts of species in hedges along the old lanes around the village which were marked on the 1587 Survey, such as Dyffryn Crawnon Road, Heol Rhiwgarn, Claisfer Lane, Cyffredin Lane and Ffrwd Lane, showed an average of between 6 and 7 species per 30m. By Dr Hooper's rule this might indicate that these hedges dated from between AD 1300 and AD 1400. However other interpretations are possible. In each lane were a few samples which had 9 or more species present. These may indicate places where the lane ran alongside a wood in earlier times and woodland saplings were used to make the hedge. Similarly, when pastures were created by clearance of woodland, rows of saplings might have been used to make hedges composed of several species. Many stretches of old lanes are bounded by derelict stone walls. Perhaps shrubs can colonise these tumble-down walls more rapidly than they can invade well-managed hedges.

Counts of shrub species in internal field hedges corresponding to field boundaries shown on the 1587 Survey produced an average of 5.3 species from 50 samples. It appears likely, from the absence of wall remains in most sections, that these hedges were planted, and not the result of natural colonisation. If a single species was used to make the hedges, Dr Hooper's formula would indicate a date of about AD 1500. We do not know whether the boundaries shown on the 1587 Survey represented living hedges, dead hedges or walls. Walls were commonly built along lanes and to mark farm boundaries, especially on higher ground where there was plenty of stone available. In medieval times dead hedges, constructed of cut branches interwoven around stakes, were commonly used to divide fields. A document[1] dated 1588 relating to the sale of land called Cae Trahaern, near Neuadd in Dyffryn Crawnon, provides an early reference to a living hedge. The document is in Latin except for one phrase describing a boundary hedge in English as "a quike sete". In those days that meant a living hedge; nowadays young hawthorn plants used for hedging are often called "quicks". Such a reference may indicate that living hedges were still unusual in this area at the end of the sixteenth century. By the eighteenth century, local farmers were being encouraged to plant living hedges. The Brecknockshire Agricultural Society offered premiums to farm labourers for the collection of hawthorn berries, and to farmers for raising hawthorn, crab-apple and "...Prickly Holly Plants fit for transplanting for Fence"[2]. At this time tenant farmers on the Beaufort Estate were instructed to plant living hedges on their holdings. The 1766 lease of Walter Watkins of Aberyail required him to plant 15 perches (75m) of

'Quick White Thorn Hedge'[3] every winter. The extent of such planting suggests that dead hedges were still being replaced by living ones.

Our results offer limited support for the thesis that the number of shrub species in a well-managed hedge is directly proportional to the age of the hedge, but, as is so often the case, the survey has discovered more problems than it has solved. The lane linking Dyffryn Road and Castle Road has a shrub count averaging 7 for most of its length, but close to the junction with Castle Road the count drops to an average of 4 species. This may indicate that there has been a realignment of the lane at some date. One of the plans in the 1587 Survey covers the area at the eastern end of Castle Road near Glanyrafon, but does not show the road west of the Yail. Shrub counts, with an average of 6 species for the hedges here, at first sight indicate that the road existed in 1587; however, the hedge on the north side of the lane is noticeably richer in species than that on the south. Along several old lanes there are stretches of hedge where the shrub count falls well below the average. In some cases this is due to poor maintenance, resulting in gaps which not only lower the species count but render the hedges ineffective as barriers to livestock. There may be other historical explanations; undoubtedly there is plenty of scope for further research.

Notes

1   NLW Maybery III 6968
2   Edmunds, H, History of the Brecknockshire Agricultural Society, *Brycheiniog III*
3   Quick in its archaic form, meaning living; Whitethorn is another name for hawthorn.

Figure 66: Pack mules carrying limestone on the Abergavenny road, near Llanwenarth Arms, 1929.

Figure 67: Timber wagons from Oaklands Timber Yard collecting tree-trunks near Glawcoed about 1900.

Chapter 6

The World of Work

Introduction

With an increase in the population of the parish in the seventeenth and eighteenth centuries, the encroachment of the commons at Coed yr Ynys and Cyffredin had gathered pace. Although many of the men found work as farm labourers, there was an increase in the proportion of the villagers not directly involved in agriculture, and this trend gained momentum in the nineteenth century. Some men found employment locally with builders, timber merchants or hauliers. Others worked in the limestone quarries at Blaen Onneu, Trefil or Llangattock as quarrymen or lime-burners. Coal and iron had been mined in the parish from the seventeenth century and lime had been produced since medieval times, but in the last quarter of the eighteenth century the economy quickened as the Industrial Revolution gained momentum. In 1785 Rev HT Payne recorded:

"Considerable kilns have within these last two or three years been erected on the hill of Blaen Onneu by Messrs. Kendall & Co by virtue of their lease under the Duke of Beaufort. ... Four Kilns producing four hundred barrels of lime per diem, sold at fourpence halfpenny a barrel on the spot[1]".

The lime was usually carried away on pack-mules (see Haulage, Page 125).

Men who could not find employment locally, or sought higher wages, travelled further afield to the coal mines or ironworks in the expanding towns on the southern side of Mynydd Llangynidr, such as Tredegar and Ebbw Vale. The men walked over the mountain to their workplace early on Monday morning, lodged nearby during the week and then trudged back home on Saturday night. In bad weather the journey could be hazardous and deaths from exposure were not unknown. William Morgan recalled:

"Very early on Monday morning the men congregated at the top of the village, near the Beaufort Arms, and set off in groups to walk to work. On his return, on a night of very bad weather, the father of Maggie Williams stopped at the Grouse Inn for rest and refreshment. Although urged to remain all night, he insisted on continuing his walk home, so that his wife should not be worried. He never reached home and next day was found dead on the mountain, having died from exhaustion and exposure."

The increasing prosperity of some farmers and other professional and business men during the eighteenth and nineteenth centuries led to an increasing number of jobs in service. A small army of indoor and outdoor servants was needed to run the larger houses. At Pwll Court in 1871 Mrs Edmontina Snead and her sister and daughter were attended by a governess, cook, housemaid, scullery maid, general servant, groom, page and gardener. On most farms the family provided the main workforce, but many employed indoor and outdoor servants. At Neuadd, a farm of 140 acres in 1861, John Williams employed two labourers, two shepherds, and a carter, cowman, housemaid and kitchen maid. Although most farms and smallholdings continued to be largely self-sufficient in food production until the early years of the twentieth century, an increasing number of people possessed insufficient land to supply their needs. During the eighteenth century there had been an upsurge in cottage-based 'industries' and more households became dependent on a range of services and products provided by the weavers, stocking knitters, tailors, cordwainers and others. These rural 'industries' were concentrated in the communities which had grown up at Coed yr Ynys, Cwmcrawnon, Cyffredin and Pentre (Upper Llangynidr). The nineteenth century census returns for Cyffredin illustrate this trend. Enclosure of the common land at Cyffredin had started before 1700 and was complete by 1760. In 1841 the ten cottages were the homes of two tailors, three shoemakers, a dressmaker, a woodkeeper and three farm labourers. With Cyffredin Mill on the River Claisfer, the King's Arms and smithy at the eastern end of the lane, and the three farms, Aberyail, Pant-teg and Aberhoywe, it was a thriving community. Not counting the wives, who no doubt worked hardest of all, there were thirty people in full-time employment. The cottage industries declined during the nineteenth century as the Industrial Revolution provided alternative employment and cheaper, factory-made goods; from the mid nineteenth century the Cyffredin population has fallen steadily. The problems of scraping a living as a smallholder often led to men working on their farms in the summer but taking jobs in the quarries, mines or ironworks during the winter. In more recent times, with shorter working hours, smallholders have been able to undertake full-time employment and still find time to farm their lands. Nineteenth century census returns show how often smallholdings changed hands as families moved to more productive holdings as these became available. This was particularly noticeable in the Dyffryn Crawnon. Nancy Vaughan remembered,

"Many of the smallholders started humbly. Henry Jones, a livestock dealer, married a daughter of William Richards, a boot repairer from the Wern, and she always said that all she brought to the marriage was a ten shilling note. They moved around in the Dyffryn Valley, each time going to a slightly larger place, until eventually they were farming Llwynyfedwen on the Gliffaes lane. They retired to a bungalow in Bwlch."

This progressive pattern was followed by many other families in the valley. When Bryn Probert married he moved to Spider's Castle (Far End), then via Tyle-bach and Pentre Cottage to Pen-y-waun, crossed over to the sunny side of the valley to Ton-mawr and thence to Cae'rhendre, illustrating this upwardly mobile trend.

Occupation	Number of people engaged in this work		
	1851	1871	1891
Farmers	48	36	29
Farm Labourers	60	43	30
General Labourers	9	19	15
Domestic Servants	25	40	30
Miners/Quarrymen	10	9	7
Lime burners	6	1	2
Builders/Masons	12	15	13
Hauliers	5	5	3
Carpenters	6	9	4
Tailors/Dressmakers	12	19	11
Stocking knitters	8	1	0
Shoemakers	8	11	5
Publicans	10	8	9
Blacksmiths	4	4	5
Millers	5	4	3
Grocers	6	6	3
Washerwomen/Laundresses	6	6	14

Often several members of the family were involved in the same trade and skills were passed on through successive generations. In 1861, Llewellin Parry, a shoemaker at Coed yr Ynys, employed his sons James and Ivor as shoemakers and daughter Anne as a shoebinder. He also employed another shoemaker, George Jones, who worked and lived with them. Some census enumerators listed shoemakers as cordwinders or cordwainers. For many years a family of monumental masons lived at Wesley Cottage, opposite Persondy. Grandfather Richard Jenkins moved to Llangynidr before 1841. Two sons, John and Thomas, and three grandsons followed the same trade. The 1891 census records that John Jenkins, his sons William and Richard, and his nephew Joseph, were all living and working as masons at Wesley Cottage. Grandfather, then 85 years old, had moved next door, but was still a mason! A family of bonnet-makers lived at Coed yr Ynys in 1851; Gwenllian Morgan was assisted by her daughters Ann and Gwenllian. They had professional competition from Margaret Williams, a milliner at the Boatman's Arms. Mole-catcher Daniel Morgan lived nearby; his son James (Lock Cottage) seems to have inherited the traps and taken over the practice. There were six hucksters or hawkers (door-to-door sellers of small goods) operating from Coed yr Ynys in 1851. Two households contained widow and daughter huckster partnerships. It was probably a precarious way of making a living for two are described as "pauper huxters". Helve-makers or helve-cleavers such as Thomas Edmunds of Brightwell (1861-1871) fashioned wooden handles for tools like spades, forks and billhooks. In the 1861 census Lewis

Pritchard of Coed yr Ynys is recorded as an 'Elve Dresser', conjuring up visions of little men in green jackets and red caps with white owl's-feathers!

Some of the occupations of villagers, recorded in the nineteenth century census returns, are noted below.

Occupation	Name	Home	Date
Basket maker	Thomas Williams	Upper Llangynidr	1861-81
Besom maker	Samuel Watkins	Cyffredin	1861
Excavator	Thomas Parry	Cyffredin	1841
Nailor	John Jones	Pant - mawr	1841
Ostler	John Dokes	Coach and Horses	1841
Plate-layer	Zelophead Llywelyn	Upper Llangynidr	1871-91
Poulteress	Mary Edwards	Wern Cottage (Dyffryn)	1851
Rag merchant	Maria Watkins	Cyffredin	1861
Rail straightener	Thomas Price	Pant-llwyd	1891
Tea Dealer	John Jenkins	Coed yr Ynys	1851

The largest local business enterprises in the early years of the twentieth century were Oaklands Timber Yard (c.1850-1930), situated at Blaen y Myarth, and the building firm of Messrs Watkins and Bevan (c.1910-1948). Dorothea Watkins' account of the timber yard was based mainly on the recollections of Dewi Parry and William Morgan, both former employees of the timber yard owned by the Jones family of Oaklands (formerly the Three Salmons). In 1920 Dewi Parry, aged 13, left school to work at the timber yard which at that time employed about forty people.

"In the yard was a stationary steam engine to drive the saws. The saw mills were about 50 yards long and the engine was fuelled with waste wood and small coal. My job was to cut up wood for David Pritchard, an old man in charge of the engine. David Pritchard had been an axeman out in the woods until he got too old and stiff for that work. He lived in a cottage in Orchard Lane, had a long white beard into which his clay pipe was apt to disappear, and he kept bees. The steam engine also worked the hooter which went at 8.15 a.m. for the men to go to breakfast, having started work at 7 a.m. It sounded at intervals throughout the day to tell the workers when to start and stop work. The final hoot was at 5 p.m. on ordinary days and 1 p.m. on Saturdays. There was also a coal business at the yard, with the office and weighbridge at the Machine House, now Braeside. The coal wharf was on the canal bank by the bridge where there were often 100 tons of coal. This meant that the coal carts were loaded beside the canal, then the horses and carts had to go downhill to the weighbridge to be weighed, and then had to reclimb the hill if the coal was to be delivered above the canal. There were two wheel wrights at the timber yard and, for a short time, a smithy".

William Morgan, who was born at the Machine House, recalled;

"About twenty heavy cart horses were kept in the stables opposite the timber yard (now Burnbrae), above which there was a granary, or in the field behind the Machine House. The timber was hauled from the woods where it was felled, by a timber wagon pulled by four horses. There were four or five timber wagons at the yard. At weekends the horses were taken along the lanes to Pwll Court fields by William and a couple of other boys who rode bareback. A smaller horse, which could pass under the canal bridges, was kept at the wharf to pull barges. Coal and limestone were transported to the wharf on horse-drawn barges which carried away sawn timber and timber products such as pit props, gates, hurdles and wheel barrows made at the yard. Limestone was burned in the kilns beside the wharf and the lime sold to farmers and builders".

Figure 68: Timber wharf on the canal about 1900.

It was sometimes suggested that one had a better chance of getting a job at the Yard if one was a Baptist (as were the owners), or if one was even remotely related to the Jones family.

In their heyday, Watkins and Bevan employed about twenty men. The builders' workshop still survives at Highfield, which was the home of Wilfred Watkins, and a carpenters' workshop may still be seen in the garden behind Gwynfa, where William Bevan lived. Highfield, Ynys Villa, Can-y-gwynt and Springfield are among the houses built by the firm, which also specialised in the restoration of churches. They rebuilt Llangynidr Church after the fire in 1928 and worked on churches as far afield as Clyro and Llanbister in Radnorshire.

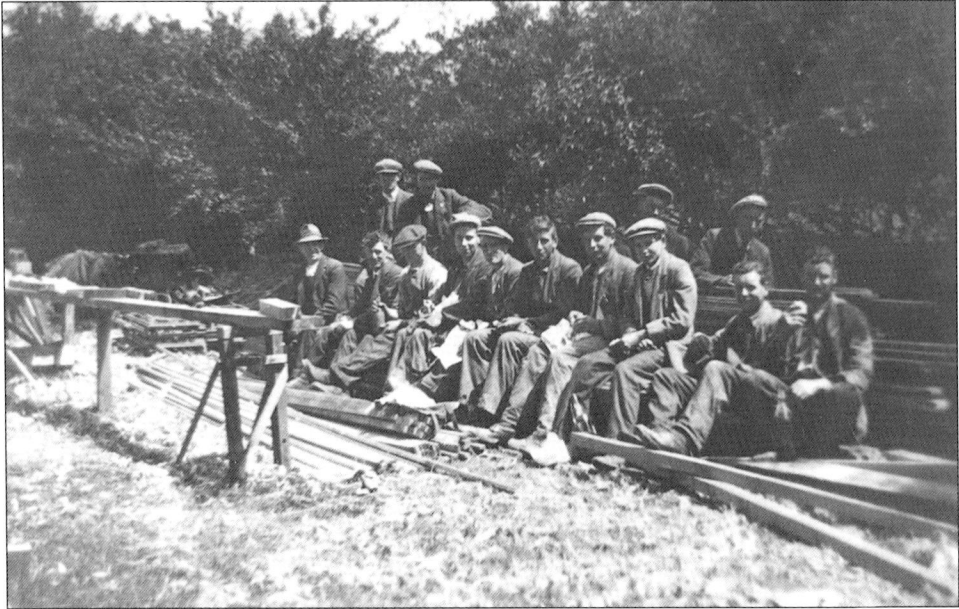

Figure 69: Staff of Watkins and Bevan, Builders, 1920s.

References

Llangynidr Local History Society Archives, Transcripts of interviews of local people by Dorothea Watkins.
Llangynidr Census Returns 1841-1891

Notes

1   NLW 4278E

Agriculture

Until the early twentieth century, agriculture was the mainstay of the economy of Llangynidr and neighbouring villages, so that the lives of most people in this area were entwined with the fortunes of farming. As the population increased in Tudor and Stuart times, numerous smallholdings were leased, which encroached upon the common land of Coed yr Ynys, Cyffredin and Mynydd Llangynidr[1]. Subsistence farming was the general practice in the sixteenth and seventeenth centuries. The land was farmed to support the family, who shared the hard work to eke out a living. Even in the nineteenth century, when there was more opportunity for education, boys went to school in the winter, but were needed to help on the farms in the summer months. Most people had a bit of land attached to their dwelling and, sometimes, extra ground further away was rented. The smallholder grew food to support his family and there was very little surplus, except in the summer, even on the bigger farms, until the end of the eighteenth century. Most livestock had to be killed in autumn and only the best beasts were kept over the lean winter months, the number being determined by the amount of winter fodder available. The Welsh for November is 'Tachwedd', which also means 'slaughter' - a reference to the animal culling which occurred at this time of year[2]. Many tenant and yeoman farmers were not much better off than labourers in the seventeenth and eighteenth centuries, judging from the inventories and wills of the time.

Until the latter part of the nineteenth century, the way of life in Llangynidr must have changed little. Rural communities had to be self-sufficient: fields, gardens and orchards provided all the food for the neighbourhood. Cattle and sheep provided milk and meat, bees produced honey, pigs were killed and salted for the winter, grain, wool and animal skins were processed locally. The products - flour, oatmeal, leather and blankets - were used in the home. The making of bread, cheese, butter, cider and beer were part of the routine of everyday life. Cloth and leather were used by local craftsmen to make clothes and shoes. In early times, the miller or craftsman would have kept part of the produce as payment. Even the Rector was a farmer. In 1720 the Bishop of St David's ordered an inventory of church possessions in Llangynidr. The resultant terrier records the crops and livestock being raised in the parish at that time on which the Rector demanded a tithe[3]. It also showed that the Church glebe, some fifty-five acres which was farmed by the Rector, contained arable and grazing land and an extensive orchard which stretched from Persondy eastwards to present-day Groesffordd. Cider was an important product at that time. Bees were also mentioned, for honey, the universal sweetener, made bee-keeping necessarily popular. Bee boles (niches for bee-skeps) can still be seen in walls at Glaisfer-uchaf, Y Neuadd, Pantypaerau and Pantllwyd-isaf (see Figure 46). The inventory of a local farmer, Jevan Thomas Price, indicates that in the seventeenth century there was probably a considerable proportion of arable land under cultivation: 'wheat, rye, barley, oats and peasen' are mentioned, 160 acres in total, on this particular farm (see page 59).

Figure 70: Pig-sties and bee-bole, Pantypaerau. This bee-bole faces east to catch the morning sun.

Some fairly large farms had developed in the parish by the eighteenth century: Neuadd, in the Dyffryn Crawnon, Aberhoywe and Pwll Court, were independent owner-occupied farms. Several farms received their present names at that time. Villagers were allowed to graze animals on the commons, but by 1760 there was very little lowland common left in the village. Archdeacon H T Payne[4], Rector of Llanbedr, reported in 1785 that, "The Right to Common for sheepwalks and the summer pasturage of small cattle is here (i.e.Llangynidr) more extensive" (than Llangattock). The parish was probably much more wooded in the seventeenth century, although clearance for arable and pasture had been going on previously and enclosure of the common land had already started in the sixteenth century. In 1704 a manorial indenture[5] of Rice Price notes, "A cottage, barn and 50 acres of ground lately enclosed by the said Rice Price being upon the hill within the parish of Llangunydr, 5/- per year". Today all that remains of both lowland commons are tiny fragments along the river, though an enormous stone marking the edge of Cyffredin Common can still be seen at the entrance to Pant-teg Farm. During the eighteenth century greater interest in breeding better stock made enclosure desirable, especially when selected bulls and rams were imported from across the Border to improve the existing herds and flocks.

In 1755, some of the wealthier land-owners in Breconshire formed the 'Brecknock Agricultural Society'. They had a vision of encouraging the new experimental ideas and of introducing modern methods, tools and crops to this area. One of the aims of the Society - the first Agricultural Society in the country - was to persuade poorer farmers of the benefits of these scientific changes. Rev Robert Wynter and Daniel Wynter, whose brother Rev William Wynter held land in Llangynidr, were among the first presidents. Farming in Llangynidr must have been directly influenced by the new ideas generated by these 'Improving Landlords'. William Thomas of Pant-teg leased 53 acres from the Duke of Beaufort in 1770[6]. His indenture required him to "plant upon some fit and convenient part of the said premises, 20 of oak, elm, beech, sycamore or poplar trees" and, "15 perches of quick whitethorn hedge". These had to be maintained over twenty one years of tenancy. If any tree were damaged or neglected, a fine of 2s 6d was to be imposed per tree and 1s 6d for every perch of hedge. The Duke was a patron of the Brecknock Agricultural Society and was carrying out its policies; in 1766 the Society caused a summary of two Acts of Parliament relating to the preservation of native trees to be pinned on church notice boards throughout the county. Charles Powell of Castell Madoc and Howell Harris of Trefeca were founder members of the Society which sought to improve, in a practical way, the economy of poorer people. A premium (6d a bushel) was to be paid to labourers and their families for collecting hawthorn berries and in 1767 and 1768 the same premium was paid for collecting acorns, beechmast, chestnut, holly and 'other timber trees'. The need for a good source of timber and the importance of its replenishment was realised.

However, change happened slowly and Arthur Young, an agricultural writer who travelled through Breconshire in 1776 and 1778, drew a distinction between farming practice in the fertile Usk Valley lowlands and the poorer land on the hillsides. He failed to see any turnips being grown in the poorer areas, and instead of rotating their arable crops in successive years, as members of the Agricultural Society advocated in order to improve production, the hill farmers were growing corn in the same field year after year. Turnips and potatoes had reached the Usk valley in the seventeenth century, but although turnips were exported to Bristol at this time, they were not grown much in the hill country until the eighteenth century. They provided fodder for animals during the winter and both potatoes and turnips helped cottagers to survive in hard times. Wheat was expensive and often suffered from wheat-smut fungus. (Potatoes were added to bread dough, in the nineteenth century, we are told by Mrs Dewi Parry - presumably to eke out the wheat flour). About 1760, the Society introduced a premium for turnips - free seed was given to small farms (rent not exceeding £40 per annum). Money awards were made to 'farm servants' (agricultural labourers) for proficiency in hoeing turnips, cutting corn, rearing the greatest number of lambs and being 'thrifty'. Training in the new methods by means of these incentives aimed to improve the lot of those who toiled on the land. Mr Thomas Thomas' (1827-1918) memoirs mention farm lads being taught to broadcast seed evenly and economically, in the nineteenth century, in much the same spirit of enlightenment as the founders of the Brecknock Agricultural Society, so they could prosper by learning, and perhaps manage their own farms eventually. Farmers were advised to buy fresh seed every year, bringing in new seed from Hereford if possible. Premiums for improving livestock came in the 1780s - indicating that animals were becoming a major source of income. There were many more people to feed in the developing industrial townships of Brynmawr, Ebbw Vale and Tredegar - the new markets gave incentives and the new methods produced a surplus with which to exploit the extra trade. There was pressure on farmer and smallholder to produce extra food to feed the rapidly expanding population in the towns. A pattern of farming stretching back to medieval times gradually disappeared. Summer abundance and winter famine became less marked as both man and his animals were better nourished during the lean season. Mr Thomas recalls fatstock being sold to local butchers or being driven over Mynydd Llangynidr to buyers in these 'new' towns at the end of the nineteenth century and no doubt these commercial links had been established for several decades.

Figure 71: Turning the hay at Ffrwd, 1930s.

All aspects of agriculture were explored by the Brecknock Agricultural Society. From the eighteenth century there was much interest in soil improvement. Good hay containing the new crops of rye, vetches and clover was acknowledged to be vital for winter and spring keep. Surplus hay could be profitably sold in the markets at Abergavenny and Brecon. The horses used in the mining industry consumed considerable quantities and helped to ensure that the price was maintained at between £3 and £7 per ton. Theophilus Jones recommended hay containing clover, rye-grass, trefoil, sainfoin and lucerne as healthy fodder for feeding cattle in spring[7]. From the same source we learn that harvest began in August and ended in mid-October but was later in 'cold vallies between the hills'. Because more animals could now be over-wintered, there was more manure available for building up the soil's fertility. This was judged to be so valuable that William Thomas' Indenture[8] of 1749 required that he 'shall and will also spend and employ all the muck, dung, soil compost and fodder that shall grow, arrive or be made upon the said demised premises upon the lands hereby demised and not elsewhere during the said term'. There are limestone outcrops on the hills above Llangynidr and Rev H T Payne recorded that 'farmers who are tenants of the Manor are allowed to build their own lime kilns'. They were not supposed to burn lime for sale, however. Lime and farmyard muck and sometimes coal ashes and headland cuttings were mixed, according to Theophilus Jones, to improve the ground. That both these historians of Breconshire should record such facts shows the interest which was taken in agricultural practice by 'Establishment' figures of those days.

Figure 72: Harvesting hay with horse and cart, near Llanwrtyd Wells, 1961.

The land in and around Llangynidr was considered good, especially along the banks of the Usk. Rev H T Payne[9] noted after one of his visits, "There is nothing particularly striking in the appearance of the place, but as it lies in the Vale of Crickhowell, where the lower lands border upon the River, it wears a Face of Fertility and from the Brecon Road, exhibits not an unpleasant contrast of Hill and Dale to the eye of the passenger". In the eighteenth century most farms grew cereals and considerable acreages of wheat, barley and oats were still being cultivated during the early twentieth century. According to his daughter Mrs Gladys Powell, William Davies of Glaisfer-isaf grew,

> "some potatoes and some corn, apart from his hay and root crops. The corn, after threshing, was taken to Llangynidr Mill by horse and gambo, where it was ground - wheat for flour and barley and oats for animal feed. Apart from his flock of sheep, Mr Davies kept milking-cows. Butter was made, also cheese, and if the early lambs were sold, the ewes were milked in order to have the milk for cheese-making".

The Llangynidr Tithe Map (1845) lists for the whole of the parish:- 891 acres arable, 3,723 acres meadow and pasture, 270 acres woodland, and 8,866 common lands. Today's acreage of arable land must be minuscule, since few farms in the parish grow cereals or root crops anymore.

Figure 73: A South Wales black cow, ancestor of the Welsh Black breed. They thrived on rough mountain grassland.

Oxen were used for ploughing in this part of Breconshire until the mid-eighteenth century, when new lighter ploughs became available. The cattle had wide horns, as the old lintel over the front door at Aberhoywe shows. We learn from the Brecknock Agricultural Society records that Welsh Black cattle (see Figure 73) were very popular. They were slow to mature, but made steady growth in summer on rough pastures and quickly recovered from the deprivations of winter. These were probably the 'small cattle' which Rev H T Payne reported being pastured on the hills. Many more cattle grazed the mountain land in the early days, being used more for milk than meat. Welsh Blacks began to be crossed with Hereford bulls in the late eighteenth century: Walter Davies[10] (Brecknock Agricultural Society) noted in 1815 that, "White-faced cattle have invaded the Vale of Usk". H T Payne says there were 160 cows being kept and fed on Llangynidr Mountain in 1805. These would have been taken to market in Brecon or Abergavenny. For centuries, cows had been the mainstay of most family farms; milk was made into butter and cheese, and whey was fed to the pigs. At Trefeca, in the mid-eighteenth century, Howell Harris kept Glamorgan Red or Brown cattle and Welsh Blacks (Pembroke or Castle Martin), carefully assessing their various points. In this part of Breconshire there was a great deal of agricultural experimentation going on, from which farming in the areas around prospered.

Horses, whether for riding or use as pack animals, for drawing carriages or to provide 'power' for farm work, were always valuable assets. When a lighter plough was invented in the eighteenth century, horses replaced oxen as draught animals: the Suffolk Punch, according to the Brecknock Agricultural Society was the favourite breed in 1800. This was supplanted by the Shire, which remained popular until tractors arrived in the 1940s. Local farmers bought and sold their horses and mountain ponies at the Talgarth Horse Fairs in the early years of the twentieth century. We are told by Mrs. Emmie Jones, who grew up in the Dyffryn Crawnon in the 1920s, that,

> "most farms kept a couple of cart horses for farm work and two or three ponies for shepherding and for going to market".

Figure 74: Harnessed horses at Ffrwd, 1920s.

Mrs Dewi Parry remembered,

> "some of the Dyffryn people went by pony to the market in Tredegar and took their produce in baskets hung in panniers made of sacking, each side of the saddle, with a third basket held in front of them".

The World of Work

Donkeys and mules were also used as pack animals. Agricultural goods were conveyed on carts pulled by horses or mules; there were also low carts and sleds used from early times to drag fodder and tools across the fields. After its construction, the canal was busy with horse-drawn barges carrying grain and farm produce as well as lime for the farms in Monmouthshire.

The sheep can be considered as a triple-purpose animal, giving meat, wool and cheese. Sheep were milked in Llangynidr as late as the 1930s. A good cheese was made from a mixture of milk from ewes and cows. H T Payne, Theophilus Jones and John Clark[11] (in agricultural writings of 1794), all admired the Welsh Mountain sheep: "they are hardy and economical to keep" and "this small Welsh sheep is extremely important in the economy of this upland area". H T Payne[12] mentioned in his notebook, "It is supposed that 3,500 sheep are depastured upon the extensive mountains of Llangynidr" and described how precarious it was to tend them in winter. In the eighteenth century, sheep were mostly distinguished not by breed, but by 'long wool' or 'short wool'. About this time, progressive farmers were trying to improve their flocks by selective breeding, using high quality stock specially imported from areas such as the Cotswolds. Cheviots were introduced to Breconshire around 1820 and began to be crossed with the small Welsh Mountain sheep; so that the sheep Tom Thomas remembered were an 'improved' type. In the nineteenth century all the farms in the parish still had grazing rights on Llangynidr Mountain. Mr Thomas stated that the larger farms kept upwards of 1,000 sheep, a large proportion of which were wethers. These remained on the hill throughout the year and were kept until three or four years old for wool and best wether mutton. The lambs were sent to lower districts 'on tack' in the mining valleys of Glamorgan and Monmouthshire and then later to the Raglan and Monmouth areas. H T Payne had noted this practice in the eighteenth century. In the late nineteenth and early twentieth centuries, ewes were bought in late autumn at the November Fair in Brecon. They were cared for close to the farm during the winter until the weather was good enough for them to be sent out onto the hill. There they were kept on the sheepwalk from sunrise to sunset by the shepherd, to prevent them from straying, until they settled. Nowadays, sheep carry their owners' individual marks and wander unshepherded for considerable periods. Today's sheep are very often corralled in huge barns for lambing, but still have to be hardy beasts and able to fend for themselves on the mountain land, where they still tend to keep to their own areas of pasture.

New tools were needed to cultivate new crops and the development of the iron industry allowed new machines to be devised. Jethro Tull had published his work on seed-drills in 1731. His ideas were introduced onto Breconshire's farms in the 1750s and 60s. At Trefeca, more efficient hoes and lighter ploughs were tried out and demonstrated to the Agricultural Society members. The 'Rotherham' or 'Whitchurch' ploughs used horses instead of the more cumbersome oxen and were more manoeuvrable on the lighter soils. Two horses abreast could plough an acre per day, according to Theophilus Jones. Carmarthenshire farmers advertised for Breconshire ploughmen at this time and perhaps their reputation was the reason why Tommy Probert (Dyffryn Crawnon), some hundred years later, went to work as a young lad on a farm near Carmarthen. In the thirteenth century, Giraldus Cambrensis[13] had noted an instrument like the blade of a knife with a wooden handle fixed loosely at each end being used to cut corn in Wales. The sickle or reaping-hook, used in the seventeenth and eighteenth centuries, was superseded by the scythe and cradle in the late eighteenth century. Theophilus Jones reported that this tool cut three acres per day. In Llangynidr, at the end of the nineteenth century, a hand flail known as a 'Philip and Mary' was used for threshing corn, although there had been threshing machines hereabouts before 1880, worked by portable steam-engines. During the First World War smaller mechanical threshers, powered by tractor, were brought in. About 1911, John Williams of Pentwyn bought the first Reaper and Binder(see Figure 76). Tom Thomas remembered him helping his neighbours at harvest-time with the new machine. Mrs Nancy Vaughan remembered her father buying a hand-worked winnowing machine in the 1920s at Waun-ddu in the Dyffryn Crawnon. Labour saving devices were constantly being tried out and some found to be worth-while!

Figure 75: Ploughing with a team of horses.

The seasons must have been very much closer to all in rural communities in earlier times, when the weather played such an important part in people's lives. Good conditions at seed-time and harvest literally meant the difference between life and death to communities, just as they still do in some parts of the world. In 1739-40 there was a dreadful winter. Many of the animals died and agricultural labourers, who would have been laid off for the winter, had no work consequently in the spring and summer. In 1795 there was near-famine in England and Wales due to atrocious weather. The government was very anxious (it was only six years since the start of the French Revolution) and the Lord Lieutenant of each county was asked to send in details of crop production. The returns were muddled; parish constables seem to have been employed for collecting these and they sent them in on scraps of paper, consequently they were of little use[14]. Famine and civil unrest were rife in 1800-1, so the frightened government sent out pre-printed forms to every parish in the land for the clergy to fill in the acreages of pulses, potatoes, turnips and grain harvested that year. However, with better weather, the harvest of 1801 turned out remarkably well. There were several later scares, in 1816, and 1817 - remembered as years without a summer and 1818 when a hot, dry summer was followed by September storms which devastated the crops. There was a move by government to take stock of the state of agriculture and its effect on the lives of ordinary people. The more detailed decennial census, started in 1841, shows that 44% of the population of our village depended on agriculture for a living. This figure rose to 47% in 1851, but by 1891 had declined to 33%. Until the mid-1840s only fragmentary information had been derived from surveys, but the decennial census and the tithe maps collated information in a much more useful form.

Figure 76: A McCormick binder drawn by three horses, 1930s. Two of the labourers are putting up sheaves to dry in stooks.

Even in the early years of the twentieth century it was necessary to make good provision for the winter. Connie Roberts, who lived at Coed-yr-ynys Farm remembered, "three cheeses, as round as a chair seat and a tub of butter", being high on the list of preparations. Cheese was made in the summer when milk was plentiful. The farms and the village could be cut off from the outside world for long periods during a bad winter. Villagers were thankful to trudge through the snow to Pentwyn Farm for milk in the winter of 1982, when the milk delivery lorry failed to get through the drifts and were thankful, too, for well- stocked village shops! However, being much less dependent upon locally grown produce nowadays, when much of our food is flown in from all parts of the world, we seem to be far from the cutting edge of those natural disasters which beset our forefathers.

In the nineteenth century the family workforce on the farm was often supplemented by some hired help, perhaps a shepherd or cowman, and a maid who would do housework or help in the dairy. As the nineteenth century census shows, these people 'lived in' as part of the family, the food being reportedly, 'mainly home-produced, plain, but good'. If there was no-one available locally, men and women were hired, for six months usually, at Brecon or Hay-on-Wye Fairs in May and November. Several came from Herefordshire and Radnorshire and settled here. In 1785, H T Payne recorded that Llangynidr villagers had a 'prescriptive right' to hold four fairs a year - April 20th, Oct 7th, Dec 1st and the Wednesday before Christmas. These fairs were principally for the sale of livestock. The sheep sale, which was always held on the first Monday in October, may have been a relic of the old Fair. In the past, the sheep sale was held from pens erected along the sides of the road through the village, on the green 'Tump' outside the parish churchyard and later in Persondy field, when Chadwicks of Abergavenny were the auctioneers. Later still, and until it was discontinued early in the 1990s, its venue was in the field in front of the Old Rectory. The old Wednesday-before-Christmas Fair has been commuted to the 'Turkey Whist-Drive', held in the evening! Tom Thomas mentioned two fairs being held in April and June in the nineteenth and early twentieth centuries, where local people often bought their pigs.

Traditionally, pigs were a fundamental part of the cottager and small-holder economy, which was the way of life in villages like Llangynidr. Almost every family kept a pig: bought at weaning, usually 8-10 weeks old, it would be kept through the summer and autumn and killed for bacon during the winter. In the early years of this century, spent hops and barley were collected after beer-making at the Red Lion' by the villagers to feed their back-garden pigs. Connie Roberts also remembered,

> "All the small potatoes were boiled for the pigs, and without draining them, barley meal was added to the water and also skimmed milk. It tasted wonderful!"

No doubt the bacon was also quite tasty! Pig-killing was a social event in the calendar. Emmie Jones, who lived as a child at The Wern in the Dyffryn, described her mother going to help neighbours who had killed a pig. Her grandmother, Mrs. Phillips, who lived at Yew Tree Cottage,

> "went to the farms where pigs were being killed, with the men who were doing the killing, to help with the making of the lard (melting down the fat from around the kidneys). She also washed the intestines and did this in the river, walking down even from Bwlch-y-waun to do it. The intestines were made into tripe and chitterlings - very good cooked with fried onions!"

Figure 77: Washing sheep at Blaenau-mawr, Cwmdu. The farmer in the bowler hat is William Morris, great-grandfather of John Games. Note the cider jar at the foot of the gate-post.

Shearing time was another big event in the social year. Again neighbours and friends joined to help each other. Mrs Gladys Powell's mother at Glaisfer-isaf would,

> "cook a shoulder of veal in the bread oven; it was stuffed with thyme and parsley seasoning and was particularly good. It would be served with spring cabbage and potatoes, followed by rhubarb and gooseberry pies. About fifteen men came to help at shearing time."

Similar preparations went on at most of the other farms in the parish. The biggest pools in the River Crawnon were used for washing sheep - ten days before shearing. Connie Roberts, whose family worked both Coed-yr-ynys Farm and Tir Alson, recalled that on shearing day, "the food was prepared at Coed-yr-ynys, and taken to Tir Alson in three tea chests on a gambo. A sheep would have been killed and butchered and cooked in the big bake oven. There were cold, cooked potatoes, salad, home-made pickles, cheese and home-made bread. Afterwards, fruit tarts (red currant was very popular) and yeast cake. The food was eaten in the loft. There were three hundred sheep to shear by hand and about ten men to do it."

Mrs Myfanwy Davies added in her memoirs,

"At shearing time, a big gooseberry pie would be made on a large meat dish, as much as two feet from end-to-end".

Mrs Dewi Parry said shearing

"lasted a fortnight and the farmers went to each other's farms to shear by hand: there was no payment and it was a six-day week, with no shearing on Sundays. There were great preparations at each farm. A sheep was killed and the legs, loins and shoulders were used. A big ham was cooked for supper. All the baking was done in the bake oven - three big yeast loaves, seven sponge cakes, five tarts and rock cakes. There was home-made cheese for tea and for supper, cold ham with four or five big bowls of salad. The salad dressing was home-made - sugar, a little water and vinegar mixed, and then added to a pint of fresh cream. A cask of cider completed the hospitality."

Figure 78: Shearing sheep at Y Neuadd (1890-1900). All the family and neighbours came to help. There are 12 men using hand-shears. Mr and Mrs William Williams are standing on the right.

The World of Work

Figure 79: Seventeenth century field barn above Dan-y-wern.

Figure 80: Wall-creep (for counting sheep) in drystone wall on Lan Fawr.

Figure 81: Mrs Cliff Price, Cefn-crug, off to market in Tredegar.

Figure 82: The pigs-cot at Aberyail.

The women and children helped in the fields at harvest time, tying the sheaves and gleaning any stray grain. The village year was punctuated by these natural festive occasions which involved most of the neighbours. Farming families stood together, having a common purpose, and this co-operation led to much conviviality and sociability. Mr Monty Jones remembered at Christmas-time,

> "much neighbourly help was given to get the 'feathering' done. Numerous turkeys, geese and chickens were reared at the top of the Dyffryn Valley and these all had to be killed and feathered and dressed for the Christmas markets - no refrigerators or freezers then!"

Mr Jones could remember feathering for,

> "a whole week at various farms without once going to bed and managing with an occasional nap in the chair. Food was given, but not on the scale of the shearing gatherings. The goose wings (for dusters), feathers and down were saved, but the other feathers were burned. The birds were taken to the Christmas markets at Tredegar in baskets and bags on the ponies."

The work on the farm was hard and, in the summer months, long. All the family helped - even young children had daily jobs, feeding the poultry, collecting eggs, bringing in the cows at milking-time. According to Bryn Probert the children gathered primroses to sell at the Good Friday market in Tredegar and in the summer whinberries and blackberries were collected, all of which helped to swell the family income. There was an old established market at Brynmawr ('Y Waun') where eggs, butter, cheese, potatoes, poultry and seasonal garden produce would be taken by donkey or pony and trap each week. Thomas Thomas remembered picking so many mushrooms from Coed Cae Mael (a field below High Meadow) one bumper year that he had a suit of clothes made from the proceeds.

Until the advent of mechanisation and electricity, everyday life was physically hard for most folk. Mrs Jane Davies (nee Edwards) was born at Pentwyn Farm in 1891. She recalled going to live with her grandparents at Rhiwgarn, where she worked with the poultry, helped with the hay harvest and, at the age of fourteen, milked four cows a day. She survived to celebrate one hundred years of living in Llangynidr! Clean drinking water had to be carried from the nearest spring. This could be some distance away, as at Aberhoywe, where the best spring was down the steep river bank; washing water here came through a pipe from the canal into a stone trough in the yard.

The work of the women-folk was planned exactly on a weekly routine, according to Mrs Dewi Parry.

> "Monday meant wash-day and the washing and cleaning and putting away of the Sunday-best clothes. Tuesday was taken up with baking and ironing. On

Wednesday the house was cleaned right through. Thursday brought butter making. Mrs. Parry's mother, Mrs. Thomas, made little pats of butter to use with little cobs of bread which she made for her children, which were especially delicious. On Friday two hours were spent cleaning the brasses. There was also presentation and packing up ready to go to market on Saturday. To get to market they went to Pant-y-rhiw station and caught the train to Dowlais with butter, eggs, poultry, etc. for market. Returning, they bought groceries [and, presumably, other necessities]. Sunday brought the round of Chapel services and Sunday School."

Connie Roberts' mother at Coed-yr-ynys had a big bread-oven outside at the back of the house. They bought Indian meal, which cost ten shillings a sack, barley meal and corn meal from Llangynidr Mill. Some Dyffryn households obtained flour (and meal for the animals) at Gibson's Mill at Talybont in the 1920s. Mrs Dewi Parry gave her mother's recipe for making bread:- half a hundredweight of flour and a quarter of a pound of yeast mixed in a big bath.

"Thirteen four-pound loaves were made once a week, and they were baked in the bake oven with three big loaf cakes and an enamel bowl of rice pudding. After they were cooked the oven was reheated and sponge cakes and rock cakes were cooked."

Tuesday must have been a busy day! Presumably they would have had a good store of dry kindling wood to heat the oven, collected by the rest of the family. The flour was delivered in bags which would sometimes be washed and made into tea towels and pillow cases. One lady was known to have made them into knickers with 'Spiller's Flour' across the seat! When they lived at Clog-fawr, Mrs Probert milked the family cow, which Bryn and his brothers rounded up, before and after school.

Other memories illustrating the life of the farm household at this time came, once more, from Mrs Gladys Powell.

"The chimney was swept regularly with a gorse bush or a thorn bush being pulled up and down inside the chimney on ropes, by someone at the fireplace and someone else on the roof. All the domestic heavy work: weekly wash, cleaning of grates, scrubbing and 'housework', was done by a servant-girl hired from one Fair Day to the next: Sometimes they were overburdened and 'put-upon'."

However, a good placement provided girls with training and security when they were treated with the kindness and consideration, such as Frances Bevan described, when she worked for the Reynallt family at Llwyn-yr-ynn and Llwynyreos.

The wages of farm servants had increased by the beginning of the nineteenth century, due to the competition of heavy industry in the townships where between 2s

6d and 3s per day was earned by railway, canal, mine, lime-kiln and iron workers[15]. (In 1780 Brecknock Agricultural Society records reapers being paid between 1s and 18d per acre, with food and drink provided; for mowing hay, men received 2s - 2s 6d and females, 6d - 9d, per statute acre). This was a problem right through to the twentieth century, with agricultural labourers generally receiving lower wages than those working in other industries. Nowadays machines have largely taken over the work and a very small percentage of today's village population makes a living from the land. Even farmers' sons and daughters have to diversify and gain employment in jobs connected to farming, like hiring themselves and their machines for contract hedging, tree clearance, and land drainage or working as representatives for animal feed and fertiliser firms. Universal education has enabled youngsters from rural backgrounds to seek employment in the wider world. Both the family farm and village life are very different at the beginning of the twenty-first century.

Until recently orchards were considered a valuable asset and most of the farms and small-holdings would have had a few apple trees to provide fruit for eating, cooking and cider-making. Twenty eight acres of orchard were listed on the parish tithe map (1845). The 1903/4 OS maps show orchards at Pwll Court, Glanyrafon, Ty-canol, Pont Garreg, Dan-y-wern, Aberhoywe and Pentwyn. All of these have now gone.

Figure 83: A cider mill. A small horse provided the power to turn the stone which crushed the apples.

A new landowner, who had made money from industry on the southern side of Mynydd Llangynidr, influenced the farming scene in the Usk Valley in the early part of the nineteenth century. Sir Joseph Bailey built Glanusk and began buying up land and holdings to form an estate. Aberhoywe was sold to Glanusk in 1832 and became a tenanted farm. The land was redistributed as more local farms were taken over. We may think the practice of blocking farms together to make bigger holdings is a twentieth century phenomenon. It perhaps happens on a larger scale now, as may be seen in the Dyffryn Crawnon, where many farm-houses have been sold and the land taken over by neighbouring farmers, but the nineteenth century census records how the acreage of many farms altered from one decade to the next, as land was redistributed between holdings.

The Duke of Beaufort owned much of the land within the village until 1915, when many of the holdings were sold and many former tenants were able to buy their farms; he retained ownership of the common land.

Figure 84: Horses were versatile animals; this was the Dyffryn Crawnon Home Guard (Mounted Section) during the Second World War.

The rate of change in farming methods accelerated as marketing methods became better organised; during the First World War a weekly fatstock market was started next door to the railway station at Talybont-on-Usk and mechanised transport and better roads encouraged mobility. The two World Wars had a great impact. Farmers everywhere in Britain were compelled to plough up land and grow more corn and potatoes to feed a nation which could no longer depend on its ships to bring imported food. Between the wars little ploughing up of pasture went on in Llangynidr, when farming, like other industries, was at a low ebb. New Zealand lamb, brought in refrigerated ships in the 1920s and 30s, spelled the end of British mutton, and consequently wethers on our hills. In 1939, however, the Government introduced compulsory ploughing orders. Each farm was required to grow the acreage of crops requested by the Breconshire War Agricultural Committee. This brought more difficult land into cultivation as every available bit of land was ploughed and cultivated. Girls were drafted in to help with the farm work, joining the Land Army and the 'Dig for Victory' campaign, since many of the young men were away in the Armed Forces. Mrs Delphine Ford went to work as a Land Girl at Llangasty and the Glanusk Estate employed others. The Government maintained a keen interest in agriculture, particularly during the wars. Marketing Boards were established when food was rationed, to organise the supplies of produce like potatoes, milk and eggs. The Farmers' Unions fought for better support to ensure farm incomes became more reliable.

The link between healthy farm produce and public health was established. In the 1950s tuberculosis was eradicated and Breconshire became a 'clean' area. The pasteurisation of milk meant the end of milk sales directly from the farm. Local milk was collected in churns in the 1960s and early 70s and taken by lorry to the bottling depots, from where it was distributed over a wide area. 'Creameries' were opened and butter, cheese and cream manufactured in hygienic factory conditions a long way from the source of production. Only recently are traditional local cheeses being produced again. Stock regulations were introduced for the purpose of controlling diseases such as Swine Fever and Foot and Mouth; sheep dipping was made compulsory. Such enormous advances have been made in animal medicine in the second half of the twentieth century that it is difficult to realise that Tom Thomas recalled an animal doctor, John Richards - a 'charmer', still working in 1946 at Penybailey. Nowadays, vets have a huge armoury of drugs available for the treatment of animal disease, but fifty years ago these were undiscovered.

After the second World War, the Farmers Union was determined to keep up the momentum and not let a grateful nation forget how much was owed to farmers for stepping up production in times of need. The improvement in stable prices for produce and conditions of work were not allowed to slip as they had after the 1914-18 war. More forms had to be filled in as farming became a well-organised industry; this was part of the price of a more stable agricultural economy. Llangynidr, at the end of the twentieth century, was still a small community surrounded by farmed land. Farming families have come and gone: the 1891 Census records thirty farms in the parish; today there are about fifteen, of which several are farmed on a part-time basis. No milk is now produced in Llangynidr, although several farms raise beef cattle. Specialised farm labourers have largely disappeared from our local farms. No longer is anyone employed purely as a 'shepherd', 'cowman' or 'dairymaid'. There were nine shepherds in the census of 1871; these had dwindled to one, only twenty years later, in 1891. Very few farms keep 'poultry about the house' (or yard), but we have one poultry specialist where we can buy our Christmas turkeys. There is very little arable land now and the farms concentrate on rearing sheep, which is less labour-intensive. Some of the farms at the head of the Claisfer and Dyffryn Crawnon valleys have been overtaken by conifer plantations - their names just a memory, occasionally discovered on an old map. Most of the farm land belonging to Danydarren was afforested around 1970 and sometime later the farm-house was demolished by the Forestry Commission. Llangynidr Service Station looks after our transport in this era of the car and repairs farm machinery, being the modern equivalent of the four smithies which were operating here a hundred years ago. Very little of our food comes from local growers; the market economy dictates the trends and cycles as it has done previously, certainly since the eighteenth century.

Nevertheless, the landscape has been fashioned by agriculture. The old practice of transhumance is still reflected in the arrangement of some farm lands. Even today, especially in the Dyffryn Crawnon, some holdings have land in a strip extending from the valley floor to the hill, where there is access to the mountain common. There is no need of a 'hafod', however, and these summer homes disappeared when the herding of livestock ceased. Although the village is no longer dependent upon farming for its main source of income, the major part of the land area in our parish is still farmed. Hedges, stone walls, fields, woods, moorland and rivers provide habitats for wild-life, but we are still dependent, to a large extent, on agriculture to maintain these features, and the landscape we love, in the twenty first century.

References

Jenkins, J Geraint, Rural Industry in Brecknock, *Brycheiniog XIV*
Edmunds, H, History of Brecknockshire Agricultural Society, *Brycheiniog II & III*
Young, A, *Annals of Agriculture Vol VIII* quoted in Edmunds, H (see above)
Transcriptions of interviews recorded by Dorothea Watkins in Llangynidr Local History Society Archives,
Hughes, W, Porter, M & Archer, M S, *Survey of Llangynidr Buildings 1997-1999*, Llangynidr Local History Society Archives
Llangynidr Schoolchildren & Staff, Porter, M & Archer, M S, Cusack, I & T, *Survey of Llangynidr Hedgerows 1997-1999*, Llangynidr Local History Archives

Notes

1   NLW Badminton 7
2   Jenkins, Philip, *History of Modern Wales*
3   NLW Maybery III 4176
4   NLW 4278E
5   NLW Badminton 6733
6   NLW Badminton 4606
7   Jones, Theophilus, *History of Brecknockshire*
8   NLW Badminton 6859
9   NLW Ms 4278
10 Davies, W, *General View of the Agriculture and Domestic Economy of South Wales*, Vol 2, quoted in Edmunds, H (above)
11 Clark, J, *General view of the Agriculture in the County of Brecknock*, quoted in Edmunds, H (above)
12 Payne, H T, *Parochial Notices of the Deanery of the Third Part of Brecknock*, Vol 1 & 2, Powys County Archives Office
13 Giraldus Cambrensis quoted in Jones, T, *History of Brecknockshire*
14 Dodd, J P, The Brecknockshire Crop Returns for 1854, *Brycheiniog VI*
15 Jones, T, ibid

Haulage

Until lorries arrived in the village about 1920, horses and mules were used for transporting goods. The mills and larger firms, like Watkins and Bevan and Oaklands Timber Yard, had their own transport, but there were also several independent hauliers such as John Bevan. Cart horses provided the traction for heavy work, like drawing the wagons which carried large oak tree-trunks back to the timber yard, (see Figure 67, page 98) and for many farming operations such as ploughing and harrowing. Tommy Probert of Pyrgad recalled working as a wagoner on a farm near Talgarth:

"He was in charge of eight cart horses and one cob. Three of the cart horses weighed twenty hundredweight each. He was responsible for ploughing 85 acres, for hauling all the hay and corn, and for hauling the threshing equipment. He had free board and lodging in addition to his pay of £1 a week. Conditions were good and the food excellent".

Horses were replaced by tractors on local farms about the time of the second world war. A cob or pony was used to draw the trap which carried the farmer's wife and her produce to market, or for pulling the gambo used by the mill to deliver bags of flour or meal. According to Rev David Charles, Principal of Trefeca College in 1847, it was dangerous to travel along the roads late on the evening of a market day.

"Seldom do we meet farm-servants returning from any considerable distance with their master's waggon or cart but that we find them intoxicated, while it is quite lamentable to witness the number of drunken farmers returning from market on Saturdays[1]".

Pack horses or mules were often used for carrying materials such as fence posts over rough terrain (see Figure 85). About 1900, John Bevan of Ty Sheriff, Pant-llwyd, Glaisfer-uchaf and Ton-mawr, took over from his father at Ty-canol, a lime delivery service using mules. His mules transported the stone for building the Dyffryn Crawnon school in 1910. In 1984 Tom and Nellie Thomas of Saladin recalled some of the mule businesses in the first half of the twentieth century.

"About 75 years ago, there was keen competition in transporting and selling lime for agricultural and building purposes. Pack horses were originally used, but then mules were found to be hardier. During the 1939-45 War, the American and Indian troops stationed at Glanusk Park had many mules, which did military training on the Brecon Beacons and Black Mountains. These were tall mules; Tom Herriot ('Tom the Rag'), who travelled around the villages collecting rags, had a similar mule in his cart. The mules used locally were smaller and more agile animals- possibly a cross with Welsh mountain ponies. Mule businesses came and went; Bill Jenkins of Cynidr House, David Powell of Rhiwgarn and William Edwards of Hillgate all kept mules at various times. There was keen competition over the price of lime. Bill Jenkins charged 1s 3d for a 'barrel' of lime, which was a bag of lime weighing about 2cwt, delivered to Talybryn beyond Bwlch. The Hopkins family of Sycamore House ran the last mule business. The Hopkins' mules were often to be seen grazing at the roadside and on 'The Tump' outside the church lychgate. These mules achieved fame by appearing in a film called 'The Drum', starring Sabu, a young Indian actor. They were last seen leaving the village about the time of the Siege of Tobruk (1941)".

Figure 85: Mules were often used to extract timber or carry materials across rough terrain.

Notes

1   Symons, J C, *Report on the state of education in Wales* (1847)

Shops

Figure 86: Waterloo shop and the old Village Hall, about 1915. From the John Addis collection.

For the dressmakers, tailors, cordwainers and many others engaged in cottage industries in the nineteenth century, their home was also workplace and shop. These shops would not usually have held stocks of goods; clothing and shoes being made to measure for customers, and other items to order. Dressmakers were often young, unmarried women, still living at home, like Elizabeth Jones, aged 15 (see Figure 149), daughter of the landlord at the Three Salmons in 1851. Sometimes a trade operated from the same house for a long period, parents passing on skills to sons and daughters. Howell Rogers, father and son, worked as tailors in Upper Llangynidr for over 40 years. Isaac Phillips was a shoemaker at Cyffredin Cottage for at least 30 years, while John Prosser, another shoemaker, was in business at Penishacoed from 1851 until the end of the century.

By contrast, grocery stores usually seem to have been short-lived. No grocers' shops were recorded in the 1851 census, but for the rest of the nineteenth century between three and six were trading at any one time. They appeared and disappeared in various spots but few survived for long. Waterloo House was an exception, as it was in business for over a hundred years. It was opened by Thomas Hadley, Miller and Corn Factor, about 1855, and closed as a grocery and general store in 1980. The initiative displayed by the Misses Hannah and Sarah Prothero, keepers of Waterloo Shop in the early years of the twentieth century, is legendary; requests for 'loose tea' met by opening packets and shaking the contents into a paper bag or the precise weighing of one ounce of sweets achieved with the aid of incisors! For about a hundred years, until 1981, the Watkins family ran a General Stores and, for most of this time, this was also the Post Office. Walnut Tree Stores, at Coed yr Ynys, has been a grocery business since 1930. It was preceded by a draper's store, destroyed by a fire in the late 1920s. Notes about other shops in the village are included in the postmen's rounds.

Figure 87: Coed-yr-ynys Shop (right). In the early twentieth century it was run by the Badgett family and later by Misses Harriet and Matilda Jones.

Figure 88: Walnut Tree Cottage in 1899. At a later date the house on the right became a draper's shop and is now a General Stores.

Mills

Local mills were important in former times when all the flour for home bread-making was milled in the parish. An early reference to mills in Tretower manor occurs in the Inquisition Post Mortem of John Picard (1305), where a corn mill and a fulling mill, together worth 40 pence a year, were listed among the manorial assets[1]. In medieval times the tenants were required to keep the lord's mill in good repair. Their duties, as recorded in a Crickhowell custumal (c.1295), included rebuilding weirs after floods, scouring leats and mill-ponds and replacing worn millstones[2]. The tenants were also obliged to take their own corn to be ground at the manorial mill, and could be fined 10s if they milled their corn elsewhere. As late as 1770 the lease of William Thomas for Pant-teg Farm included a "Suit of Mill" clause requiring him to take all his corn to be ground at the manorial mill at Cwmdu[3]. The millers took a proportion of the meal in payment and were notorious for their sharp practice, or in Chaucer's words, describing the miller in The Canterbury Tales,

"Wel coude he stelen corn, and tollen thryes
And yet he had a thombe of gold, pardee."

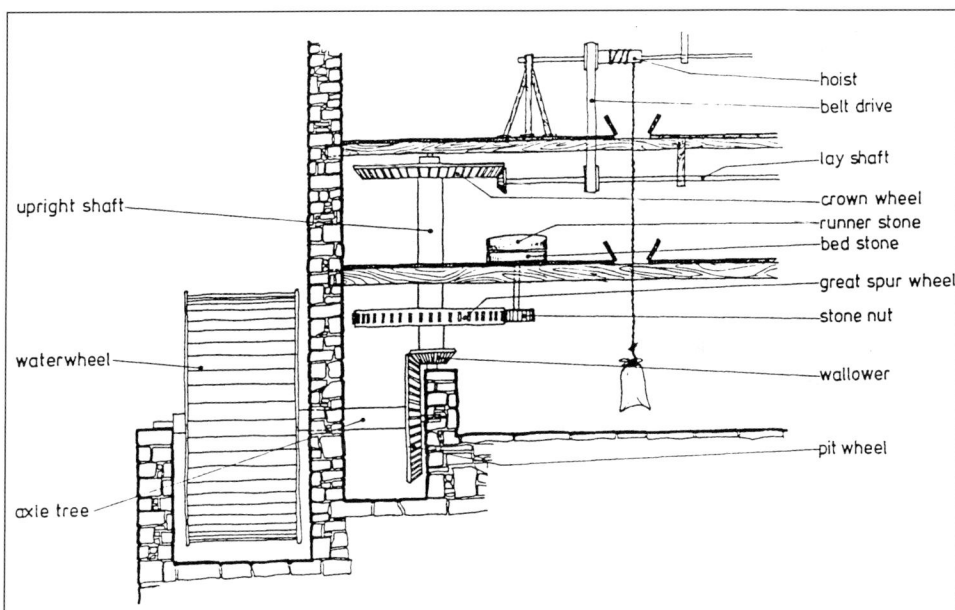

Figure 89: Plan to show the machinery of a water mill.

To make sure of his share the lord charged high rents for his mills. In 1587 the annual rent of the main manorial mill at Felindre, Cwmdu was £13 6s 8d[4], which was more than the total rents of all free and customary tenants, excluding those with indentures.   Such lucrative investments contributed to the wealth of several prominent families like the Vaughans, Prices, Williams and Gwynnes, all of whom owned local mills. Giles Nicholas, Rector of Llangynidr, (1637-1678) ensured that his youngest son, Benjamin, was well provided for by bequeathing him several parcels of land, two houses and a water mill in Llanarth, Monmouthshire, in addition to the advowson of Penderyn. Fourteen years later, Benjamin is described as a 'Chyrurgeon' (surgeon) in the will of his brother-in-law, Rev John Bowen (1691).

Six corn mills are known to have operated in Llangynidr, though probably not more than four were functional at any one period. All the local mills were water corn grist mills, harnessing water power from the rivers. Often weirs were built to impound a supply of water, which could be diverted along a leat to drive the mill wheel, geared to rotate the mill-stones which ground the grain into flour.

Figure 90: Interior of the water mill at Felin-fach, 1984. The great spur wheel can be seen on the left.

Mill wheels were of three types, breast, overshot or undershot, depending on the height at which the water was delivered to the wheel. Crops such as oats, beans, vetches and, in hard times, gorse were milled for animal fodder. None of the machinery has survived and in most cases the buildings have also disappeared, although the mill in Upper Llangynidr remains, much altered, as Mill House. In early medieval times the lord of the manor usually reserved the right to fish the weirs. At a later period the fishing rights were leased. In his will (1688) Lewis Morgan, a prominent Royalist, who became Attorney General for South Wales after the Restoration, bequeathed to John Watkin "the residue of my terme in Glawcotts weare", his fishing on the River Usk at Buckland Mill.

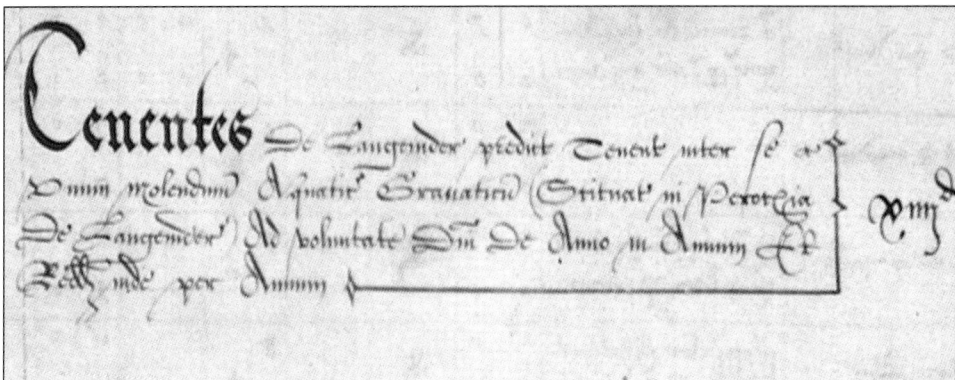

Figure 91: The reference to Llangynidr mill in the Manorial Survey of 1587.

Llangynidr Mill

In the sixteenth century the free tenants of Llangynidr had their own mill, for which an annual payment of 14 pence was made to the manor in 1561[5] (see Figure 91). This water corn grist mill with overshot wheel, no doubt repaired and rebuilt from time to time, probably occupied the same site on the River Claisfer in Upper Llangynidr for several centuries. It was owned by the Vaughans during the seventeenth and eighteenth centuries[6]. In 1675 it was held by Henry Williams, and he was succeeded by Rice Price (1700) and Thomas Watkins (1726).

The tithe map schedule (1845) shows William Prosser as owner and Thomas Hadley as miller. The Hadleys, who also had a grocers shop at Waterloo House from 1860, continued as 'Millers and Corn Factors' until 1891[7]. This was the last working mill in the parish, operating until the 1930s when Watkin Watkins was the miller[8].

The leat, about 350m in length, on the south bank of River Claisfer, ran underground for part of its course, and supplied two mill ponds about half way along. The upper mill pool was also fed by a spring known as Hadley's Well.

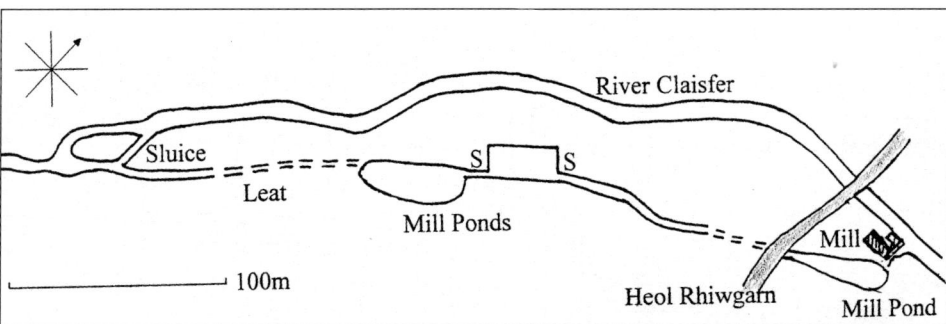

Figure 92: Plan of the watercourses associated with Llangynidr Mill, 1842.

Clog-fawr Mill

A mill with an undershot wheel is shown on the 1587 survey on the River Crawnon near Clog-fawr. At that time it was the only manorial mill in the parish, leased to Thomas David for £2 a year. Thomas David also rented[4] the Clog-fawr holding of 15 acres for £2. Clog-fawr Mill was probably the mill referred to as Melin yr Arlwydd (*Lord's Mill*) in the 1675 dispute (see page 60) In 1663, "now in decay", it was leased to Hugh Powell for 21 years at an annual rent of £2 and six loads of coal worth 4s[9]. The previous tenant had been Charles Vaughan. The mill is not shown on the 1760 Beaufort Estate map[10] and, according to local people, the mill had been derelict for thirty years in 1675.

In the sixteenth century there was another water corn mill less than 1km below Clog-fawr Mill. It was owned by Howell Phillips in 1588 and situated below Y Wern near the place where a little brook, called Nant Angharad in medieval times, enters the Crawnon[11].

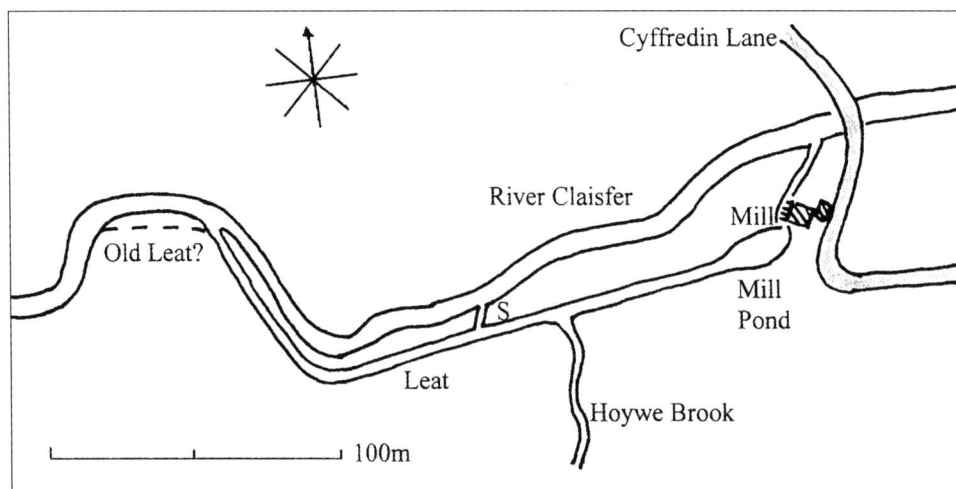

Figure 93: Plan of the water-courses associated with Cyffredin Mill, 1842.

Cyffredin Mill

This is shown, with overshot wheel, on the 1587 survey (Figure 33), located on the River Claisfer near its confluence with the River Usk. At that time it was owned by William Vaughan of Tretower Court. The adjacent land, and probably also the mill, was bought by Thomas Price in 1609/10[12]. The mill was held by the Prices of Aberhoywe until the farm was sold to Glanusk in 1830[13]. In the 1851 Census, Henry Saunders is recorded as farmer and miller at Aberhoywe, employing a miller, William Jenkins, and a mill carrier, Thomas Watkins who was 15 years old. The mill stopped working about 1860. Some tumble-down walls remain and the leat, running for some 250m along the south bank of the Claisfer, and the tailrace can still be traced on the ground. A millstone in a garden nearby seems to be made of the local conglomerate (millstone grit).

Figure 94: Cyffredin Mill photographed by Mr Sparrow about 1890.

Felin-genol (*Middle Mill*)

Felin-genol was probably situated on the River Claisfer near the point where the canal crosses the river. In 1675 the mill was bought by Edmond Jones of Buckland from William Phillip Powell for £40 and within a year it was the focus of a 'Suit of Mill' dispute between the lord of the manor, the Marquis of Worcester, and three local farmers (see page 60). William Phillip Powell lived at the farm now known as Tyr William Richard. Felin-genol may not have lasted very long, for it does not appear on a Buckland rental of 1745. About 1756 the Buckland estate was purchased by Roderick Gwynne of Glanbran Park, Carmarthenshire. Plans (c. 1910) of a proposed canal feeder from the River Claisfer near Pontganol bridge show an existing leat which might have been associated with the mill.

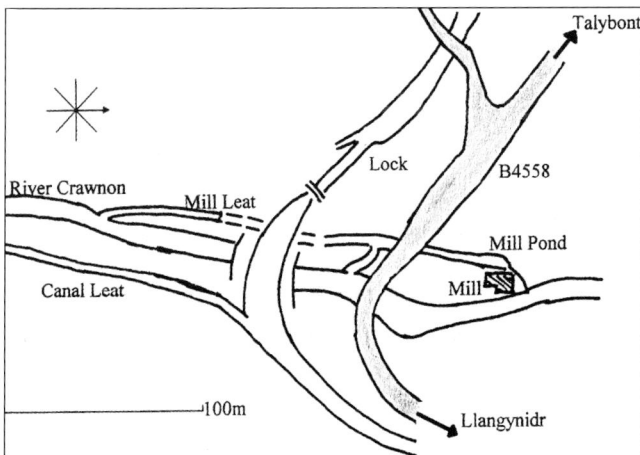

Figure 95: Plan of the water-courses associated with Cwmcrawnon Mill.

Cwmcrawnon Mill

Located on the west bank of the River Crawnon near its confluence with the River Usk, this mill was in Llanddetty parish until recent boundary changes. Both Cwmcrawnon Mill and Melin Maes-y-gwaelod (Buckland Mill) on the north bank of the River Usk nearby, were owned by the Gwynnes of Buckland in the eighteenth century. In 1802 Cwmcrawnon Mill was sold to the Brecon and Abergavenny Canal Navigation Company for £682 10s 0d[14]. The sale included other property and the right to abstract water from the River Crawnon. In 1799 an attempt to sell the mill for £200 had failed to attract any bidders[15]. The mill was not working during the construction and early years of the canal[16], but in 1806 the Agent reported,

"... the canal from Brecknock to Llanelly is become so tight that it is likely the Crawnon water will but seldom be again wanted and that he thinks the Crawnon Mill might now be worked without prejudice to the Navigation".

The Canal Company decided the mill could be leased, but reserved the right to secure future supplies of water from the Crawnon. In 1820 it was recorded that Thomas Prosser gave up the mill and David Jones rented it from year to year at 15 guineas per annum. Two years later he was prepared to renovate the mill and buy a new pair of millstones at his own expense, if the Canal Company would grant him a 21 year lease. The mill appears to have closed down in the 1870s when Edward Williams was the miller.

Figure 96: Buckland Mill photographed about 1875. The undershot wheel can be seen, though the mill is clearly derelict.

Fulling Mills

The name Pandy nearly always indicates the location of a fulling or tuck mill, which was involved in the production of woollen cloth. Pentwyn Pandy was the name of a small holding which formerly occupied the site of the Twyn Pandy estate, but no further evidence has been discovered of a fulling mill on this site.

Notes

1 Cooke, M, *The Family of Picard*, p 35
2 NLW Badminton 379, 380
3 NLW Badminton 4606
4 NLW Badminton 3
5 NLW Badminton 406
6 PCAO Marriage settlement of Charles Vaughan (1726/7) B/D/JPO/18/1
7 Census Records for Llangynidr (1851-1891)
8 Notes for Introduction to History of Llangynidr Reminiscences of Mrs Jenny Morris (Llangynidr Local History Society Archives, File 7)
9 NLW Badminton 6679,6670
10 NLW Badminton 7
11 NLW Maybery 6968
12 NLW Badminton 58
13 NLW Twiston Davies, Vol II 3533
14 Poole, E, *Illustrated History and Biography of Breconshire*
15 NLW DTM Jones Collection Vol IV p 427
16 Records of the Brecon and Abergavenny Canal Navigation Company per John Norris

Smithies

Blacksmiths, like millers, were important figures in the community in earlier times. They forged armour and weapons in times of war, shod horses and cattle, replaced metal tyres on cart and carriage wheels, and made and repaired household implements and farm machinery. Occupations are not generally noted in manorial records before the eighteenth century; exceptions were priests, denoted by cleric, and blacksmiths, identified by gof (*smith*) after their names, as in the Welsh Jury for the 1587 Survey[1] (see page 49).

Parish field names from the sixteenth century attest the activity of local blacksmiths in former times. Ero gove (*Smith's Acre*) and Kay'r Oden (*Kiln Field*), recorded in the 1587 Survey, indicate the presence of an early forge somewhere between Cyffredin Lane and Pencommin. At that time the blacksmith there was William Watkin. When his son Watkin William took over, the smithy doubled as an alehouse[2]; operating a forge was always thirsty work, and there were 'captive' customers waiting for their horses to be shod. Watkin William died in 1634 and in the instructions in his will to Maud, his wife and executrix, he asks for his, "Shopptools Andevils bellows and all other implements pertaining to a smyth shoppe to be sould ... for the uttermost penny". The proceeds were to be paid to his daughter Ales (*Alice*). In his inventory the tools were valued at £4.

Philip Thomas Llewelyn is the first Llangynidr blacksmith to figure in the manorial records, leasing a house and eight acres in Cwm Claisfer in 1530[3]. By 1587 another smith, Hoell David, was renting the same holding, so probably the forge was also there[4]. In 1682 a village blacksmith, Henry Thomas Nicholas, described as 'a poore man' petitioned for parish relief at the Quarter Sessions[5]. A field where Groesffordd now stands was known as Cae dan yr Evell (*Field below the smithy*) in the eighteenth century[6], so there must have been a forge near the Red Lion from an early date. There was also a forge at the top of the village, then called Pentre, opposite the Beaufort Arms, in the eighteenth century[7]. At a later date that forge seems to have been moved across the road into Mardy Lane.

Nineteenth century census returns show that there were four or five smithies in business in Llangynidr at that time. Almost every inn had a forge nearby, operating in a kind of symbiotic association catering for the needs of passing traffic; while their horses were being shod or their carriages repaired, travellers could be refreshed at the inn. Pentre forge was handy for both the Beaufort Arms and the Mason's Arms. Beside the churchyard and 'Byways' was the forge of John Edwards, son of John Edwards landlord of the Horse Shoe across the road (see Figure 97). There was a smithy next to the King's Arms at the eastern end of Cyffredin Lane, while another on 'The Square' near the canal wharf at Coed yr Ynys was well-placed for the Three Salmons and the White Lion.

Figure 97: Horse Shoe Smithy about 1890, situated next to Byways and across the road from the Horse Shoe Inn. The blacksmith was John Davies.

Figure 98: The repair and replacement of horse-shoes and iron tyres for cart-wheels was a regular source of work for the blacksmith.

In 1851 five members of one family were working as blacksmiths in the village: John Owen, his three sons and his grandson. Grandfather John(1), helped by his son Rees, operated the Coed-yr-ynys smithy. John Owen(2), eldest son of John Owen(1), was a master-blacksmith at the Pentre forge in Upper Llangynidr (see page 223). Thomas Owen, brother of John(2) and Rees, was at the King's Arms smithy where his nephew, John Owen(3) aged eleven, eldest son of John Owen(2), was his apprentice.

As motorised transport developed and tractors replaced horses, the smithy trade declined. Wyndham Davies, the last blacksmith operating in Llangynidr, closed down his forge near Pencommin about 1970. His father John Davies was a blacksmith in Upper Llangynidr from 1870 until about 1900 when he moved to the forge at Pencommin. Wyndham was the youngest of four blacksmith brothers. Late in life he took up the scissors and plied the trade of barber, outside the forge in all weathers. His re-assembled smithy can be seen at Brecknock Museum (see Figure 171).

Notes

1   NLW Badminton 3
2   NLW Badminton 58
3   NLW Badminton 408
4   NLW Badminton 3
5   CRO Quarter Sessions Order Book B/Q/St/1
6   NLW Maybery III 4176
7   Deeds of Bridgend, by courtesy of Mrs Radcliffe

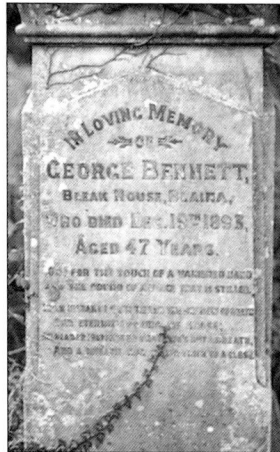

Figure 99: A link with the industrial towns.

Chapter 7

Hills of fire and iron

Llangynidr's links with the Heads of the Valleys towns

Thomas Kitchen's 1785 map of Brecknockshire shows the southern boundary of the county at that time running east to west from south of Llanelly Hill, high above the Clydach Gorge, to Ystradgynlais in the waterfall country at the top of the Neath Valley. This southern part of Brecknockshire includes the highest land in the county - the Brecon Beacons, mainly mountain and moorland, but an area of great beauty and diverse ecology. Llangynidr Parish extended to this southern boundary of the county from the Ebbw River at Rhyd-y-blew on the northern outskirts of today's Ebbw Vale, westwards to the Rhymney River. Between the two rivers - the Ebbw and the Rhymney - flowed the Sirhowy River, with today's town of Tredegar standing on it. In 1785, there was just one farmstead, Milgatw, on the upper reaches of the Sirhowy River and falling within the Parish of Llangynidr.

However, by 1800, the roads from Crickhowell and Llangynidr to Merthyr Tydfil and the Brecon and Abergavenny Canal from Gilwern were enabling coal, lime and iron products to reach the Usk Valley more easily and the population around Milgatw - just north of today's Heads of the Valleys Road above Tredegar - had grown to 200. Dukestown on the northern edge of Tredegar was in Llangynidr Parish as were Rhymney Upper Furnace, Dukestown Iron Mine and Penmark Colliery - all with their workers' cottages nearby, as shown on the 1832 Ordnance Survey Map and on the Tithe Map of a decade later.

The Heads of the Valleys area was one of the centres of the Chartist unrest in the 1830s, when the Chartists were agitating for political and social change. Chartist Lodges flourished in Dukestown, at the Horse and Jockey Inn, and in nearby Rassau. During the spring of 1839 there were nightly meetings to organise marches and to hear guest speakers. For example, William Edwards, a colleague of Chartist leaders John Frost and Zephaniah Williams, spoke to a gathering of 800 in a field at the Star Inn, Dukestown, on 1st May 1839. The Chairman of the Dukestown Chartist Lodge was a Tredegar sawyer, Richard Jones.

We do not know what the villagers of Llangynidr, on the far side of the mountain, would have thought of Chartism - would they have had awareness of, or even sympathy for, the aims of the Chartist movement, or would their attitude have been more agricultural than industrial, more placid than fervent? We know that some of Llangynidr's villagers are recorded in the census returns as miners or quarrymen and that the ferment of ideas and aspirations of the Chartist Lodges did infect some of the villagers. John Owen (see page 138 and 223), for example, had a smithy on the tram road near Ebbw Vale; he was said to have made fifty pike heads for the Chartists which he deposited in the Rassau Chartists Lodge not far from his smithy. He was later to settle in Llangynidr where he had family connections.

The tithe returns of this time list only one named occupant for each dwelling - the head of the household, usually male. In the Dukestown and Rassau returns the name of the household head is followed by 'and others' - so we can estimate that the 151 dwellings in 1840 could well have housed fifteen hundred people. The population of this part of the Heads of the Valleys area continued to expand, reaching a peak of well over 3000 people in the 1870s. At the same time, Llangynidr Village's population dropped as people moved to the industrial area in search of higher wages (see page194).

Slater's Directory of 1858 lists 13 retailers of beer and 6 Inns in Dukestown - the Bush Inn, the Duke Inn, the Mechanics Arms, the Rising Sun, the Royal Oak and the Star - so obviously beer featured strongly in the community. In fact, an earlier parliamentary speech on the problems of drunkenness in industrial areas, delivered in February 1840, credited Dukestown with 5 public houses and 28 beer-houses! There were also chapels in abundance - in 1858 there were 4 - English and Welsh Baptist, Independent English and Wesleyan Methodist. But 'dignitaries' were thinner on the ground - only two were listed - Mr Walter Miles and the Duke of Beaufort's Agent, Mr Lewis Powell. There was a shop, owned by Thomas Bennett, two tailors and two shoemakers and, inevitably, the inhabitants met many of their other needs in the larger communities of Ebbw Vale and Tredegar. Indeed, probably their only link with Llangynidr, several miles due north over Llangynidr Mountain, might have been to pay a tithe apportionment and, at the end of their days, to be buried in Llangynidr churchyard (see Figure 99). Likewise, the life of Dukestown held little interest for many of Llangynidr's villagers - who tended to shop, pray or drink locally, or if their means permitted, went to Brecon or Crickhowell for goods or services.

There was, however, one economic advantage that a number of Llangynidr smallholders gained from their proximity to this rapidly growing, and relatively prosperous, population - they could walk or ride over the mountain to sell dairy and farm produce at the weekly markets of Ebbw Vale and Tredegar, a practice that continued well into the twentieth century, long after Dukestown, Rassau and the other communities of the area had been officially absorbed into Brynmawr, Ebbw Vale or Tredegar. Another linkage across the mountain was the quarries of Trefil - quarrymen walked daily to Trefil from homes at the top end of Dyffryn Crawnon or walked weekly from Llangynidr Village, staying in Trefil from Monday to Saturday and only being back home on a Sunday. In the quarries they worked alongside colleagues who travelled up to Trefil from Dukestown and shared the same hopes and dreams that they did. From the Trefil Quarries the Brinore Tramroad ran round the top of Dyffryn Crawnon and along the ridge north towards Tor y Foel, also linking the community of Talybont with the mines, quarries and ironworks of these 'hills of fire and iron'.

Chapter 8

Services

Figure 100: Water-seller Davey
Buckle outside the Mason's
Arms about 1910. He collected
water from local wells and sold
it to the villagers.

Figure 101: The 'ty-bach' was
often sited at the end of the
garden.

Water

In the past most dwellings were situated near a well or spring and many of these are
marked on nineteenth century OS maps. Wells are shown for instance at Pontganol,
Cwmcrawnon, near Ty'rywen and Brook House, and beside Llwyncelyn track near
Cilfynydd. Many of the older farms, such as Cefn-crug, Ty Sheriff and
Aberhoywe, have a well or spring nearby. Some of these are very old: a field near
Glaisfer-isaf, in which there was a well renowned for its healing properties, had been
named Kaye yr Funnon (Spring field) before 1587[1]. Another field called Cae'r
Ffynnon is shown east of Tyle-bach on the 1760 Beaufort Estate map[2]. Strong
springs such as Ffynnon Cae-rhos near the top of Cwm Claisfer and Ffynon Hoywe
on the hillside above Llwyncelyn are often named on the OS maps. The spring near
the Wern, named Ffynnon Sion-Mead on the map, was called Ffynnon Shoni Mud
(*Dumb John's Well*) by local people. Its water, like that of the spring near
Worcester Cottage, was always very cold and in hot weather was used for butter-
making. Those cottagers without a spring drew their water from the nearest brook,
like many of the villagers in Mardy Lane, who reached the Claisfer along small

alleyways (see Figure 167) which can still be seen, for example near Bridgend and alongside Pentre Cottage in Claisfer Lane. Some farms also received a supply of water from the canal. At Aberhoywe canal water was piped into a stone cistern in the yard. Dick Powell, who was brought up at Aberhoywe, remembers washing in this cistern, and referred to the supply as 'compensation water'. According to '*A History of the County of Brecknock*' by Theophilus Jones, written only a few years after the canal was opened,

> "Where the works interfered with any river or watercourse hitherto used for supplying any mills or dwelling-places, or watering any farms near the canal, then the company should convey to those places water for those purposes at their own charge".

The catalogue for the auction of the Duke of Beaufort's land (1915) shows that water was also supplied from the canal to Aberyail, Pant-teg and Worcester Cottage under an annual arrangement with the Great Western Railway Company for a payment of one guinea per annum.

In 1903 Jehoshaphat Powell of Rhiwgarn completed an easement with Crickhowell Rural District Council relating to the Rhiwgarn spring. For an annual rent of £4 and a free water supply to Mr Powell, Crickhowell RDC - and later their successors SE Breconshire Water Board - took over the maintenance of that spring and installed a piped water supply to the village. Taps were built into walls and pillars in various places around the village, (see Figure 169) from Ash Cottage to Oaklands and Persondy to Worcester Cottage. These taps may still be seen outside Ash Cottage and in the wall at Persondy (marked as T on the maps). In 1934 this supply was augmented from further springs in Rhiwgarn Lane and the piped supply extended from the old school to Cwmcrawnon. Before 1930, the Bevan family of Dan-y-wern carried their household water from a spring down by the River Usk (sometimes covered by flood water), or from a well along the Crickhowell Road near the Dyfnant. After 1930, a piped water supply, from a spring on the hillside above Dan-y-wern was installed by the Glanusk Estate to supply the houses at Aberhoywe, then owned by the Estate. Aberhoywe Cottage and Dan-y-wern still depend on this supply.

The water main from Talybont Reservoir to Newport, which runs through the village, was completed in 1927. Delphine Ford (nee Bevan), who lived at Dan-y-wern Cottage, recalled that all the trench-digging and man-handling of the big iron pipes was done by labourers, mainly Irish workmen. Her young brother was a tea boy who had to carry water from the well. At mealtimes the men would clean their shovels and cook bacon and eggs on them, holding them over an open fire. The men found lodgings in houses along the route of the pipeline. Local masons did the stone-work of the bridges for the pipes, e.g. Pontganol. On their way home from school, the children were often asked to run back to Waterloo House shop to fetch the men five 'Woodbines' (cigarettes), which cost 2d.

The village was transferred to the Talybont mains supply in 1949, after analysis had shown that the Rhiwgarn spring water was not fit for human consumption.

Figure 102: Laying the water main from Talybont Reservoir to Newport about 1927.

Sewerage

In the nineteenth century many householders installed a toilet in an outhouse, or 'ty bach'. Later, with the development of bathrooms, indoor WCs were installed, with waste piped to cesspits or septic tanks in the gardens. Most villagers depended on this arrangement until sewerage mains were laid in 1967. The provision of the piped sewerage system, combined with the pump-house close to the River Usk near Penishacoed, allowed the building of the new housing estates, such as Twyn Pandy, Pencommin, Church Close and Erw Bant.

Electricity

The Mains electricity supply was brought to the village in 1950. Before this houses depended on candles and oil lamps for their lighting. Vans from hardware stores came around each week to deliver paraffin. A few of the larger houses had their own electricity supply powered by generators. Glanyrafon and Worcester cottage were among the first with electricity, powered by diesel generators, installed by Mr Hodgkiss about 1947.

Telephone

Telephone lines were erected during the first decade of the twentieth century and the telegraph service reached Llangynidr Post Office about 1911. The school logbook has the following entries:

"24 February 1915, Headmaster telephoned Dr Williams, Senior Medical Officer, and received a wire from Dr Williams to close the school".

"28 March 1916, Snow, Telephone wires down and the roads closed."

A mobile phone mast has been sited at Pencommin, opposite the old school - taking Llangynidr into the twenty-first century with a new type of telephone service.

References

Llangynidr Local History Society Archives: Transcripts of interviews with local people by Dorothea Watkins.
Records of Crickhowell Rural District Council
Records of South East Breconshire Water Board

Notes

1   NLW Badminton 3
2   NLW Badminton 7

Chapter 9

Law and Order

Figure 103: Arrival of the Circuit Judge at the Shire Hall, Brecon, about 1880.

The Acts of Union (1536/43) resulted in the formation of the new shire of Brecknock and the establishment of the common law of England and Wales in place of the regime of the Marcher Lordships. From among the ranks of the gentry unpaid Justices of the Peace, also known as Magistrates, were appointed to administer the law through the Court of the Quarter Sessions in Brecon. The jurisdiction of the court was far-reaching, ranging from supervision of the management of prisons and militia to the upkeep of roads and bridges. The courts were responsible for the administration of the Poor Law, receiving petitions from paupers seeking relief, like the Llangynidr blacksmith, Henry Thomas Nicholas, in 1682, or villages seeking funds for building workhouses. The Justices dealt with cases involving assault, theft, vagrancy and public disturbance. In 1745 "Margarett Phillip otherwise Watkin and others of Llangynidr were indicted for a Riott" and fined 6d apiece. Punishment meted out by the courts in the sixteenth and seventeenth century was often harsh and ruthless. On several occasions men and women found guilty of petty larceny at the Quarter Sessions in Brecon were stripped to the waist, tied to the back of a cart and whipped as the cart was driven through the streets. In 1788,

Richard Rees, convicted of larceny, was flogged at the cart's tail, receiving 60 strokes of the cat-o-nine tails[1].

Transportation was another barbaric punishment. Convicts from Brecon were taken to Bristol, where ship owners were paid £10 for each person transported to America or Australia. Herded together in cramped, insanitary conditions aboard ship, many died of starvation or disease during the long voyage. In 1789 Catherine Williams of Llangynidr was transported to Australia for 7 years for stealing a sheep. In practice this was a life sentence, for a woman would not be able to work her passage home. In 1853 David Lewis was given the same sentence for stealing a flock of geese. Walter Watkins of Aberyail was promised a reward of £5 for helping to catch the thief. The money was raised by the parish through the sale of Heol Dwr, the old lane along the Yail from Castle Road to Waterloo House. The Duke of Beaufort bought the lane for £10 and closed it. Transportation ceased soon afterwards.

Following the Toleration Act of 1688, the Court of Quarter Sessions maintained a register of houses licensed as places of worship for Nonconformists, like the house of Lewis Prydderch in Dyffryn Crawnon. At a later date charities and printing presses were registered. The Clerk of the Peace kept a record of the Court's decisions in his Order Book; the earliest local records which survive date from 1670. Very serious crimes, such as murder and treason, were dealt with by the Court of Great Sessions held twice a year in Brecon, presided over by a travelling Judge (see Figure 103). From 1843 this court sat in the Shire Hall, now Brecknock Museum, where the courtroom can still be seen. At this time prisoners were detained in the County Gaol, built at Llanfaes about 1780; many years earlier they would have been incarcerated in the castle[2]. Mr Tom Thomas (1902-1988) recalled a story passed down through his family of a man convicted of murder who had been hanged on the mountain beyond High Meadow[3].

The magistrates appointed unpaid chief constables, often well-to-do yeomen farmers, who served for one year and acted as intermediaries between the courts and the parish officials. In 1717 William Price of Aberhoywe was chief constable for the Crickhowell Hundred, which included Llangynidr. Jenkin Lewis of Pyrgad held the post in 1723 and Walter Watkins of Aberyail in 1839. They directed the parish constables who checked on alehouses, quelled riots and apprehended poor vagrants, who were assigned to the House of Correction, in the same building as the County Gaol. The constables were despatched by the magistrates on special missions, as in 1634, when they collected money to help disabled soldiers; David Williams of Llangynidr received £5 on that occasion[4]. Sometimes, perhaps, their instructions were not adequate, as in the case of the crop survey of 1795, when the information returned on scraps of paper "... formed such a heterogeneous muddle that the Select Committee set up to report on the evidence, could make little sense of it."[5]

As a result of the Tudor re-organisation, the parish had become responsible for the local administration, undertaken by such officers as the constables, highway surveyors and overseers of the poor. These parish officers were selected by the magistrates from a short-list presented by the Vestry, a meeting of parishioners which was responsible for management of local affairs. The Vestry was empowered to levy rates for expenditure on such matters as relief of the poor, maintenance of roads, pest control and provision of ale for parish meetings. The Llangynidr Vestry Books, from 1803 onwards, which record minutes, orders and accounts, are a mine of information and highlight the diversity of functions controlled by the local community. Relief of the poor took a large part of the resources. In the early nineteenth century, particularly the years following the Napoleonic Wars, the number of destitute people had risen, due to such factors as an agricultural depression, unemployment, poor harvests, inflation and an increase in the population. The number of paupers in the parish rose from 21 to 41 between 1806 and 1820. The parish was responsible for their maintenance and as their numbers increased the parish rates became a burden resented by many tax-payers. The Vestry resolved to procure a workhouse in 1817, but it was not until 1826 that Ty Newydd, in Mardy Lane, was bought for that purpose. It only functioned for 10 years and when the Poor Law Amendment Act led to the establishment of the Union Workhouse at Crickhowell, Ty Newydd was sold.

Figure 104: The village workhouse, Ty Newydd (1826-1836), was situated on the right of Mardy Lane at the back of Bridgend House.

Whilst provision for the poor took the lion's share of the parish rate[6], other items of expense provide insight into village life at that time. The machinery of parish administration was lubricated with liberal supplies of ale. The accounts of overseer

James Watkins (1803) included £1 5s 0d for ale, including 8s 4d for ale at Vestries. The following year 7s 6d was spent on 'Ale for cleaning churchyard', and in 1806 ale for parish meetings cost 13s 6d. With such inducements it is perhaps surprising that there were seldom more than a dozen parishioners present at Vestries.

A statute of 1566 enjoined parish officers to provide bounty payments "for the destruccion of noyfull[7] Fowles and Vermyn". These included crows, kingfishers and birds of prey such as kites and buzzards, as well as mammals like otters, wild cats and foxes. 4d was paid for killing a fichock (local name for polecat) on two occasions in 1804. There was also a payment of 13s 0d for killing 3 foxes - lucrative employment, considering a labourer was paid 2s 0d a day for breaking stones to maintain the highway. Another parish expense that year was 14s 6d for wood for making stocks, so presumably these were still being used for troublesome parishioners. In 1808 the Vestry made a contract with John Jones Painter "to paint the Decalore[8] and other sentences on the walls of the said church in workman-like manner". A series of entries in 1844 relates to repairs of the vestry room:

	s	d
200 tile stones for new roofing of vestry room and repairing church	6	0
Turnpike toll for 2 horses and cart hauling the tile stones from Bwlch quarry	1	0
David Morris for hauling	4	0
Thomas Reynallt for 5 bags of lime @ 13d	5	5
5 pecks[9] of mortar hair	2	6

During the same year William Evans, carpenter, was paid £1/5/0d for making a new bridge over the Claisfer at Cyffredin. Five years later this was replaced by the present stone bridge.

In 1850 the Vestry paid Mr Powell, 'Tinman of Brecon', £1/5/0d for a new tin case for the Parish Tithe Map.

In the first forty years of the nineteenth century the population of the parish had doubled through the development of the industrial area south of Mynydd Llangynidr, so in 1841 the vestry decided to appoint a third overseer in the 'Upper district'. Indications of some local lawlessness emerged at a vestry in 1843 when it was decided to equip all eight parish constables with 'constables clubs'. The following year the Vestry resolved that,

"the owners and occupiers of farms or lands within the Parish of Llangunider be called upon to associate themselves together, for the purpose of preventing and suppressing as much as possible every kind of Felony within the said Parish, and for maintaining and supporting a Fund for the apprehension of all Persons so offending within the said Parish".

A second resolution respectfully solicited the inhabitants of Llangattock to join in to form an "association for the prosecution of Felons". Subscribers to this early form of 'Neighbourhood Watch' came from all corners of the parish. Later the same year a pair of handcuffs was purchased for Daniel Jenkins, a constable at Tafarnaubach.

Discontent and civil disturbance, which had been simmering for years in many parts of South Wales, due in large measure to the squalid and oppressive conditions of workers in the industrial towns, exploded in the Merthyr Uprising of 1831 and the attack on Newport by the Chartists in 1839. The Municipal Corporation Act of 1835 obliged boroughs to establish police forces financed by the rates, but it was not until 1856, following another Act of Parliament, that the Brecon County Police Force was formed. Villages were assigned resident policemen. In the 1861 census 'William Morris, Police Officer', was living near the Mason's Arms, in Upper Llangynidr, and in 1881 a police constable called William Oram lived at Cwmcrawnon. Sometime later Pontganol became the police station, but after 1919, Springfield (Coed-yr-ynys Road) served as the official home of the resident policeman until about 1975.

References

Most of the information in this chapter has been gleaned from either the Quarter Sessions Order Books (1670 onwards) at Powys County Archives Office, or Llangynidr Vestry Books (1803 onwards) at the National Library of Wales.

Notes

1   Quoted in Jones, Theophilus, *A History of the County of Brecknock*
2   Davies, D, *Brecknock Historian*
3   Watkins, D, *An Introduction to the History of Llangynidr*
4   Thomas, W S K, *Brecon 1093-1660*
5   PRO, HO 42/36-37/- Quoted in Dodd, J P, The Brecknockshire Crop Returns for 1854 in *Brycheiniog VI*
6   Lewis, S, (1840) *Topographical Dictionary of Wales* records that the Llangynidr parish rate for 1837 was £380, of which £331 was relief of the poor.
7   Noyful is an obsolete word meaning troublesome or annoying.
8   No doubt a misspelling of Decalogue (Ten Commandments), often painted on walls inside churches.
9   A peck was an old measure of capacity used for grain, flour, etc. 1 peck = 2 gallons = 9.0921

Figure 105: Llangynidr Church. Sketched by Rev H T Payne about 1800.

Figure 106: Baptist Chapel outing, early 1900s, on a canal barge near Llangattock Wharf.

Chapter 10

Religious Life

The names of many Celtic Saints, such as Bilo, Cadog, Cynidr and Teilo, live on in the names of our communities. Llangynidr is named after St Cynidr, who, with artistic licence, is represented as a bishop in the east window of the parish church. Henry Thomas Payne, Archdeacon in the latter half of the eighteenth century, asserted that Llangynidr Church may have been dedicated to Cynidr and Rheingar in the Dark Ages, but when the Normans conquered this area of Wales in the late eleventh century, Mary was substituted for Rheingar and the church became known as 'Eglwys Fair a Chynidr'[1]. Cynidr is reputed to have lived in the sixth century, but after fifteen hundred years it is difficult to tease historical fact from the myths and legends. Of Cynidr's parentage it is impossible to be certain. A Latin tract of early-medieval times, 'Cognatio de Brychan', of which there are two versions, appears to contain the first written record of Cynidr's ancestry[2]. Five hundred years of oral tradition had elapsed before the evidence was documented. Cynidr is supposed to have been the son of either Gwladus or Rheingar (alias Kehingayr), daughters of Brychan, king of Brycheiniog in the fifth century. According to Baring-Gould's 'Lives of the British Saints', Gwladus was said to have been married to Gwynlliw Filwr, king of Gwynllwyg - the area around Usk and Newport, but the claim of parentage cannot be substantiated. Rheingar is thought by scholars, such as T Thornley Jones and H T Payne, to have a greater claim as Cynidr's mother. Payne based his judgement on the books of Welsh pedigrees which Hugh Thomas, the 'Welsh Herald', compiled about 1700. Here Cynidr was said to have inherited considerable lands from Rheingar, including Llangynidr, Aberyscir, Llanywern, Cantref and Glasbury, where it is thought Cynidr formed a small monastic community, or 'clas', in the sixth century. Ffynnon Gynidr (Cynidr's well) is marked on today's OS map on the north side of the River Wye at Glasbury. Further afield, Cynidr is associated with Llangennith on Gower, which has Cynidr's symbol of a cock bedecked with ribbons on its Church, and Kenderchurch in Herefordshire. Traditions of parentage are often associated with inheritance, so Rheingar was probably Cynidr's mother, but his father remains obscure.

The neighbouring church at Llangattock is dedicated to St Catwg, whom Baring-Gould and H T Payne believed was Cynidr's brother. The evidence is tenuous, but maybe there was some relationship. It would be rather appropriate if it were true, since these two parishes are now served by the same Rector. Today St Cynidr is celebrated with the Blessed Virgin Mary on December 8th, although he was 'anciently commemorated' on August 1st and in 1785, according to Payne, the 'Parish Wake' was held on February 1st.

In 1288, Pope Nicholas IV granted King Edward I a tenth of the tithes from every parish for six years, to help fund an expedition to the Holy Land. Between 1288 and 1291 a list of parishes, together with their valuations, was compiled, called the Taxatio Ecclesiastica. We know from this that the annual income of Llangynidr (named Egluseyll) was £4 6s 8d. In the Llangynidr Church guide (1987) Roger Pritchard is noted as the first recorded rector (1291), but no evidence has been discovered to substantiate that claim. An error may have arisen through misinterpretation of a reference to Roger Pichard (Lord of Straddewy) in the margin of the Taxatio.

A century later, an interesting snippet from the Episcopal Registers of the Diocese of St Davids[3] records a letter, sent in 1398 from the Bishop of London to the Bishop of St David's, "William Witham [Wykeham, according to Llangynidr Church guide], rector of the church of Llankgenedire of your diocese and John Tony, rector of the parish church of Great Braxstede intend, as they assert, to exchange benefices canonically one with another". Lady Joan de Bohun, Countess of Hereford, Essex and Northampton, was the patroness of Llangynidr at this time so maybe this proposed exchange was connected with other benefices of which she was patroness, since the Bohuns held land in Brecknock and Essex.

Tantalisingly, there is no more known and we are left to guess the reason why someone from the south-east corner of England might wish to come to Llangynidr at the turn of the fourteenth century. The exchange did take place, because the Bishop of St David's Register records that 'William de Wickam' resigned from the benefice of Llangynidr in 1397 and was succeeded in 1398 by 'John Toby'. The patroness was Joanna de Bohun, and it has to be assumed that spelling was not totally dependable then. Near Great Braxsted on the present-day map, two villages appear - Witham and Wickham Bishops.

The first picture we have of a church building is that in the Beaufort Estate Survey of 1587 (see Figure 35). A simple stone church, which had no division between nave and chancel, and a square stone tower with pitched roof, was shown[4]. There was the roundish churchyard, as we have today, which some historians claim denotes great antiquity. This may well be a reasonable likeness, as other buildings in the Survey are known to have been accurately depicted.

Fifty years before this map was produced, during the period of the disestablishment of the Anglican Church, Henry VIII had caused the financial worth of each parish in England and Wales to be valued. 'Valor Ecclesiasticus' was the basis for tithe assessment. In the 'King's Book', or 'Liber Regis'(1536), when Lewis Jones was Rector, Llangynidr church was valued at £13 14s 7d. (cf Llangattock £31 13s 9d).

A relic of the seventeenth century can be found enclosed in a small glass frame, near the twelfth century water-stoup, on the south wall of the present-day church. It contains a plaque bearing the same coat-of-arms as that above the front door at

Aberhoywe. It was probably found in the rubble, when the Church was rebuilt after a fire in 1928. Its history was unclear until recently. In a Harleian Manuscript c.1700[5] Hugh Thomas described a wall monument in Llangynidr Church to Jevan Thomas Price (died 1639), bearing this coat-of-arms (see Figure 36). Unfortunately the little plaque is all that remains of his wall-stone. It is now known that Aberhoywe was the home of the Price family for more than two hundred years.

During the Civil War, Giles Nicholas was the Rector (1638-78). His incumbency survived the reign of Charles I, the period of Commonwealth Government and a further eighteen years when Charles II returned. Many priests in neighbouring parishes, Matthew Herbert and Matthew Williams (Llangattock), Richard Williams (Llanddetty), Rowland Gwyn (Llangorse), Thomas Lewis (Llanfeugan) and Thomas Vaughan (Llansantffraed) lost their livings during the Interregnum, often on dubious charges of 'scandal and delinquency'[6]. In this area the clergy were checked and approved by Colonel Jenkin Jones of Llanddetty, one of the Welsh Puritan leaders. He was himself a Baptist preacher, who licensed itinerant preachers in Breconshire in the 1650s. Somehow Giles Nicholas held on to his living. In 1650, an Act 'For the Better Propagation and Preaching of the Gospel in Wales' was introduced in an attempt to impose the Puritan way of life. The Act allowed church tithes, profits from rectories and rents to be sequestrated in an attempt to distribute the wealth of the established Anglican Church between other denominations.

Perhaps Giles Nicholas was one of the more tolerant clergy. His living was certainly not as lucrative as those of some of his neighbours, so perhaps its confiscation was not as attractive. He seems to have been an independent character because in 1664, together with six other clergymen, he was charged to appear at the Court of the Exchequer for refusing to pay the visitation fees of the Archdeacon of Brecon, Dr William Nicholson, who was also Bishop of Gloucester. By taking this position, the seven had allied themselves with the Bishop of St David's, William Lucy, who had a long-standing disagreement with Dr Nicholson. A well-preserved gravestone, now brought inside the church for protection, commemorates Giles Nicholas' son, Richard who died in 1666. Margaret, daughter of Giles Nicholas, married John Bowen, the incumbent of Llanddetty, in 1663. In 1678, John Bowen succeeded his father-in-law as Rector of Llangynidr. When he died in 1691, he left Giles, the eldest of his eleven children, his study of books, his clock and his furnace. Giles succeeded his father as Rector, continuing a family line described in an old register as 'The Hereditary Rectors of Llangynidr' (see page 166 onwards).

Since the sixteenth century, anyone who refused to attend the established Protestant church had been fined 12d; this had been changed to £20 per month for obstinate offenders, with the additional sequestration of two thirds of the rent of lands belonging to the offenders. After the Restoration of the Monarchy, those refusing to pay Church Rates had to do public penance, for example, being dressed in a white sheet, walking in procession through the Church with the Churchwarden during a service and confessing while kneeling before the congregation. These were testing times for non-conformists, both Roman Catholic and Puritan; during the 1660s, it was not wise for Catholics, Baptists, Quakers or Independents to keep any record of their meetings. As time went by, the idea of conforming to one form of worship was questioned more frequently. In 1662 several Llangynidr parishioners were cited with others from Crickhowell for 'Non-Conformity'. They did not appear before the Court and were excommunicated. Six years later, in 1668, 302 people from Breconshire were under sentence of excommunication: 53 of these came from Llangynidr and 31 from Llanddetty. Baptists, Independents and Roman Catholics were included as 'non-conformist'. The years of the Commonwealth period had seen a tremendous growth in religious dissent in this area: Llanigon and the Olchon valley, in the Black Mountains, were particularly well-known as places where Baptists gathered to worship. Baptists were also establishing themselves at Llantrisant, near Usk, and this influence spread up the Usk Valley later in the seventeenth century. In 1671 the Declaration of Indulgence was passed by Parliament, giving all shades of dissenters the freedom to worship how and where they wished. Although this Act was revoked in the following year, the seeds for tolerance had been sown. In 1676 a countrywide Census of Conformists, Papists and Non-Conformists was taken: 164 Roman Catholics were named in Breconshire. In 1680, 20 Roman Catholics from Llangynidr were named in a list presented to the House of Lords after the Popish Plot had unnerved the Authorities; Gabriel and Catherine Thomas, who lived at Pantypaerau in the Dyffryn Crawnon, were on this roll. So besides having many Non-Conformists, this area was strongly influenced by Roman Catholicism too; that the Lord of the Manor's son Henry, 1st Marquis of Worcester (son of the 4th Earl of Worcester), was a devout Roman Catholic may have given confidence to this cause. However, Henry accepted Anglicanism in 1672, in order to take up the office of President of the Council! After the strength of support for Roman Catholicism during the seventeenth century, it is perhaps strange that no church was built locally. Sympathisers would have been allowed to hold services in licensed houses like the other dissenters, but were viewed with suspicion during the eighteenth century, when Jacobite plotting tried to destabilise the established Government. Nowadays Roman Catholics have to travel to Brecon or Crickhowell to go to church.

At the other end of the religious spectrum were another two interesting characters. The first, Lewis Prytherch, who lived in the Dyffryn Crawnon, refused to attend the Established Church to take Holy Communion and was 'held in contempt' in 1678, 1682, 1683 and 1684, together with fifteen others from Llangynidr. The Consistory Court in Brecon was charged with bringing such people to justice. Lewis and his wife Mary were excommunicated on each occasion. This was a serious punishment for it meant their property was forfeit, nor could any property be conveyed by will. Lewis Prytherch refused to execute the office of Overseer of the Poor, to which he had been 'lawfully elected'. He was replaced by John Rosser and proceedings were taken against him. The Court of Quarter Sessions deemed him to be, 'a most intractable Non-Conformist' in 1683/84 and threatened to outlaw him[7]. When James II, Charles II's Roman Catholic brother, died and the Protestants, William and

Mary, succeeded to the throne, the Act of Toleration was passed in 1689. At the first Quarter Sessions after this Act became law a licence for holding religious services was given to 'The House of Lewis Prytherch at Llangunider'. In 1700 the house of Thomas Powell also received a licence. Unfortunately, no house names are given, so we do not know the exact location of these early places of Non-Conformist worship.

The second notable character was a woman, who was born at Pyrgad in 1670. In 1711, there is a note of, 'Sarah Price of Aberhoywe, Llangunider ' registered as a member of Tredustan Chapel , which lies between Llangorse and Talgarth[8]. Sarah was married to William Price of Aberhoywe, who at that time was Churchwarden of Llangynidr Church! She must have travelled 24 miles to worship at Tredustan, a licensed meeting place for Dissenters. She, too, must have been a strong character to gainsay her husband and her father, Jenkin Lewis, who had also been Churchwarden of Llangynidr. Sarah's mother, Mary Lewis, was included in a list of 43 people from Llangynidr presented to the Brecon Quarter Sessions in 1686 for 'not coming to Church for three Sundays last past' - so no doubt Sarah must have been influenced before her marriage by the Dissenters of the Dyffryn Crawnon.

We know the extent of the property of Llangynidr Church in the eighteenth century from a terrier which the Bishop of St Davids caused to be drawn up in 1720, after his visitation[9]. Charles Griffiths, the husband of Anne Bowen, Giles Nicholas' grand-daughter, was the incumbent at that time. In addition to naming all the fields making up the glebe, he recorded that there was, 'a Mansion House comprising four rooms upon thc floor and three chambers, with a barn containing three bays, stable and outbuildings'. There is no mention of any building on the glebe land where the present Rectory was later built, so the 'Mansion House' clearly refers to Persondy. The village was served by curates in the eighteenth and nineteenth century, when it was not unusual for the Rector to have the benefit of more than one living. According to the deeds of Bridgend House, opposite Beaufort House, one of these curates, John Griffiths, son of the previous rector, agreed to purchase the cottage and forge for £40 from the owner, Howell Thomas. John Griffiths died, and the new curate, David Davies, having been renting the property since 1738, bought it in 1741 for £59 15s 0d from the executor, William Griffiths of Ystradfellte, and Howell Thomas. In 1785, when Archdeacon Henry Thomas Payne made his visitation report, Persondy, the parsonage house, was described as 'an irregular building, tolerably roomy but inconvenient. The situation of it is near the Church, low and gloomy. The barn, stable and other outbuildings occupy a court adjoining the house'. Payne added that it looked as if it had not been used as a 'place of clerical residence for many years past'. William Lucas, who had been Rector of Llangynidr since 1784, 'enjoys the Rectory of Peterstow, Herefordshire, where he principally resides'. Llangynidr (obviously not a living of consequence) was served at that date by a licensed curate, Rev David Phillips, who lived in the village. We do not know if he actually resided at Persondy. Lucas was reported to be considering making the house more 'amenable'. We do not know that he did, however, and when William

Davies became Rector of Llangynidr in 1821 he built a rectory at his own expense. This is the fine house we know now as 'The Old Rectory'.

Figure 107: Rev William Davies, Rector 1821-1861.

Figure 108: Augustus Roberts, Farmer and Rate Collector who rode a horse called Black Bess. He was 90 years old when this photograph was taken in 1945.

Archdeacon Payne described Llangynidr Church in some detail in his visitation report of the 'Rural Deanery of the Third Part of Brecon, 1785'. Part of this was used by Theophilus Jones in his 'History of the County of Brecknock', published some twenty years later. Payne's account has two versions. The report sent to the Bishop described the exterior of Llangynidr Church as 'firm and strong, with a small shed erected on the west end in which are three indifferent bells'. In his notebook, 'Parochial Notices of the Deanery of the Third Part', he wrote, 'The Fabrick is of mean construction consisting of a single Ile and Chancel with a shed erected upon the west end of the roof for the preservation of the small bells. The roof coved with coarse timber frame and cover'd with the heavy tile stone of the county. The Church Wardens have a mind to ceil in with lath and pleister and to new-lay the floor, which has been rendered very uneven by repeated burials'. There were three entrance doors, one at the west end, 'guarded with a tiled porch' and two doors on the south side, one of which is 'likewise guarded with a porch. One porch is converted into a store-room for materials of repair'. Payne told the Bishop that "The Parishioners humbly beg permission from the Ordinary to convert one of these porches into a school-room or vestry". He suggested that this might be achieved 'without inconvenience'. It was about this time that Sunday Schools were being established in our village. At his first visitation there was rubbish in the corners of the interior of the Church and some windows were broken. On a subsequent visit things were a little better, but there was still room for improvement. A very worn carpet lay at the Communion Table and this latter was covered with shabby linen cloths. The Table was 'an indifferent piece of furniture'. There was a battered silver chalice, perhaps that mentioned in Llanddetty Church notes as being inscribed 'Edward Williams: Jenkin Lewis: Churchwardens: Anno Dom 1671'. A stone font, probably the twelfth century one which now stands outside the west door as a plant container, was used for baptisms[10]. The parish also possessed a bier for burials, but no 'Parish Hearse cloth'. A table of the prohibited degrees of marriage was displayed. The churchyard cross stood outside and the public footpath, which ran through the churchyard, was provided with stiles and a gate in the stone walls which bounded it. It must have been very similar to today's churchyard, although the stone base is all that remains now of the preaching cross. Two services in Welsh were held each Sunday and Holy Communion was celebrated at 'Michaelmas and the three Great Festivals'. On Christmas morning it was the custom, Payne said, to hold the traditional Dawn Service, or 'Plygain', when the congregation gathered at five or six o'clock to pray and sing carols and hymns until dawn broke.

In 1815 the Rector of Llangynidr's income was £350. This rose to £430 in 1845 when the tithes were commuted to a money payment. In 1911, according to the Glanusk edition of 'A History of the County of Brecknock', the value of the living had fallen to £270. After 1900 Llangynidr parish became smaller when the rural part was separated from the industrial townships.

Three Charities are noted in Theophilus Jones:

      1. Mr Griffiths,
      2. Jenet Powell,
      3. Sarah Prytherch.

The oldest, noted as 'lost' by Theophilus Jones, was that of Jenet Powell (verch John), who died in 1626. Recent examination of her Will, however, shows that she bequeathed twenty shillings per annum to be divided between the poor of Llangynidr and Llanddetty each Christmas. The money was to be raised from the profits of a farm which she left to her son Hugh Powell. The reference to the 'Mr Griffiths' Charity is confusing. Theophilus Jones gives no date. Rev Jenkyn Edwards in 'The History of the Dyffryn Crawnon, Llangynidr and Llanddetty with their lore and Legends' credits Rev Charles Griffiths (died 1728) with leaving a 'Bread Charity' to the poor. H T Payne mentions a 'Mrs Griffiths' Charity. Samuel Lewis in the 'Topographical Dictionary' noted that in 1761 Mrs Frances Griffiths bequeathed £10, the interest on which was to be divided among the poor on Easter Eve. Later, in 1880, Edwin Poole noted in his 'Charities of Breconshire' that, 'Francis Griffith, by his will in 1761 (not proved), left the interest on £10 to be annually distributed in bread amongst the poor. This sum, which had been deposited in the Brecon Savings Bank, had increased to £11 7s 9d, when the Charity Commissioners reported in 1836. At that time no distribution had taken place during the last four years, in consequence of the absence of the rector, who had the bank book with him, without the production of which no interest could be received'. In a further update of its status in 1880, Poole stated that 'the £10 bequeathed by Francis Griffith to the poor of Llangynidr is at present deposited in the National Provincial Bank at Brecon, where it has been for several years past, and the interest is distributed annually as directed by the founder's will'.

The Sarah Prytherch Charity, set up in 1787, allowed £8 per annum to be paid from the profits of Llwyncelyn, by the Churchwardens and Overseer at Llangynidr:

40/- to be distributed among poor persons not receiving parish relief at Michaelmas (William Price of Aberhoywe, Miss Prytherch's cousin, was to nominate these).

£4 to supply poor persons with clothes at Christmas.

40/- for poor persons at Candlemas.

After William Price's death this was to be distributed by the proprietor of Aberhoywe or, in his default, the Churchwardens and Overseer were to appoint trustees. The Parish Vestry Book lists 36 people sharing the money in 1835; amounts allocated ranged from 2s to 9s. Margaret Williams (Castle) received a share every year from 1828 to 1852. 150 years later there was just one applicant for the Charity, which continued to be paid until 1988.

The parish church and chapels were often the focal points for the social activities of the village and were in a position to render practical help to needy parishioners. William Davies (Rector 1821-1861) set up a committee in 1822 to try to help the paupers in the parish of Llangynidr. It was proposed that poor children should not be put into the Workhouse, but billeted amongst the landowners in the parish. Davies chaired the vestry meeting of 1823, when the committee agreed to pay thirty shillings for clothing. A Poor House, 'Ty Newydd' in Mardy Lane, behind the present Bridgend House, was set up in 1826[11]. A Board of Guardians, working from Crickhowell, administered the Parish Relief and acted under the aegis of the Poor Law Commission. When the Crickhowell Union Workhouse was built in 1836, Ty Newydd was sold. William Davies was a pluralist, who held the livings of Cathedine, Llanddewi Rhydderch and Llangynidr. He filled in the Religious Census form in 1851 and remarked that the parish church services were held alternately in English and Welsh.

Perhaps the need for individuals to be able to worship according to their own inclinations was the main reason for the growth in Non-Conformity, but Tudor Griffiths, who was Rector of Llangattock and Llangynidr in the 1980s, also noted in his Church guide (1987)[12], 'It is one of the sad facts that the Anglican Church did not respond to the growing populations of the industrial valleys and did not build churches where the people lived'. The Religious Census illustrates this:

District	Population	Denomination	Places of Worship	Sittings
Llangynidr	3,246	Church of England	1	205
		Independents	6	1724
		Baptists	6	1680
		Wesleyan Methodists	2	198

The population in the upper reaches of the Sirhowy Valley had vastly increased so that in 1900 Dukestown and Rassau were included as part of the parish of Tredegar.

When Llangynidr parish extended over Mynydd Llangynidr as far as Blaen Rhymney, the coffins used to be carried on the men's shoulders, over the mountain, down to Llangynidr Church. Often fine singing could be heard as the funeral procession approached. Most of the memories of this were perhaps third-hand by the time they were committed to record, but what an atmospheric picture they evoke!

The growing group of Independents in Llangynidr decided, in 1780, to build a chapel on a plot of land leased from the Duke of Beaufort by the River Usk. The Minister, John Jenkin of Llangattock, collected money for this, but he absconded with the money, long before the building was completed. The site and the unfinished building had to be sold to pay off the debts already incurred. However the local Baptists, who had to travel to the Llanwenarth Chapel, at Govilon, at this time, agreed to take over the project. The Independents, after this unfortunate set-back, had to continue holding services in local houses until 1829, when a Mr Thomas from Carmel Chapel, Beaufort, rented a house which was converted into the Independent Chapel. Mr W Jones, also from Beaufort, became the first Minister. This Chapel, which stood next to the lower graveyard of the present-day 'Top Chapel', was known as 'Sardis' like the Baptist Chapel, and was built in 1838, as the plaque on the present building affirms. A note on the 1851 Religious Census return for Sardis Independent Chapel remarked, 'the present Chapel has 240 'free' seats, 30 'standing' spaces and a gallery which 'contains 120 sittings', according to the Minister Rev Sam Phillips, who filled in the form. Mrs Nancy Thomas' father remembered village lads peeping in through the windows, which were below the level of the lane, during services! In 1845 a 'Tea Meeting' was held to help pay the debts of the chapel. Tickets were one shilling each and 'Tea on the tables at 2p.m.' was announced. Mr David Thomas came from Carmarthen to Llangynidr to be Pastor in 1856 and encouraged the building of the present 'Top Chapel', which was opened in 1890, having been built across the road from its predecessor. David Thomas remained here for forty years.

Figure 109: Sardis United Reformed Chapel, opened in 1890, and Rev Gomer Harris in the gateway.

In 1898 Gomer Harris, a student from the Memorial College in Brecon, was ordained and served as Pastor until 1938. Both men, who provided this Chapel with such continuity of service, are buried in the Chapel's lower graveyard. The Independents became known as Congregationalists. The chapel drew its members from quite a wide area and Mrs Thomas remembered members who lived in the village would walk a little way with those who had come some distance, to 'send them' on their way. Pastor Dilwyn Williams, who came in 1952, was provided with a Manse. His wife started the Ladies Guild which still thrives today and with its November Sale of Work provides the village with a good venue for buying its Christmas presents. In the mid twentieth century, until his death in 1984, the Rev E Powell looked after Sardis and Dyffryn Chapels, although commuting from Gilwern. This link with Gilwern Chapel was maintained when Rev Julian Jones also ministered from there to the United Reformed Church in Llangynidr, formed when the Congregational Church united with the Presbyterian Church in 1972.

The formation and early history of the Baptist Church at Llangynidr were outlined at a centenary service in 1912. The Baptists had established a Chapel at Llanwenarth in the seventeenth century, when religious persecution and intolerance made life hard for all non-conformists. Records there show that members were drawn to Llanwenarth from a wide area, including Llangynidr. 'A certain Jenkin Thomas from Llangynidr came to be baptised here in 1749 and Baptists travelled to Llanwenarth from our village for worship and Communion until 1812'. It was quite a long journey and meetings were organised in private houses like Cae'r-ddol, in the Dyffryn Crawnon. In 1792 the baptism of John David is recorded, 'just above the new bridge in Llangynidr, in the presence of a multitude of spectators'. The baptism of William Thomas took place in the River Crawnon in the same year. At a church meeting in 1794 in Llanwenarth it was agreed to lease a piece of land from the Duke of Beaufort, for the purpose of building a meeting house at Llangynidr. Presumably they were taking over the Independents' uncompleted Church. John Edwards, William Garrah and Joshua Lewis were to undertake the work, together with 'seven other brethren', and were to complete the building at their own expense. They were to be reimbursed later. It took until 18th March 1812 for this new Baptist Chapel, named 'Sardis', to be built. David Naunton was its first Minister, with seventeen male and twenty four female members. These people had been given 'Peaceable Dismission' from the Mother Chapel at Llanwenarth. One of the preachers at the opening service was Dr John Jenkins of Cefn Hengoed, a remarkable man who had been brought up at Clog-fawr in the Dyffryn Crawnon. He taught himself to read the Welsh Bible after buying a school book for three pence. He said he had practised his 'pastoral arts' by declaiming to a tree stump at Clog-fawr! Collections for the building of Sardis had been taken at Llanwenarth and in 1797 had totalled £50 16s 0d. Full payment was completed by 1811, which indicates the dedication of all involved. In 1851 the Religious Census form was completed by 'Lewis Evans, Baptist Minister', who lived at 'Bishops Cottage', a small house between Glandwr and Usk Cottage, in Cyffredin Lane. In the census return 'Sardis Coed-yr-ynys Particular Baptist Chapel' had 400 'free' seats and 40 'standing' spaces. The earliest recorded marriage took place on 5th December 1863, when John Perkins of Beaufort married Gwen Peters of Gliffaes.

Figure 110: Sardis Baptist Chapel. In spring the churchyard is full of wild daffodils.

The Chapel was rebuilt in 1858, with the addition of a vestry, at a cost of £230. It took David Roberts, a local carpenter whose family farmed Coed-yr-ynys, six months to complete. Rev Enoch Jones at the reopening affirmed in Welsh, 'There were plenty of ministers, plenty of listeners, plenty of refreshments, plenty of money and an abundance of the Lord's Glory and Grace'. In the early years members were baptised in the River Usk near Penishacoed (a small baptistry is shown at this spot on the 1889 OS map), but later in the Chapel. On 1st September 1886 Augustus Roberts recorded in his notebook (in Welsh, translated by Tom Thomas) *"Paid three-quarters for seats"*. These would have been seats in the Baptist Chapel for which worshippers paid an annual 'rent'. By means of these payments the Duke of Beaufort was paid the ground rent for the land on which the chapel stood. Eventually a big Sale of Work was held and enough money was made to pay off the price of the land.

In the nineteenth century. there were two other Non-Conformist chapels within the village. A lease, dated 1824, establishes that a 'Welch Wesleyan Methodist' chapel had been erected in 1808[13]. A lease was granted from the owner of the land,

"Llewellin Prosser of Pwll in the parish of Llangunider, Esquire",

to the chapel trustees,

"William Batten of Merthyr Tydfil, Minister of the Gospel, John Burfield of Crickhowell, ironmonger, Henry Saunders, farmer, of Dan-y-wern, Thomas Williams of Panteague, John Badgett, tailor, John Williams of Aberhowy, yeoman, and David Saunders of Llangattock, yeoman"

upon the,

"surrender of a former lease granted by Thomas Prosser (father of the said Llewellin Prosser) in 1808, of a piece or parcel of land therein described and on which the Methodist Chapel hereinafter described and hereby granted and demised is erected".

This document not only shows when the chapel was founded, but by including the names of villagers who figure elsewhere in our village history, it deepens our knowledge of the lives of people who lived here nearly 200 years ago. Thomas Prosser and his wife Ann owned the land beside Dyffryn Road where the chapel was built and their initials can still be seen on the stone plaque on the front of Pwll Court farmhouse. (see page 213) The lease of 1824 grants Llewellin Prosser and his heirs, 'The pew in the chapel, for which he will pay 1d on 4th December each year'. It also stipulates that the members 'adhere to the dictates of Rev John Wesley' and send a representative to the Methodist Conference. David Saunders was the only survivor of the 1824 lease, when a new 'Wesleyan Chapel Model Deed', approved by the Charity Commissioners, was drawn up in 1883. A new set of trustees was appointed, including John Jenkins, mason, William Jenkins and Richard Jenkins, labourer. We know the Jenkins family lived at Wesley Cottage. Perhaps the house was so named either because of their Wesleyan connection or because it had been used as a Meeting House in earlier times. Unfortunately no documentary evidence has yet been found to verify either suggestion. In the chapel's final lease of 1923, all the trustees were members of either the Williams (Pant-teg), or Prothero families and by the 1930s the chapel was run by Miss Hannah and Miss Sarah Prothero, the sisters who kept the shop at Waterloo House. After their deaths, the chapel was neglected, so in 1957, following representations from the Parish Council concerning the unsafe condition of the building, it was partially demolished. Later the stone was used to build the garage at Penrheol. The Religious Census (1851) listed another Wesleyan Methodist Chapel in the parish; erected in 1847 to serve the newly developing industrial area, its preacher Lewis Evans lived at Tafarnaubach, Rhymney.

The Independents of the Dyffryn Crawnon established the Soar Chapel in 1841. Mr John Williams, who moved to the Neuadd, Dyffryn Crawnon in 1840, felt it was too far to go to church in Llangynidr, so he and others in the vicinity decided to build a chapel at the Wern. In the 1851 Religious Census, Sam Phillips, the Independent Minister, recorded there being 120 "free" seats at this Chapel. Howell Bevan and Watkin Parry were its first Deacons. John Williams became the Secretary of the Dyffryn Chapel in 1842 and continued until his death in 1887. "He kept every account carefully and correctly all the years and read them every quarter to the perfect satisfaction of each benefactor and debtor." (His great grand-daughter Margaret Davies, inheriting this trait, does a similar task today, as treasurer of the new Village Hall!) He was also the Sunday School superintendent. His son, William Williams succeeded him at the Neuadd and as Secretary of the Dyffryn Chapel. It was due to his direction that in 1870 a new chapel was built to replace the earlier building. William Williams was a well-known singer and he conducted a thriving choir. This Chapel is still remembered for its musical activities and the Eisteddfodau held there in the nineteenth century were important occasions in village life. It ceased to be a chapel in the 1980s.

The chapels appear to have taken a lead in education in the nineteenth century, particularly in the industrial towns. In 1850 there were said to be twelve Sunday Schools in Llangynidr parish.

Mrs Emmie Jones remembered the part played by Soar Chapel in the 1920s. In those days, every farm employed a servant girl and a servant boy, so that the Dyffryn Chapel was full for its services. The standard of singing was high and Mr Will Evans, Glasgwm-isaf, played the organ and trained the choir for the Singing Festival held in the Plough Chapel, Brecon. There was morning service, or prayer meeting, afternoon Sunday School and evening service or prayer meeting. The Minister, Rev Gomer Harris, came up from Llangynidr village. On Whit Monday there was 'Tea and sports'; tea served in the Chapel and sports held in the next field opposite Wern Cottage. The village people arrived in numbers for this occasion, some on bicycles, some walking. Mrs Dewi Parry vividly remembered Harvest Festival time at the Chapel. Visitors coming from elsewhere for the afternoon service went to the farms for tea. Then everyone went to the evening service at the Chapel and back to the houses for a ham supper. The people walked to chapel in their heavy shoes and changed into 'best' shoes in Mary Phillips' cottage under the yew tree opposite the Chapel. It was so dark in the cottage, due to the tree and the small windows, that Mrs Phillips kept a candle burning in the kitchen.

Dyffryn Crawnon was also the site of an ancient chapel called 'Gwain y Capel' by H T Payne in 1785, 'Capel y Waun' by Theophilus Jones in 1809 and 'Eglwys Vesey' in Samuel Lewis' 1833 'Topographical Dictionary'. Theophilus Jones noted the site was 'marked by an amorphous mound of rubble'. The chapel lay on Neuadd land, below the farmhouse and today's road, on the side of an old lane leading to the River Crawnon. Today its ruins are hardly visible and its history is as uncertain as in 1809.

Figure 111: Llangynidr Church. Photographed about 1890 from the field, north-west of the church, which is now Church Close.

After the spate of chapel-building in the nineteenth century, the parish church was given a 'face-lift' in 1873. In fact it was rebuilt on the old foundations, to plans by Clifton West, an architect whose father owned Gliffaes (see above). The cost was £2,074, of which £800 was paid from a Parish Fund and a large amount given by the Rector, William Hughes Sinnett. The present pulpit is dedicated to him. This new 'Victorian Early English' style building was destroyed by fire on 13th December 1928. The lower half of the walls was retained and the rest rebuilt by the local firm of Watkins and Bevan, so most of our present Church dates from 1929. In the 1850s and 60s there had been a move to close the ancient footpath through the churchyard, but we can thank the villagers of the time for ensuring that this did not happen.

The Anglican Church was disestablished in 1920 and became the 'Church in Wales'. Most of the glebe lands passed into the hands of the Breconshire County Council. The land now designated for a burial ground, near the New Village Hall in Cyffredin Lane, was owned until 1989 by the Representative Body of the Church in Wales, when the land was bought by the Community Council, on the understanding that it was to become a village cemetery. The Coach House of the Rectory was used in the Second World War as the headquarters of the Llangynidr Fire Brigade. The volunteer firemen took turns to sleep there, on duty in case of incendiary bombs. The Church Room was originally the Rectory stables and cowshed. It was altered in 1926 and was used for services for a while when the Church was burned down. It was sold in the 1980s and has returned to private ownership as part of the 'Old Coach House' property. The Rectory was sold in 1972 when the two parishes of Llangattock and Llangynidr were linked; the Rector now lives at Llangattock. In 1987 the churchyard wall was lowered by Powys County Council, to improve visibility for traffic.

Religious and social life are often intertwined; the Church and Chapels providing venues not only for Services, but for other social activities. Co-operation between denominations has resulted in the formation of a Council of Churches group; each denomination continues its own type of religious service, but four times a year joint services are held, hosted by each church in turn.

Figure 112: Rev William Lewis with the Llangynidr Church Choir about 1974.

The Rector is no longer required to inspect the village Primary School, but the schoolchildren come to Church for their Harvest and Christingle Services. Sardis Baptist Chapel has held a thriving Sunday School for more than 160 years and the Chapels and Church have supported each others' Harvest Festival celebrations for an even longer time. Services which have a common purpose, like Remembrance Sunday in November, Women's World Day of Prayer and Mothering Sunday in March and the Village Carol Service in the Village Hall, organised by the WI and the Council of Churches, bring the community together, which is an optimistic way to start the new Millennium.

Incumbents of Llangynidr Parish Church

Year	Incumbent	Notes
1397	William Wykeham *	Exchange of benefices with John Toby
1398	John Toby *	Badminton Catalogue
1420	John ap Howell *	
	John Styles, died 1431	
1431	John Claye	Badminton Catalogue
1432	John Evan ap Gruffydd *	
	Philip ap John *	Mentioned as 'late Rector of Llangynidr' in John Herbert's presentation
1486	John Herbert *	Presented by Ann, wife of William Herbert late Earl of Pembroke, Thomas Morgan, Kt William Morgan and Thomas ap John, Esq.
1536	Lewis Jones	Listed as Rector at the time of the 'Valor Ecclesiasticus'
1550	William Vaughan *	
1570	Morgan Powell*	Presented by the bishop after dispute between William, Earl of Worcester and William Vaughan of Tretower
1588	Hugh Powell*	Presented by Queen Elizabeth 'per lapse' (right of patronage went to the Crown by reason of the lapse)
1610	Thomas Williams*	Presented by Edward, Earl of Worcester..
1637	+Giles Nicholas*	Presented by Andrew Nicholas, by grant of the Rt Hon Earl of Worcester. Another dispute over the right of presentation (caveat entered by William Vaughan) - hence the enquiry
1677	+John Bowen	Son-in-law of Giles Nicholas
1691	+Giles Bowen	Son of John Bowen.

1706	+Charles Griffiths,	Grandson-in-law of Giles Nicholas, presented by Henry Williams.
1729	William Sheward, or Seward (according to Payne)	Presented by Lord Arthur Somerset.
1784	William Lucas	Presented by the Duke of Beaufort
1809	William Prosser	"
1813	John Rumsey	"
1816	John Harries	"
1821	William Davies	"
1861	George Irving Davies	"
1863	Henry Thomas Harries	"
1867	William Hughes Sinnett	"
1912	David John Evans	"
1919	Richard William Jones	Presented by the Bishop of St David's.
1925	John Edward Lloyd	"
1937	Henry Thomas Parry Lewis	"
1973	William Lewis	"
1978	Robert M E Paterson	"
1983	Tudor F L Griffiths	"
1989	Kelvin Richards	"

+   Hereditary Rectors

*   Research notes relating to the disputed Patronage 1637, (NLW Badminton 166 and 167 taken from the Bishop of St Davids' register in 1637)

References

Payne, H T, NLW 4278E and Powys County Archives Office A 104/1/1

Jones, Theophilus, *A History of the County of Brecknock*

Religious Census 1851

Watkins, Dorothea, *An Introduction to the History of Llangynidr*

Llangynidr Local History Society Archives: Transcriptions of interviews recorded by DW.

Notes on Llangynidr Parish Church (Mr Eric Brown); Sardis United Reformed Church (Mrs Nancy Thomas); Sardis Baptist Church (Mrs Linda Games); Soar Chapel, Dyffryn Crawnon (Miss Margaret Davies)

Notes

1   Jones, T Thornley, The Daughters of Brychan, *Brycheiniog XVII*
2   Cognatio de Brychan Vespasion A XIV & Domitian I (2 versions) quoted in Jones, T Thornley, The Daughters of Brychan, *Brycheiniog XVII*

...continued

Notes continued

3   Cymmrodorion Record Series I, *Episcopal Registers of the Diocese of St David 1397-1518*
4   NLW Badminton 3
5   Thomas, Hugh, *Genealogical History* (Harleian Mss NLW)
6   Jones, R, Tudor Religion in post-Restoration Brecknockshire, Brycheiniog VIII
7   Powys County Archives Office: Quarter Sessions Records B/Q/SO/2
8   Powys Family History Society: Tredustan Chapel Record
9   NLW Maybery III, 4176
10 It is not known when the thirteenth century font was damaged, but in 1848 the Vestry authorised payment of 4s 4d to James Williams, quarryman, "for 8 feet of stone for a baptismal font"
11 Hankins, Fred, From Parish Pauper to Union Workhouse Inmate (Part1), *Brycheiniog XXXI*
12 Griffiths, Tudor, *The Parish Church of St Cynidr and St Mary, Llangynidr: A History and Guide*
13 NLW The Welsh Methodist (Wesleyan) Archives 670

Figure 113: Children of Llangynidr School, 1879.

Chapter 11

Education

Education is the means by which knowledge is passed from one generation to the next. In medieval times education was provided by the monasteries and was mainly of a religious nature. After the Dissolution of the Monasteries in 1536, grammar schools were established, like Christ College at Brecon, founded by Henry VIII in 1541, which promoted the rise of a broader, formal style of education associated with the Renaissance Movement. Sometimes clergymen set up small schools to educate the sons of gentlemen. For six years (1632-1638) prior to going to Oxford, the poet Henry Vaughan and his brother Thomas were educated at a small school at Llangattock Rectory run by the Rev Mathew Herbert[1]. The twins probably travelled through Llangynidr, crossing the Usk by the new bridge, on their way to and from their home at Newton in Llansantffraed. During the eighteenth century Rev Griffith Jones, with the enthusiastic financial support of Mrs Bridget Bevan, set up more than 150 Circulating Schools in Breconshire[2]. Teachers were employed to organise temporary schools where adults and children were taught to read, and given religious instruction, in Welsh. A map in Atlas Brycheiniog shows Circulatory Schools at Cyffredin, Cwmcrawnon, Penybeili (Dyffryn Crawnon) and Upper Llangynidr. Sunday Schools were founded in the the late eighteenth century for the education of the poor. Young and old were taught in Welsh by volunteers who held classes for 3-4 hours on Sundays in the churches and chapels. After visiting Llangynidr Church in 1785 Archdeacon Payne recorded that the parishioners had asked permission of the Church Authorities to extend the porch on the south side of the church to make a schoolroom[3]. In the same year a Llangynidr schoolmaster, Thomas Jones, is recorded in the manorial court roll[4]. By 1809 there were 12 Sunday schools in the parish, according to *A History of the County of Brecknock* by Theophilus Jones. In 1838 Thomas Thomas of High Meadow started attending Sunday school in the Baptist Chapel in Lower Llangynidr. He was fortunate in having the opportunity of being taught reading, writing and arithmetic, but, like many of the children, he had a long walk to chapel and home again. In 1846 the population of the parish, which then included the industrial townships, was 2715. Only 117 children attended day school, but 45 went to the Church Sunday school and 1429 attended Chapel Sunday schools.

As a result of public disquiet, in 1846 the Government set up an Inquiry into the state of education in Wales. The report of Jelinger Symons, Commissioner for the counties of Brecon, Radnor and Cardigan, published in 1847, aroused considerable resentment, being considered by many to be biased and patronising, but it does shed some light on various aspects of education at that time.

"A Welsh Schoolmaster of the ordinary description thinks himself well-supplied if he is provided with two long tables and one short table, two or three forms for the children, a chair for himself, a score of Bibles, slates, and Vyse's spelling books, a few copy books and plenty of primers. Two or three Walkingham's Tutors' Assistants, an old newspaper, a rod, and if it be winter, a heap of peat in the corner complete the sum of his wants and of the recognised requirements of the scholars."

Only 12% of teachers in Brecknock had received any training and their salaries ranged from £18-£25 a year.

"The position of the majority of schoolmasters is one midway between a pauper and an able-bodied labourer ... a common labourer at the rolling mills or puddling furnaces at the iron-works can earn more in a week than an average schoolmaster in my district can earn in a month"

Teaching methods were roundly castigated:

"With a few exceptions, there is no system of teaching in the schools in my district. The general plan is precisely that of the old-fashioned village dame-schools. The children sit in rows on forms, and save the master all sort of trouble by "reading their books"; and in order that he may assure himself of their industry, they all read aloud. ... Thus a Babel of tongues is kept going on all subjects, from Leviticus to the alphabet, in which any attempt to correct, or even to distinguish individual performances, would be perfectly hopeless."

With reference to Llangynidr, Symons reported:

"The only schools, except dame schools, in this extensive parish, are those erected by Mr Bailey MP, near his seat and in the neighbourhood of the church. ...The schoolhouses, and the master's and mistress's dwelling-houses, form an ornamental and commodious building, situated by the side of the road from Crickhowell to Brecknock. Nothing can well exceed the solidity and neat exterior of the building, or the utter incompetency of the instruction within. The total salary of the master and mistress is £30 per annum, with house and garden rent free. The system of teaching is that of the dame schools. All the children read together, and aloud, by way of preparing their lessons. ... In few country schools have I met with more profound ignorance than in these. I could obtain no account of who were the Apostles; of what miracles meant they had no idea. Two boys only knew a little arithmetic, the whole of the rest of the school knew nothing of it. ... No single boy in the school knew the number of weeks in a year, though pence were constantly offered and given for correct answers. This country, they said, was Breconshire; Wales was far away; and Asia was the chief town in England."

Symons estimated that less than half the population of Brecknockshire spoke English, and several of the clergymen and magistrates he consulted expressed the opinion that the standard of education could only be raised by teaching entirely in English. In spite of fierce criticism of several aspects of the report, the educational authorities followed this path. As a result, from that time children were taught in English and obliged to speak nothing but English in school, and this must have contributed in large measure to the decline in Welsh-speaking during the following century. This decline was eventually arrested by the formation of Welsh Schools after the second World War, and the setting up of the Welsh TV channel in 1982.

Llangynidr School

The old village school near Pencommin, which is referred to above, was built between 1843 and 1846. Rees Davies and his wife Mary were the first schoolmaster and schoolmistress, recorded in the 1851 Census returns. In 1861 four pupils were boarders in the schoolhouse. In 1855 the village school was established as a Church School, known as Llangynidr Alms School. During the nineteenth century schools set up by churches, chapels or private benefactors received no financial support from ratepayers. Education did not become compulsory until Forster's Act of 1870. Elementary Schools were set up and managed by School Boards, and children from the age of 5 to 14 years old taught in English.

Figure 114: Llangynidr School and children, 1882.

A Board school was established at Beaufort, supported grudgingly by the taxpayers of Llangynidr parish. Mrs Nancy Thomas recalls that her mother, born in 1872, paid one penny a week for schooling. She walked down from Golden Castle Farm, taking sandwiches for lunch and had a drink of water from a pump in front of the school. Girls and boys had separate playgrounds. Llangynidr School had difficulty administering the school on voluntary contributions, grants and school pence. In 1889 one assistant teacher was discharged to save £10 5s 0d. In 1893 the Education Department withheld a grant until certain improvements had been made to the school buildings, including the provision of new lavatories on the school premises to replace those in the field across the road. In 1897 the school was let to managers and enlarged by public subscription, the alterations, costing £483 13s 6d, were made and a water supply connected. During that time 'school' was held in the clubroom at the Boatman's Arms, rented for 13s 6d a week.

Punishment in school at the end of the nineteenth century consisted of caning, thrashing with a birch and whipping. Fifty years later corporal punishment had been reduced to one or two strokes with a cane on each hand and today there is no corporal punishment in school. The County Education Authority came into being in 1902 and the school was then classified as a Non-provided Church School. It was run by six managers and the Headmaster had to be a practising churchman. David Roberts was Headmaster from 1904-1931. By 1913/14 there were 120 children aged from 5-14 years, who were taught in three classrooms by the Headmaster and his two assistants. The Headteachers of the new grammar schools in Brecon, built after the Welsh Intermediate Education Act allowed County Councils to levy a halfpenny rate for the provision of secondary education, recognised that Llangynidr children would be 'well up to standard'.

Figure 115: School certificate awarded to Dydfil Parry in 1881.

School log books, which had been made compulsory by the Education Act of 1870, are an invaluable source of information. Attendance figures were recorded punctiliously as the level of school grant depended on them. Registers were examined at frequent intervals by local dignitaries. Each year the school was closed for Sunday school trips, local festivals, fair days in Brecon and Crickhowell, Eisteddfodau and royal events. The Headmaster also closed the school in bad weather or when there were epidemics of childhood diseases. In 1906 the school was closed for five weeks because of an outbreak of scarlet fever and in 1915 there was a closure of over six weeks because of measles. As the century progressed medical care improved. In 1911, when a Llangynidr child stuck a needle in her finger, she was sent home with instructions to put turpentine on it! The School Nurse examined the children every month and pupils received orthopaedic and dental treatment. The school provided lectures on the prevention of TB and 'the evils of drink'. In 1942 six children were immunised against diphtheria; by 1962 there was skin testing for TB for all pupils, and every child was vaccinated against smallpox.

Figure 116: Llangynidr School and children, 1904. The headmaster (right) was David Roberts.

At the start of the first World War, on 11th November 1914, a former pupil, William Lloyd, was wounded at Aisne River and died in Liverpool Hospital. After his burial in Llangynidr the Headmaster wrote 'Dulce et decorum est pro patria mori' in the school log book. On St David's Day 1916 a list of 38 ex-pupils serving with the flag was read out. An entry in the log book for 22nd March 1918 reads 'Gunner Tom Richards was killed in France - the twelfth from this school'.

Between the wars the school curriculum was broadened and Welsh, gardening, needlework, nature study, geography and music were studied, though arithmetic, reading , writing and scripture remained the core subjects. In 1919 the Inspectors commented favourably on the state of the school garden and the practical approach to the teaching of gardening and needlework.

Figure 117: The gardening class, 1922. The girls did needlework while the boys cultivated the school garden.

Mrs Nancy Thomas, who started school in 1915, recalled that

"The Governors inspected the school once a year. We were taught the three Rs and sewing or gardening. There were two holidays each year for Sunday School outings and children had time off for, say, shearing or killing a pig. Our games were marbles, hopscotch, skipping, spinning tops and chestnuts. The classroom was heated by a black combustion stove; pupils were either hot or very cold, depending on their distance from the stove"

Children were encouraged to take the Scholarship examination, held in Crickhowell. Those who passed attended the Grammar Schools in Brecon and lodged there during the week. Just after the 1914-18 war pupils cycled to Brecon on Monday morning in time for lessons at 9a.m. Mervyn Watkins won his scholarship in 1920. He remembered that, when he started

"The children walked to Pantybeili on Monday morning to catch the bus, carrying spare clothes and enough food to last a week; these were taken in a basket container with a lid fitting completely over it and secured with a strap going all the way round. On Monday morning school did not start until

11a.m. because no 'country pupils' could get there any earlier. To make up for this, school did not finish until 5p.m. on Mondays and Tuesdays. Pupils lodged with families in Brecon during the week and returned home on Friday evening, and the parents paid the cost of the lodging. About 1922 Thomas's of Brecon started running a lorry, with a canvas cover over the back, and three benches running the length of the back, to provide public transport along the "back road" to Brecon, and the Grammar School children travelled in that. At the beginning of each term, Thomas's sent a postcard to the children's families setting out a list of rules of behaviour to be observed. The general public also used the lorry, especially market people, and for that reason, the lorry didn't leave Brecon until 7p.m. on Friday evening."

Mrs Ford started school in Brecon in 1924 when Thomas's lorry had been replaced by a bus operated by the Great Western Railway Company.

"Weekly bus tickets, about ten shillings each, had to be bought at Brecon railway station, and paid for by parents. School fees were provided by the scholarship and there was a ten shillings and sixpence allowance for books each term. If there was a school or form party in the evening after school, Watkins and Bevan brought the children home in the back of their open lorry."

From 1939 those who did not pass the examination proceeded to Crickhowell Secondary Modern School, which they left at the age of fourteen. In Brecon there were sixty scholarship places for girls but only thirty places for boys. Parents had to pay supplementary school fees until the 1944 Education Act.

In Llangynidr children started school when they were five years old, where "Little ones make good progress in an atmosphere of freedom and sympathy" according to the Inspector's report of 1926. During music lessons Mr J A Wellwood, Headmaster from 1932-1949, and father of Dorothea Watkins, taught the older children to make recorders out of bamboo pipes. A pupil who later became a TV presenter told the Headmaster, "they all sounded like cows mooing". In those days there was little road traffic, so the Headmaster painted hopscotch markings on the road, as the play ground was surfaced with black ash. This ex-pupil, who remembered riding to school on a pony, also recalled the 1937 Coronation, when the children performed a play about kings and queens in the village hall.

At the start of World War II, 3rd September 1939, all the schools were closed for a week. Seven evacuees were enrolled at Llangynidr School, with more following in 1940. The school log notes an inspection of gas masks in January 1943, when the 'Micky-mouse' types were changed. Former pupils remembered American soldiers passing the school and throwing Wrigley's chewing gum to the children. No doubt this was considered a wonderful treat as almost everything was rationed. Food ration books were issued, with coupons for shoes and clothing. Every schoolchild was given a small bottle of milk each day. In the Autumn term there was a week off school for potato-picking.

In 1943 Mrs Phyllis Tyler was appointed as the first school cook; a storeroom with no water supply became her kitchen, and the meals were cooked on a solid-fuel 'Army-type' stove. The Infants Room served as the school canteen. Cooked meals were sent to Dyffryn Crawnon school.

During the war the Home Guard paid a rent of £1 per month for the use of the Infants Room which, later, became known as the Home Guard Room. The newly-formed Women's Institute also held meetings in that room - but at a different time!

As Llangynidr was a Church School it was subject to Diocesan Inspections; in 1942, after an inspection, four Roman Catholic children were excluded. After the war the status of the school was changed so that it became a Controlled School. A former pupil who was at school in the 1940s recollects that there was a bell hanging on the outside wall, rung by pulling a rope in the classroom. There were still separate, ash-covered, playgrounds for boys and girls, and games such as cricket and rounders were played on Pencommin field opposite the school. Electricity was installed in the school in 1952, three years after Mr Vivian Thomas had been appointed Headteacher, and two years after the School House had been connected to the mains! In 1970, with 70 pupils on the roll, there were two classrooms in the main building and the infants were taught in a demountable classroom in the playground. The old, grey, corrugated-iron Home Guard Room was used by the top class for Science lessons. It housed a binary adding machine and was considered to be at the cutting-edge of Technology at that time. Swimming lessons were introduced when a new pool was opened in Brecon. Every year, in March, the children were encouraged to compete in the local Eisteddfod and, at Christmas, they sang in the Village Carol Concert organised by the Women's Institute. Both events were staged in the old Village Hall (1910-1995).

New school buildings were opened in Upper Llangynidr in 1976 and the old school sold in 1980. The number of pupils has increased as new housing estates have sprung up in the village. The school curriculum is wider nowadays; the teaching of Welsh has been extended and pupils may be taught to play musical instruments by visiting musicians. The school was involved in the formation of the local Primary School Orchestra. There is a wide range of extra-curricular activities designed to broaden outlooks; parents and teachers support these enterprises through the Llangynidr Friends of the School Association.

As part of their environmental studies, Llangynidr School pupils helped in a project to estimate the age of hedges in the parish, as a contribution towards the compilation of this book (see page 95).

Dyffryn Crawnon Primary School

Figure 118: Dyffryn Crawnon School, about 1912.

On 2nd November 1910 a primary school with accommodation for forty children was opened in Dyffryn Crawnon. The first pupil on the register was Edwin Phillips, aged 14. By the end of the first week 22 children had been enrolled by the Headteacher, Miss Mary Jones. Village schools seem to have enjoyed plenty of extra holidays in that era. In the summer of 1911 the Coronation of King George V was celebrated with a week's holiday in mid-June, there was a day off on July 10th for the Investiture of the Prince of Wales and another holiday on August 2nd for the whole school to attend a tea given by Lord Glanusk in the Deer Park. In May 1913 the school was granted permission to close "for special services in all the chapels and Aber chapel". In May 1914 there was a week's holiday for the Brecon Fair. Special teas were arranged on Sports Days and at Christmas. On one memorable occasion the children were given an afternoon break to gather chestnuts. The school log book does not specify whether these were sweet chestnuts or horse chestnuts, but they were probably the latter for the time-honoured game of conkers.

There seems to have been a happy atmosphere in this small school and pupils must have felt their schooldays flew past. Unfortunately, on 12th July 1912, a visiting Inspector also noticed. He reported that "the clock gains half-an-hour a day"!

In 1920 there were 27 children on the register, but from that date numbers fell, largely as a consequence of the population decline in the valley, until, in 1957, when Miss Linda Bufton was appointed Headteacher, there were only 5 children in school. Three years later her red Vespa scooter provided transport for 25% of the school population. In 1961 the school was closed and eight children and their headteacher moved to Llangynidr. At a stormy meeting to discuss the closure one irate parent commented, "Damn good school with a damn good teacher!" "Moderate your language, please " replied the Chairman of the Education Committee. In 51 years 174 pupils had been educated at Dyffryn Crawnon Primary School, and during that period there had been the astonishing total of 17 headteachers.

Figure 119: The teachers and children at Dyffryn Crawnon School, 1912.

References

Davies, J, A History of Wales
Llangynidr School Log Books (1911-1976)
Dyffryn Crawnon School Log Book (1910-1961)
Minute Books of Llangynidr School Board (1889-1893, 1897-1903, 1903-1954)
Symons, J C, Report of the Commissioners of Inquiry into the State of Education in Wales: Part II Brecknock, Cardigan, Radnor, and Monmouth
Notes on Llangynidr School (Mrs Moyra Ball) and Dyffryn Crawnon School (Mrs Linda Games)

Notes

1   Hutchinson, F E, *Henry Vaughan, A Life and Interpretation*
2   Atlas Brycheiniog, p78
3   NLW 4278E
4   NLW Badminton 361

Chapter 12

Social Life

Figure 120: Duke of Beaufort's tenants at the Red Lion for the annual Court Leet lunch, about 1905.

In times past leisure was a rare experience for local people. Most social gatherings were associated with farming occasions, such as shearing time, or events connected with places of worship. People derived much pleasure from going to Church or Chapel two or three times on a Sunday, and there was a great interest in choral singing, especially in the Dyffryn Crawnon, which was noted for its choir. Organisations like the Mothers' Union and Girls Friendly Society were sponsored by the Church, Ladies Guild by the Congregationalists and Band of Hope by the Baptists. The weekly meetings of these groups provided a welcome break from the "daily round and common task" of villagers, whose six-day week was intense and demanding.

For many years music has played a significant part in village life. In earlier days it was mainly associated with the churches and chapels. Rev Jenkyn Edwards claimed, in his history of Dyffryn Crawnon, that Tonic Sol Fa was introduced to the valley in 1869 by Edward Davies, who had learned this art during the time he was working as a clerk in Dowlais. The method brought the reading of music within the reach of the ordinary person. By the end of the nineteenth century Tonic Sol Fa was being taught in Sunday Schools, churches and also in day school, where the Modulator and the hand sign Curwen method were used well into the twentieth century. During this period competitive meetings thrived and grew into full-blown Eisteddfodau held in Dyffryn Crawnon Chapel. A letter discovered recently at Glasgwm-isaf provides a flavour of such events. It was written by Jenkin Williams to his daughter and dated 20th February 1867.

Dear Daughter,

I do right this few lines to inform you that the eisteddfod is over and how did it pass Miss Jenkins Aberfarm did come by ourhouse and your Mother did go down with her tea was at Edward Whatkins owl house your sister Margaret and Mary Phillips Ann Williams Margaret Williams Margaret Phillips Mrs Phillips Llanarchybudy waiting at the table.

the meeting began at six oclock Mr Davis Talybont was the chareman the children did go throw thier tasks very good all of them your uncle of Noyadd had two price Edward Davies two prices Thomas Jones had one price Thomas Phillips had one price your uncle Cevencrig had the sovrin for the best song to Mr Davis and another two price the singing was verry good Mr Thomas Tredegar was with them.

the first thing in the meeting your uncle Cevencrig did sing a very pretty song to the nice tea and cak all the people was placed very much the chapel quite full Mr Thomas Penynorth was there William Edwards Cevenyllwinau is at our house I hope your foot is much better place to answer this letter as soon as you can

I am your affectionate Father

Jenkin Williams

A noted competitor at local eisteddfodau was William Richards (Cyw Cloff), who opened a shoe maker's shop at the Wern in 1873. "He was a great eisteddfodwr and always won prizes for the 'Impromptu Speech', even when William Pugh and Robert Baglin competed"[1]. From 1898 eisteddfodau were held in fields (Cae porth and Erw bant) in Llangynidr on Whit Monday, with an open-sided tent erected over the stage in the early days, to give shelter to the competitors. In 1911 the event was moved into the newly built village hall, but after the First World War the eisteddfod was back in a marquee hired from Stephens, the caterers from Abergavenny. The stage was supported by empty beer barrels from the Red Lion, as were the planks on which the audience sat. At this time competitors came from a considerable distance; one year nine male voice choirs attended, one of which had sixty voices. The winning choir sang "Martyrs of the Arena". There was hymn singing by the villagers in the marquee on the Sunday evening following the eisteddfod.

ZOAR ❖ CONGREGATIONAL ❖ CHAPEL,
DYFFRYN CRAWNON.

AN

EISTEDDFOD

IN CONNECTION WITH THE ABOVE PLACE, WILL BE HELD

AT LLANGYNIDER,

On Whit-Monday, May 27th, 1901.

President—M. P. JONES, Esq., J.P., C.C., Pwll Court.

ADJUDICATORS :

MR. J. CRAWNON JONES, G. & L.T.S.C.
REV. OWEN GRIFFITHS, GILWERN.

Treasurer :
MR. TOM EVANS,
GLASGWM.

Secretary :
MR. JNO. C. MORRIS,
GELLY FARM, LLANGYNIDER.

MEETINGS to COMMENCE at 1 and 5-30 p.m.

ADMISSION—*Front Seats, 2s. ; Second Seats, 1s. ; Children under 12,
Half-price.*

PROGRAMMES, 1d. each, per post, 1½d., may be obtained from
the Secretary.

Printed by ELLIS OWEN, *" Express" Printing Works, Brecon.*

Figure 121: Programme of the third Eisteddfod in Llangynidr, 1901.

The Eisteddfod was an annual event until 1935, when it lapsed - possibly due to a lack of guarantors. The local male voice choir, which had prospered in the early part of the century, under the baton of Penry Thomas, was also disbanded, but was reformed in 1957 under the leadership of David Handley. This was the inspiration for the present series of eisteddfodau, which in 1999 celebrated its fortieth anniversary, with three of the founder members still serving on the committee.

Figure 122: Llangynidr Mixed choir at the Eisteddfod held on the field at Cae Porth, 1902.

Annual Concerts were held on Boxing Day at Sardis Baptist Chapel. For over a hundred years a tea-party and concert was held on Easter Monday at Sardis Congregational Chapel.

Just before the Second World War, in 1939, a branch of the Women's Institute was formed. One of the first tasks was to collect the special ration of sugar for jam-making from Talybont station. Topics of talks and courses in the war years were mainly of a utilitarian nature, ranging from Nursing to Poultry Keeping. Similar courses, held in the 1920s, were recalled by Mrs Dewi Parry (nee Dilys Thomas). She cycled down to the village hall from Brynmelyn for butter and cheese-making classes and to learn how to dress poultry. She remembers coming down the Neuadd pitch too fast, running the bicycle up the bank and flying over the hedge into the field. The best pupils were chosen to compete in shows. They learned to make about 16 sorts of cheese. At one Brecon Show, her neighbouring competitor had failed to clip the lid onto her churn and the butter flew out into the crowd: Mrs Parry was the winner! In more recent times, as the WI membership expanded with the growth of the village population, leisure pursuits such as Scottish Dancing, Bridge and Keep Fit classes took centre-stage and a choir was formed which took part in concerts and eisteddfodau. The WI has provided refreshments at all the main village events for over 30 years. Its interest in environmental concerns led to the erection of an Information Board, which has been twice updated since it appeared in 1970.

In response to the government's 'Dig for Victory' appeal the Gardening Association began in 1940. The annual Garden Show is held in September and a programme of talks on gardening topics occupies the winter months. The Sheep-Dog Trials were originally held on Glanyrafon field on the same day as the Garden Show. The last trial was held on 11th September 1993, when the winner was awarded a special trophy marking the fiftieth anniversary of the event.

Figure 123: Llangynidr Football Team, cup-finalists in 1952.

Sport has always been popular in the village, with football taking up Saturday afternoons and, more recently, Sunday mornings. Llangynidr has always fielded a formidable team, often carrying off the honours in the local leagues. Until recently cricket too has enjoyed popular support. In the earlier part of the twentieth century tennis was enjoyed by a privileged few. 'Bobs Field' near The Grove and later a court behind Sonoma were used until the public tennis courts were built on the new playing field about 1950.

During the 1950s, in the relaxed aftermath of World War Two, youth clubs and dancing classes were successful. Dances have been held occasionally in the Village Hall since the 1930s and nothing shows better the changes in fashion of both music and dress than these - from the 'Charleston' to 'Ballroom', 'Rock and Roll' to the 'Twist' and 'Disco' to 'Line Dancing'. For some years now it has been the custom to see-in the New Year with a Ceilidh, which is popular with all ages.

In the latter half of the twentieth century the village population soared to over 1000 and new societies have flourished. Scouting and Guiding with all their attendant groups are popular. Both ends of the age-scale are catered for, from Toddlers and Playgroups to the 'Over 60s', who have a varied programme of events. In 1965 an enterprising group, led by Henry Small, introduced 'Gala Day' on August Bank Holiday Monday. This annual jamboree attracts hundreds of people from a wide area and thousands of pounds have been raised over the years, with many local groups benefiting from the proceeds each year. In the 1970s a remarkable personality, Joan Hughes, settled in the village. A professional accompanist, she immediately established an Opera Group, using in the main local talent. The first production, 'The Magic Flute', was a great success. Since then Joan has produced, directed and accompanied approximately twenty operas, her enthusiasm and expertise sustaining a high standard of performance. The local drama group, which started in the 1960s, produces an annual pantomime, its special brand of humour entertaining villagers on three evenings each Spring. When the new village hall opened in 1995, it provided improved accommodation for a range of sporting and cultural pursuits. There was plenty of space for indoor games such as badminton to be played and the Bowls Club was able to expand its activities and host county matches. Nowadays, with increasing leisure time, the hall has become a hive of activity. The long-established Workers' Educational Association arranges courses on a wide range of topics during the winter months and enthusiastic groups of dancers, gymnasts, quilters, artists and flower arrangers keep the hall busy throughout the year.

Figure 124: The old Village Hall, scene of most social events from 1910 to 1995.

In the twentieth century most of the social events took place in the village hall. The first hall was erected by the local firm of Watkins and Bevan on land leased from the Duke of Beaufort, beside the Yail, by Waterloo House. It was a corrugated zinc building, internally wood-panelled, consisting of an auditorium with ante-rooms at each side of the fixed stage. There was a wooden sliding partition so that it could be divided into two rooms. The whole building was heated by two black 'Tortoise' stoves before electricity was installed. This style of hall was found in many villages and proved versatile and durable.

Funding came from donations totalling £428 8s 7d. At the official opening in October 1910 there was a balance of £9 8s 3d, of which £5 2s 1d came from the opening concert and £2 2s 6d from the 'Penny Reading' held in the Games Room. The hall was managed by a panel of Trustees consisting of the County Councillor, a Parish Councillor, a representative of the Duke of Beaufort and three representatives from each of the three places of worship. The freehold was bought in 1952.

As the village grew in size, from c.1975 thoughts turned to the provision of a larger, modern hall, and a committee of hall trustees, councillors and representatives of user groups investigated ways in which that could be achieved. In 1986 a Reconstruction Fund was set up and in 1993 it was agreed to establish a new Charity encompassing the old hall, playing fields and new hall, allowing the old hall to be sold to fund the new building. In March 1995, at the last meeting of the old village hall committee, the chairman, John Games, marked the historic occasion by praising the foresight shown by our predecessors in 1910, in providing a hall which had served the community so well in the twentieth century; he also commended the efforts of present villagers in providing a new hall worthy of the twenty-first century (see Figure 172).

References

Information provided by many local people has been collated by Llangynidr Local History Society
Llangynidr Local History Society Archives: transcriptions of interviews recorded by Dorothea Watkins.
Edwards, J, *History of the Dyffryn Crawnon*

Notes

1   Edwards, J, *History of the Dyffryn Crawnon*

Figure 125: Bardic Chair made by David Thomas for the National Eisteddfod at Pont-nedd-fechan (1910). Mr Thomas, who was born at High Meadow, was still making bardic chairs at the age of 81 in 1947.

Figure 126: The Coach and Horses Inn, Cwmcrawnon, about 1900.

Chapter 13

Inns

Figure 127: The Coach and Horses Inn, 1985.

In former times it was practically impossible to enter or leave the village without passing an inn. The 1851 census records ten inns or public houses in the village. Probably some of these had evolved from alehouses, often associated with smithies, like that kept by the blacksmith Watkin William in the first quarter of the seventeenth century[1] (see page 136). In addition to the public houses run by officially 'Licensed Victuallers', there were many unlicensed houses where beer was brewed such as Ty Zillah[2], the ruins of which can still be seen on the hillside above the mountain wall, near the point where the rough lane from Llwyncelyn meets the open hill. There Zillah sold food, accompanied by free beer, to travellers crossing the mountain on foot or horseback. Larger inns developed beside main roads to supply refreshment and lodgings for travellers and their horses. The Red Lion no doubt benefited from the traffic along the Brecknock Way, and later the Turnpike, whilst trade was boosted at the Coach and Horses and the Boatman's Arms by the construction of the canal.

From Tudor times the provision of licences for selling ale, and fines for contravening regulations, appear to have provided the authorities with a steady income. Before they received their licences, alehouse keepers had to enter into a bond, or recognisance, before the justices. At the Quarter Sessions in 1672 Angaradd verch John and Gwenllian John received licences for their alehouses in Llangynidr[3]. Each woman entered into a recognisance worth £10 to guarantee that they would maintain good order and not permit illegal games. A reputable local person, Thomas Meredith, stood surety for both with another bond of £10. By this time licences had to be renewed each year. Four Llangynidr alehouse keepers were licensed in 1673, but it is not known how many premises were operating illegally.

Figure 128: Horse Shoe Inn, 1903.

Alehouses provided convivial surroundings where men could relax, share a joke over a mug of ale, but not, legally, enjoy games. Games were prohibited; not only gambling games of cards and dice, but also bowls, quoits, ninepins or any others. In early records of the manorial court at Tretower (1572)[4], the names of several Llangynidr worthies such as John Gunter and Howell David may be detected in a long list of people fined 3d each for playing illegal games. In the 1608/9 court proceedings the names of five Llangynidr alehouse-keepers are recorded[5]; two of them were fined for allowing card-games to be played in their houses.

Until the nineteenth century each tavern would have brewed its own ale or beer. In medieval times the ale was flavoured with herbs like ground ivy (ale-hoof), but in the fifteenth century the Dutch are credited with introducing beer-ale flavoured by hops - which rapidly overtook ale in popularity. An old iron vat, probably used for brewing ale, has been found at The Boathouse (formerly the Boatman's Arms, Cwmcrawnon). When the ale or beer was ready for drinking it was advertised by an ale-bush, simply a pole with a bundle of twigs on the end, hung outside the house.

Figure 129: Hunt meet at the Red Lion.

Badly-run alehouses were always causing problems. The church warden or later, the parish constable, was responsible for checking that the local taverns were not selling beer during the Church services! In Llangynidr the alehouse of Howell Morgan was so notorious that, at a Quarter Sessions in 1679, it was suppressed for disorderly conduct. It appears that, in spite of the court ruling, the landlord's son Morgan Howell carried on business, and in such a disreputable manner, that in 1680 the magistrates, clearly somewhat peeved, ordered

> "...that the said alehouse be absolutely suppressed and it is hereby suppressed and the petty constables of the said parish are hereby required to repare to the said house forthwith after receipt hereof and to require the said Howell Morgan Morgan Howell and every other person inhabitinge or that shall in future inhabit in the said house from selling any longer any beere or ale within the said house as they and every of them shall answere the contrary att their perills".

In 1681 Maud Howell's alehouse was suppressed after she had been indicted for keeping a disorderly alehouse and committed to the House of Correction for twelve months. The saga continued, for, in 1714, Gwenllian Howell Morgan's tavern was suppressed because she was "... keeping a disorderly alehouse and suffering idle persons to tipple and play at unlawful games at his (sic) house upon the Lord's Day"[6]. Probably she was carrying on the family business but, although alehouse keepers required licences, the names of their establishments were not recorded at that time.

Disorderly alehouses continued to be a problem during the nineteenth century, especially in the industrial towns. It was claimed in 1840 that 33 out of the 151 houses in Dukestown sold beer[7]. The beer houses were virtually the only places of refreshment and relaxation available to the working men in the industrial towns, and must have seemed like oases in the desert after hours of strenuous labour in hot, filthy mines or ironworks. Although the magistrates blamed most of the ills of local society on the fact that the beerhouses were open at all hours and that drunkenness was rife[8], the ironmasters and colliery owners, and other influential bodies such as the Church, were slow to provide alternative facilities.

Figure 130: Red Lion Inn with the landlord, James Philpotts, 1885.

In 1839 there were eleven cases at the Quarter Sessions in which Llangynidr publicans were fined for offences such as selling beer after hours or permitting "Drunkenness, tippling and disorderly conduct in their houses"[9]. Nearly all of these cases involved beerhouses in Dukestown or Rassau, at that time still within the parish of Llangynidr. The landlords of the Cross Keys, Beaufort Castle, Rising Sun and Star were among those penalised; most were fined £2 for selling beer after hours, plus costs, ranging from five shillings to twelve and sixpence, which were often awarded to the informers. But more sinister events were afoot. Several of these public houses, notoriously the Star at Dukestown, were bases for the organisation of the Chartist uprising later in 1839; indeed the Star field was one of the muster points for the ill-fated march on Newport on November 4th, 1839[10].

Of the ten public houses in the village named in the 1851 census, six were still in business at the start of the twentieth century. Joshua Jones was landlord of the Three Salmons (now Oaklands Residential Home) in the middle of the nineteenth century. He must have been a busy man; in the 1851 census he was listed as a 'Timber merchant, Farmer of 20 acres employing 7 men, Land proprietor, Inn Keeper and Carpenter', while his wife

Anne, is described as 'Hostess'. After his death, about 1860, she managed the inn until it stopped trading in the 1880s (see Figure 132)

Figure 131: Mrs Mary Philpotts, Hostess at the Red Lion.

Figure 132: Mrs Anne Jones who was landlady at the Three Salmons in the mid-nineteenth century.

Figure 133: Beaufort Square, Upper Llangynidr; Beaufort House, formerly Beaufort Arms Inn with Ash Cottage (right) and Bridgend House (left).

The White Lion opposite had closed about twenty years earlier. Here Sarah Morris was the 'Hostess' in 1851. The exercise apparently kept her fit for she was only three years older by the 1861 census! The Mason's Arms (now Penrheol) finished in the 1870s and the Grouse at Blaen Onneu about 1880. The Grouse was reputedly the scene of occasional gambling. Situated on the mountain outside the village, it would probably not have been visited very frequently by the local police constable. In 1851 the publican William Saunders and his three unmarried sons were lime burners. There were lime kilns situated nearby at Blaen Onneu and along the escarpment towards Llangattock.

This century has seen further closures. "Time!" was finally called at the King's Arms in 1917 and at the Beaufort Arms (now Beaufort House) about 1940; these, like the Horse Shoe, opposite Persondy, and the Boatman's Arms, are now private houses. At Beaufort House many broken clay tobacco-pipes were found during alterations a few years ago - a reminder of past times when tobacco smoke was a major constituent of the 'atmosphere' of a pub. Nowadays only the Red Lion and the Coach and Horses still welcome thirsty travellers, but spare them the smoke!

Notes

1   NLW Badminton 58 (1608/9), 67, 68 (1623)
2   The source and date of this DW reference are unknown. From the description Ty Zillah may be the half-acre smallholding named Ty Charlotte (SO 165183) on the parish tithe map schedule (1845). The holding was leased from the Beaufort Estate by Charlotte Lewis, who, as a pauper child had been 'settled', by the parish, at High Meadow in 1812. (Llangynidr Vestry Book 1 at NLW, quoted in Hankins, F, From Parish Pauper to Union Workhouse Inmate (part1), *Brycheiniog XXIX*). Census returns record a Zillah Lewis living on Lan Fawr from 1841-1861, but are not precise enough to locate her dwelling. In 1861 she was described as a spinster aged 59, an outdoor pauper with no occupation. Alternatively the person referred to may have been Zillah Lewis, aged 22 in 1891, daughter of John Williams, landlord of the King's Arms. Zillah was quite a popular name in the village at that time.
3   Powys County Archives Office: Quarter Sessions Order Book B/Q/St/1
4   NLW Badminton 25
5   NLW Badminton 58
6   Powys County Archives Office: Quarter Sessions Order Book B/Q/St/2
7   Speech by Sir John Packington in House of Commons (1840) quoted in Hammond, J L & B, *Age of Chartism*, p 61
8   Symons, J C, Report on the Counties of Brecknock, Cardigan and Radnor under the Commission of Inquiry into the State of Education in Wales
9   Powys County Archives Office: Quarter Sessions Order Book B/Q/SO/9 and Sessions Rolls B/QS/SR/1839E-1840M
10 Jones, D J V, *The Last Rising*

Chapter 14

Population

Accurate population records are available from 1801 when the decennial census began. Estimates of the size of the parish population in earlier days are based on manorial surveys, tax returns, court rolls and tables recording the number of men of working age, but the 'evidence' becomes progressively sparser and less reliable as we go back in time. Our earliest source is the Inquisition Post Mortem following the death of the Lord of Straddewy, John Picard, in 1305, when it was noted that there were 99 tenants, including freeholders, in the manor. Based on later information about the relative sizes of the populations of the parishes of Llangynidr and Cwmdu, which together formed the Manor of Straddewy, 180-210 might be an approximate figure for the population of Llangynidr at that date. This is probably a low estimate, although it is likely that the local population had been depleted by the levy of 50 men that the Lord of Straddewy (Roger Picard) had taken to fight in France in 1297. Roger Picard had not returned from the war and perhaps few of his men survived. Various historians[1] have suggested that, as a rough guide, when calculating population sizes in the seventeenth and eighteenth century, it may be assumed that there were an average of 4.5 people per household in rural areas.

The English chronicler Geoffrey le Baker[2] stated that a third of the people in Wales were killed by the plague during the fourteenth century and John Davies noted in '*A History of Wales*' that the population of Wales fell from 300,000 to 200,000 between AD 1300 and AD 1400, and that it took until AD 1600 for the population to reach 300,000 again. Estimates for Llangynidr suggest a rather faster local recovery rate, for by AD 1600 the population appears to be double that of AD 1300. Evidence from manorial surveys and court rolls indicates that the local population rose steeply at the end of the sixteenth century and early part of the seventeenth. Few manorial records have survived from the period of the Civil War but Hearth Tax returns are available later in the century. These list the number of fireplaces in all the dwellings in the parish, though only householders with property worth 20 shillings a year or more were liable for the annual tax of 2 shillings per hearth. In 1664, 58% of the local households were exempt; by 1675 the proportion had risen to 80%. 34 of the 158 households were headed by women in 1664, probably many of whom were widows living on their own. Calculations based on the number of households indicate populations of 710 (1664) and 730 (1675), but these are probably over-estimates. If the population were calculated on the number of households headed by men the figures would be 560 (1664) and 576 (1675). Both estimates are high when compared with the figure of 433 recorded by the Archbishop of Canterbury's Commission of 1673[3]. Between 1600 and 1760 the population of Wales rose by 66%, from 300,000 to 500,000[4]. During the same period the population of Llangynidr increased by just over 40%.

Tretower manorial court returns from the eighteenth century which note the number of men in the parish of working age (generally between 12 and 60 years old) have been used to estimate the parish population. Numbers were recorded in Spring and Autumn every year and there are fairly complete records for 1743-1760 and 1778-1788. These estimates indicate that the population rose by 33% during the second half of the eighteenth century, reaching 800 by 1790. This matches fairly well with the figure of 775 (with an average of 4.5 people per household) recorded in the first census in 1801. From this date the population figures shown in the table are those given in the decennial census.

Between 1770 and 1850 the population of Wales doubled, while that of Llangynidr rose by 400%. That was due to its position on the fringe of the industrial area and the migration of people to the collieries and ironworks. By 1871 the population of Llangynidr parish had risen to 3928. The increase was entirely due to the growth of the industrial townships which had sprung up on the southern slopes of Mynydd Llangynidr; Llechrhyd, Dukestown, Rassau and part of Beaufort were all in the parish of Llangynidr at that time. From 1875 Beaufort and Rassau were incorporated into the Urban District of Ebbw Vale, Dukestown became part of Tredegar and Llechrhyd joined Rhymney. They became separate civil parishes in 1894.

The 1891 census gives the population of the industrial townships as 3154 and the agricultural part of the parish as 488. Following a trend apparent throughout Mid-Wales, there had been a decline in the rural population during the nineteenth century. Attracted by the higher wages in the collieries and ironworks, many of the local people had moved to the industrial fringe. During the period 1850 to 1914 the population of Wales had increased by 117%. Whereas in 1851 35% of the working men were engaged in agriculture and only 10% in the coal industry, by 1914 only 10% were working on the land and 35% in the collieries. In the twentieth century the population of the parish hovered around the 500 mark until 1970, when the first of the housing estates was built. Now (AD 2000) the population has reached 1000, having doubled in the last 30 years.

Summary of changes in population of Llangynidr

Date	Number of men	Estimate of total population	Source
1305	45	200	IPM of Lord of Stradewy
1561	69	310	Manorial Rental
1587	74	330	Manorial Survey & Rental
1608	95	430	Manorial Court Roll
1664	124	560	Hearth Tax Return
1675	128	576	Hearth Tax Return
1740-50	133	600	Manorial Returns of men
1750-60	128	576	of working age
1780-90	165	742	(average figures)

Population of Llangynidr parish from Census Returns[5]

Year	Population	Agricultural part of parish
1801	775	
1811	1008	
1821	1192	
1831	1296	
1841	2775	662
1851	3000	664
1861	3594	660
1871	3928	659
1881	3625	538
1891	488	Industrial townships became separate civil parishes
1901	479	
1911	497	
1921	528	
1931	508	
1951	491	
1971	520	
1981	908	
1991	982	

References

Census returns
Davies, J, *A History of Wales*
Jones, T, *A History of the County of Brecknock*
NLW Badminton Estate Records: for individual references see previous page

Notes

1   Noted in Iredale, D, *Discovering Local History* and *Enjoying Archives*
2   Quoted by Carr, A D, *Medieval Wales*
3   Quoted by Payne, H T, *Parochial Notices of the Deanery of the Third Part of Brecknock*
4   Davies, J A, *History of Wales*
5   From 1841-1891 local households had an average of 4.2 people.

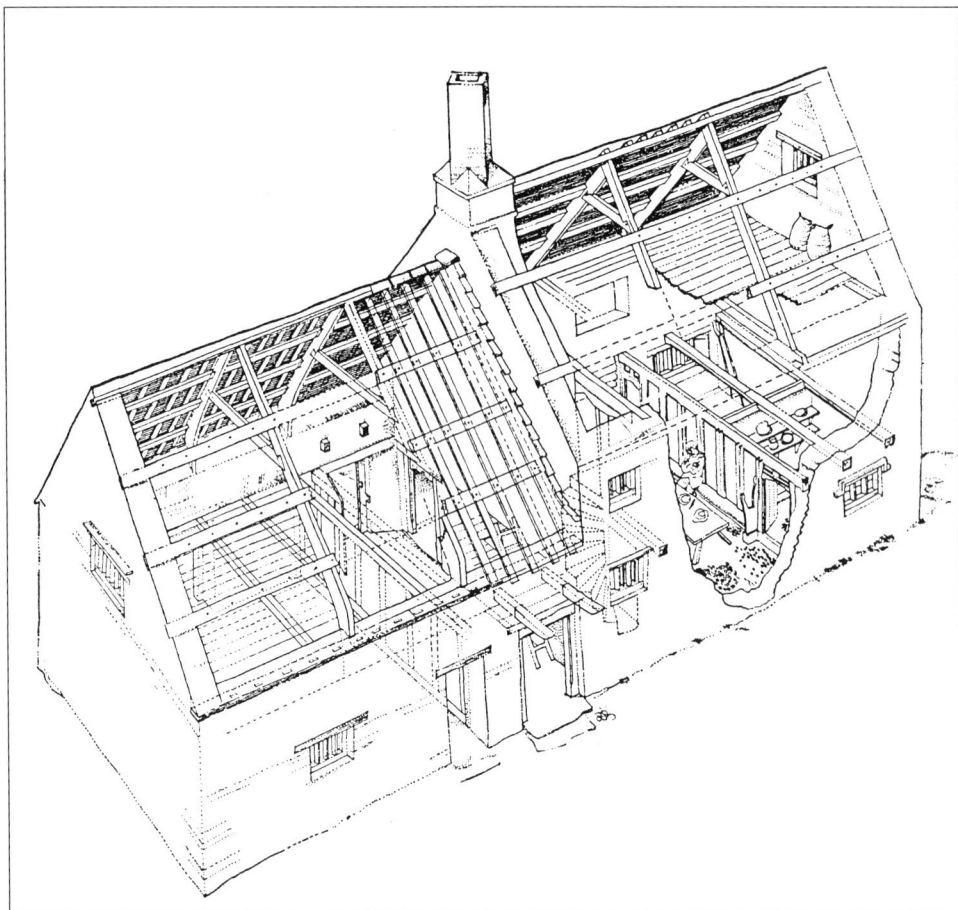

Figure 134: Drawing to show the structure of a seventeenth century farmhouse, based on Pen-y-bryn, Llangattock from Brycheiniog XII.

Chapter 15

Houses

This chapter contains a short account of the architecture and history of some of the old houses in our community. The selection ranges from modest homes, like the small cottage of Widow John and the croglofft of Rosser Prosser, to the relatively grand gentry houses such as Pwll Court and the Old Rectory. As would be expected, almost all the houses show agricultural connections. James Snead farmed 250 acres at Pwll Court in 1850, though he may not have become actively involved in the daily chores, and even Widow John probably kept a cow. None of the houses described were built before the sixteenth century, though some possibly may have earlier foundations. A close relationship between structure and function is clearly demonstrated in the architecture of the Elizabethan and Jacobean farmsteads of this area. Most of the farmhouses follow the pattern which has been described as a regional house type B in *'Houses of the Welsh Countryside'* and a modified long house in *'The Houses of Breconshire'*. The salient features of this type of house are illustrated in this drawing from *'The Houses of Breconshire, part IV from Brycheiniog XII'*. (see Figure 134, opposite)

A cross passage behind the main fireplace on the gable end of the house separates the hall from an adjoining byre and gives access to both. Entry from the cross passage into the house is from a doorway next to the fireplace, usually up a couple of steps. In many cases the byre has been converted into, or rebuilt later as another room, usually dairy or kitchen. Occasionally the byre has fallen into disrepair and been demolished; sometimes it has been replaced by a more recent farm building. Most modified long houses are aligned down-slope with the house at the upper end. The roof-line of the byre was usually lower than that of the house.

Inside the house the main room downstairs was the hall which had a large open fireplace where, in former times, all the household cooking was done. On one side of the fireplace was the entrance door and on the other narrow spiral stone stairs led to the first floor. Opposite the hearth the hall was separated from one or two smaller inner rooms, usually by a wooden post and panel partition. A long bench was fixed to the partition on the hall side. In front of this stood a trestle table with a top made from a single stout oak plank. The table board has usually disappeared, but an example, which survived until recently in a Llangattock farmhouse, measured 12 x 3 feet and was almost 4 inches thick. Unfortunately in many farmhouses of this period the original fine wooden structures, such as the post and panel partition, bench, doors, ornate doorheads and mullion windows have been lost through the ravages of fire, decay and modernisation.

The first six of the houses described below fall into the regional house type B category. Unless otherwise specified the houses are built in random rubble of sandstone, occasionally with gritstone or limestone incorporated.

Figure 135: Aberhoywe. Photograph (1965) from the Smith and Jones collection at Brecknock Museum.

This tall farmhouse is situated high above the River Usk, where the south bank is precipitous and wooded. The Hoywe is a small stream which flows into the Claisfer some 200m from the house. Aberhoywe was built in the second half of the sixteenth century as a modified long house or regional house type B, but was altered and enlarged early in the seventeenth century. At first a cross passage behind the main fireplace separated the house from a byre and provided access for people and cattle. From the cross passage the house was reached up two steps, through a doorway south of the fireplace leading into the hall. On the north side of the hearth a spiral stone stairs led to the first floor. Opposite the large open fireplace, with chamfered stone jambs and oak lintel, there used to be an oak post and panel partition with a long low bench in front, and doorways at both ends. All the hall doorways have slots in the chamfered jambs to take ornamental door-heads. The ceiling beams have deep chamfers with simple stops.

The inner rooms or parlours on the other side of the partition had fireplaces similar to the one in the hall. At the side of the hearth in the south parlour stone stairs provided access to the granary which extended over both parlours and had a door on the west side leading out to the orchard. The granary was separated from the other first floor rooms by a second oak partition.

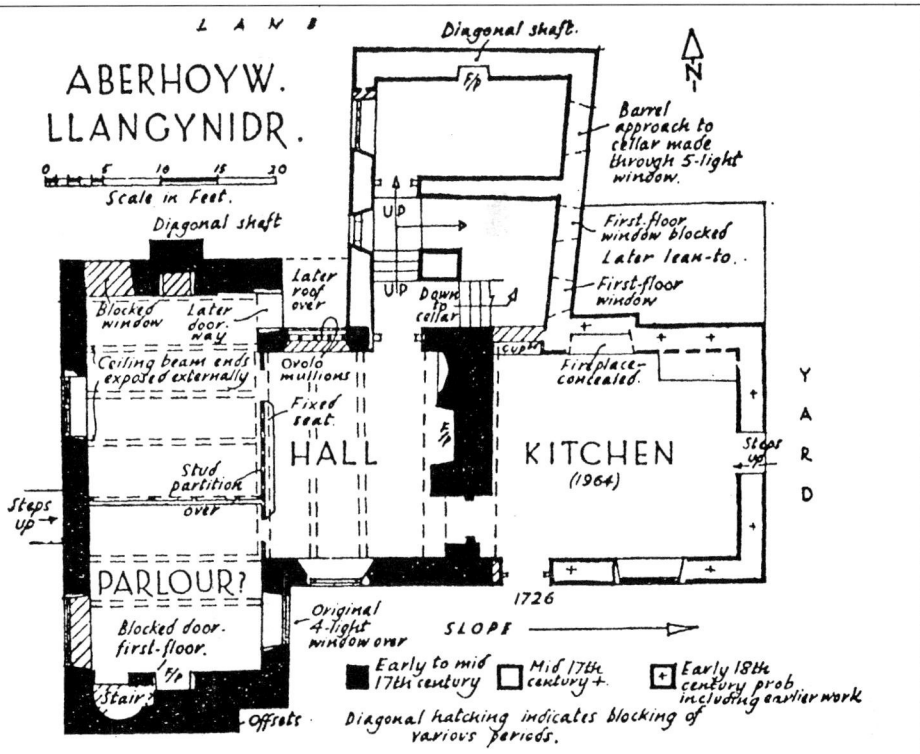

Figure 136: Aberhoywe. Groundfloor plan (1965) from Brycheiniog XII.

The plan from 'The Houses of Breconshire', reproduced here, suggests that the parlours and granary were contemporary with the hall and byre, although as the authors point out, it was unusual for inner rooms to have fireplaces at such an early date. The parlours were also much larger than was usual at this period. They were certainly heated by 1664, as Hearth Tax returns show five fireplaces in use, taxed at a rate of 2s 0d per hearth per annum. Possibly the cross wing containing parlours and granary was added about 1600. Early in the seventeenth century a north wing was added, which involved the construction of a new stairway, consisting of six flights of solid oak steps rising round a rectangular column of masonry from the ground floor to the attic. This new stairway made the original spiral fireplace-stairs redundant. A new room on the first floor, open on one side except for a simple balustrade, may have been used for the storage of cheeses. During the alterations a cider cellar, consisting of two chambers lit by a mullion window on the east side, was excavated. This required the blocking of the doorway at the north end of the cross passage. It is likely that the cows were moved to a cow house across the yard at that time, allowing the original byre to be converted into a kitchen. Until then all the windows of the house had wooden mullions and were protected by drip-stones. (see *Houses of the Welsh Countryside,* page 288).

In 1726, Mary, the eldest daughter and heiress of William Price, then owner of Aberhoywe, married William Prydderch of Llandefaelog House. Perhaps the front of the house was modernised by the insertion of sash windows, and the Price coat-of-arms replaced by a newly engraved version, to mark that occasion. In 1968 there was a serious fire and the west wing containing the parlours and granary was subsequently demolished. The post and panel partitions were removed at this time.

A range of farm buildings across the yard, consisting of a byre, hay loft and stable, built between the seventeenth and nineteenth century, was converted into a dwelling in 1986. In the eighteenth century a set of new farm buildings at Upper Barn, some 500m from the house, became the centre of farming operations.

The Prices, and the Vaughans of Tretower, had freehold land in this part of the parish in the sixteenth century, the time of the earliest available detailed records, but it is more likely that Aberhoywe was built by the Prices. Money was raised on the house of Rice Thomas ap Rice, among others, for a settlement of 1,000 marks on the marriage of William Vaughan of Tretower in 1556. Aberhoywe remained in the ownership of the Price family until its sale to the Glanusk Estate in 1830.

Aberyail   SO 159199

Figure 137: Aberyail. Photograph of the homestead showing farmhouse and threshing barn, with stable and byre (right) and wagon shed (left).

Aberyail Farmhouse and its associated farm buildings form an attractive homestead beside the Yail brook near the point where it flows into the River Usk. This parcel of land, called Tyre Owen ap Griffith in the sixteenth century, had been leased by John Herbert the Rector prior to 1533, but in that year Watkin ap Rosser ap Mericke was granted a 40 year lease of the ground at 13s 4d per annum. After his death his sons Jevan and David held the lease jointly. In a rental, about 1560, it is recorded that the holding then included a house, barn and cottage, and 8 acres of arable and pasture land, though estimates of acreage were unreliable at this time.

By 1579 more land had been taken into cultivation and two farms formed. In 1587 Jevan ap Watkin was living at Aberyail and renting 30 acres of arable and pasture land, while his brother David farmed Pant-teg, though neither house was named at that time. In the manorial survey a house built on an L-shaped plan, probably of a single storey, with the chimney on the end of the northern wing, is shown at Aberyail (see Figure 33). The dwelling was rebuilt, probably early in the seventeenth century, as a modified long-house (regional house type B) with a cross passage behind the chimney on the western gable-end. The passage separated the living quarters from a byre. The hall, which was entered from the cross passage by a door on the south side of the fireplace, was divided from the adjacent inner room by a timber-framed wall, infilled by lath and plaster, instead of the more usual post and panel partition. There is a centrally placed doorway with an ornate doorhead (see *Brycheiniog XII*, page 69). The upper rooms were reached by stairs right of the fireplace in the hall. A seventeenth century window with wooden diamond mullions survives on the eastern gable-end. At a later date the byre was converted into a dairy. The eastern wing was rebuilt and extended to provide the barn shown in the 1760 Manorial Survey.

The barn, renovated or re-built again in the nineteenth century, has vertical stone ventilators, and two pairs of large doors on opposite sides of a threshing floor to provide a through draught for winnowing the grain. In 1998 it was converted into living accommodation, but most original features have been kept.

North of the threshing barn, at the eastern end of the farmyard, is a well-built pig's cot, until recently roofed with stone tiles. West of the house is a byre and stable, and, across the yard, a nineteenth century cart shed with granary above (now also living accommodation). Under the external gable stairs to the granary there is a dog kennel, or goose pen.

From the manorial records it would appear that the Watkins family, probably descendants of Watkin ap Rosser ap Mericke, may have farmed Aberyail for over 400 years. For several successive generations in the eighteenth and nineteenth centuries there was a Walter Watkins as head of the household. In 1760 a Walter Watkins leased almost 100 acres from the manor at a rent of £35 per annum. The terms of his 1766 lease forbade the ploughing of any meadow or ancient pasture land, and required him to establish 20 trees each year and 15 perches of quick hedge. "The liberties and royalties of Fowling, Hunting, Hawking and also all Timber trees and Trees likely to become timber and all coppice" were reserved to the Lord of the Manor. All corn had to be ground at the lord's mill at Felindre, Cwmdu. The farm was sold by the Beaufort Estate in 1915.

FRONT ELEVATION – facing East   Cae'r Hendre

Figure 138: Cae'rhendre. A modified seventeenth century longhouse. The barn was rebuilt in the nineteenth century.

Cae'rhendre is situated on the north side of the Dyffryn Crawnon, formerly in the parish of Llanddetty. The farmhouse, of two storeys plus attic, is built on a modified long house plan, aligned down the slope. On the ground floor, before recent alterations, the hall was separated by a wooden partition from two unequal sized inner rooms, also divided by an internal partition. The open hearth in the hall has a wooden lintel and an oven inserted on the right side.

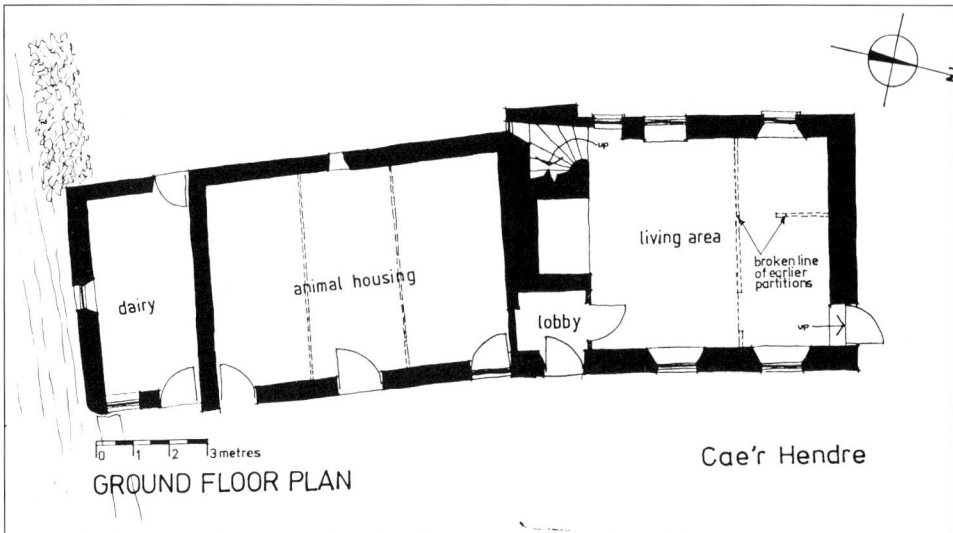

GROUND FLOOR PLAN   Cae'r Hendre

Figure 139: Cae'rhendre. Ground floor plan, AD 2000.

There are ceiling beams with shallow chamfers and simple run-off stops which appear to be of the seventeenth century. The stone stairs to the right of the fireplace have been widened by rebuilding the outer wall. Formerly the upstairs rooms had floors of elm planks. The windows have been replaced with sash casements or nineteenth century 'Brecon Hopper' windows. Probably a cross passage behind the fireplace, giving access to both house and byre, was replaced in the nineteenth century by the barn and byre which now form part of the range connected to the house. A barn above the house probably dates, like the house, from the seventeenth century, while across the yard is a barn built about 1850.

Nantyllaethdy (formerly Tir Howell Sais)   SO 130183

High above the road on the south side of Dyffryn Crawnon are the ruins of a seventeenth century farmhouse built on the plan of a modified long house, with farm buildings aligned down the slope. The cross passage behind the chimney stack afforded access to the house up a step through a doorway on the west side of the fireplace. On the other side of the large open hearth were the stone stairs leading to the bedrooms. In the hall are the decaying remains of a post and panel partition, with doorways at either end, which separated the hall from the two inner rooms. Upstairs a cruder form of wooden partition divided two bedrooms. There are horizontal window openings protected by drip-stones and remains of several wooden diamond mullion windows (see Figure below).

Figure 140: Wooden-mullion windows at Nantyllaethdy (Tir Howell Sais).

About 1800 the house was substantially altered by an extension in the form of a small gable wing on the east side of the hall, which allowed the stairs to be widened. A gable window was added on the east side to provide more light and headroom in the main bedroom. The house was reroofed in slate and the open fireplace in the hall was reduced in width and furnished with a mantleshelf. The cross passage was converted into a dairy during the eighteenth century when the west doorway was blocked up and replaced by a window. Probably access to the house continued to be through the dairy. Another doorway (later blocked), which gave direct access to the hall on the west side, may also date from this period.

Figure 141: Nantyllaethdy. The ruined seventeenth century longhouse from the east.

The dairy was divided from the adjacent byre by a stone wall and another stone wall separated the byre from the stable. The entire range of farm buildings had a stone-tiled roof lower than that of the house. Detached, and further down the slope, there is a small corn barn with a stone-tiled roof, and threshing floor with opposed pairs of winnowing doors protected by canopies. There are vertical ventilators on east and west walls and triangular ventilators on the south wall. Tir Howell Sais was the land of Howell the Englishman sometime before 1587, when the land (but no farmhouse) was shown on the Manorial Survey as the freehold of John William David Griffith. It was owned by Mrs Margaret Games in 1760. The holding was known as Tir Howell Sais until about 1870, but sometime during the late nineteenth century exchanged names with Nantyllaethdy, a neighbouring farm on the opposite bank of the nearby stream.

Figure 142: Y Neuadd from the west in a photograph (1965) from the Smith and Jones collection at Brecknock Museum.

The farmhouse was built about 1600 on a ground floor plan akin to that of the regional house type B. A cross passage behind the main fireplace probably separated the house from a lower byre which has not survived. In the north gable of the house is a blocked doorway which would have lead from the cross passage into the house. Slots in the chamfered oak door frame show that there was once an ornate door head. There are square window openings with wooden mullions at first floor level in the north gable end. Possibly these were inserted at a later date, or they may indicate that no byre was ever built. In the hall the ceiling beams are stopped and chamfered. Some early oak floor planking survives upstairs. A wooden staircase has replaced the stone stairs to the L of the fireplace in the hall. Early roof timbers, incorporating a raised cruck and collar, indicate that the roof has been raised.

Across the yard to the east of the farmhouse there is a rare local example of a 'tyddyn-y-traian', a small dwelling providing a home for an aged relative - the forerunner of today's 'granny flat' (see Figure 143, overleaf). At a later date a barn has been built adjoining the house at the upper end. In the eighteenth century another barn was built at right angles to the house, and just below it on the north-east. This barn, which has recently been converted into a dwelling, shows a range of stone ventilators and at the west end there is a set of six square recesses (? for bee skeps), with a larger shelter for geese or dogs below. The extent and quality of the buildings, and remaining woodwork, indicate that this was an important farm. A holding called Tyre Nyadd is mentioned in the 1587 survey but is not shown on the plans because it was not part of the Beaufort Estate. At a manorial court in 1610 it was reported that Charles Vaughan had sold Tyre y neadd to Tobye Payne. In 1850 Neuadd, then managed by John Williams, was a farm of over 200 acres.

Figure 143: The Tyddyn-y-traian at Y Neuadd in 1965.

Figure 144: Mr & Mrs Williams, photographed about 1883.

Ty Sheriff   SO 158183

Overlooking the village, at an altitude of 300m, on the northern flank of Llangynidr mountain, Ty Sheriff is another late sixteenth century or early seventeenth century farmhouse built on the pattern of a modified long house. The farmhouse and attached byre are aligned down the slope, with the gable end of the byre heavily battered at the lower (north) end. The house was entered through a doorway in the north gable from the cross passage behind the chimney stack. The hall, with large open fireplace, was originally separated from two inner rooms or parlours by a post and panel partition. Although the partition has not survived, the ceiling beam into which it was set has been re-used as a lintel above the fireplace. A curved stairs to the left of the fireplace leads to the bedrooms. During the eighteenth century the lower end of the byre was converted into a stable. Recently the house has been extensively modernised. For three hundred years, from the sixteenth to the nineteenth century, this small farm was owned by the Prices of Aberhoywe. It was known as Tir Penrwgan in the seventeenth century and Ty-fry in the nineteenth century. Last century it reverted to Ty Sheriff, a name acquired in the mid-eighteenth century, when the house was inherited by William Prydderch in the same year that he served as High Sheriff of Brecknockshire.

Widow John's Cottage   SO 141166

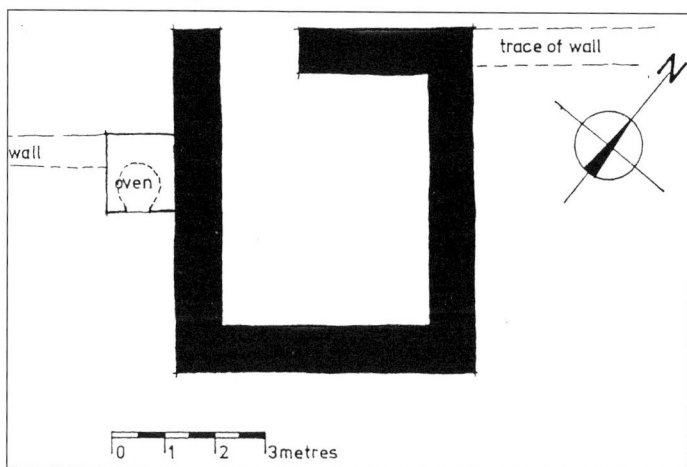

Figure 145: Plan of Widow John's cottage.

At the head of Cwm Claisfer, beside the great boundary wall which separated the highest meadows from the upland mountain common, stood a tiny cottage. In 1587 it was the home of Widow Sciscily John, and is shown in the manorial survey as a small gabled cottage with no chimney. It is now a ruin. Externally the building measures 6.7m x 6.1m at ground level. The walls, of dressed stone with traces of mortar, are almost 1m wide so that the internal floor space is only 5m x 4.2m. The interior is cluttered by rubble, but no remains of a fireplace or chimney have been detected. There was a doorway in the north-west wall. Although the walls on the south-west and north-east survive to a height of 1.5m in a couple of places, no window openings have been found. On the outside of the south-west wall are the remains of a stone oven about 1.5m in diameter. There is insufficient evidence to tell whether this was a 'croglofft' cottage.

Croglofft, Cwm Claisfer   SO 139165

A small derelict dwelling at the head of Cwm Claisfer is a rare local example of a 'croglofft' cottage. It was a simple stone gabled cottage of one and a half storeys, built in the eighteenth century, possibly by Rosser Phillip Prosser who was living there in 1760. The dwelling measured 8.3m x 5m (externally at ground level). There was probably a single room on the ground floor measuring 6m x 3.75m. On the west side there was a centrally placed doorway and two windows on both east and west walls. At the north gable end was a fireplace with a bread oven on the right. A low loft opposite the fireplace might have overhung about half the room and been reached by a short ladder. Four small enclosures adjacent to the cottage were leased by Rosser Prosser in 1760.

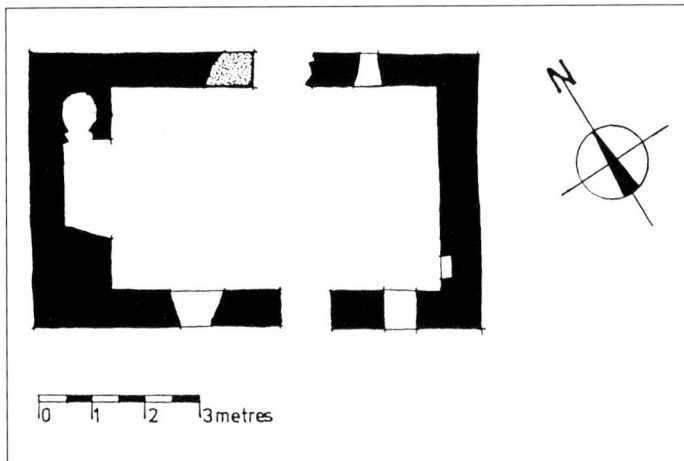

Figure 146: Plan of the Croglofft of Rosser Prosser.

Mowfield/Rose Cottage   SO 152201

This small Georgian house was built on Coed yr Ynys Common in 1782 for John William, a tiler. A circular date-stone, originally on the north wall, has been reset on the east wall of the house. John William's indenture (1783) states that he has, "At his own costs erected one good new and substantial stone and tiled dwelling house upon the said Lord Duke's wast [sic] or common called Coed yr Ynis and inclosed in a garden thereto". His garden, of one rood (quarter of an acre) was bounded by part of the common, the turnpike road, the gardens of Thomas William Powell and William Evans and a "building now erecting and intended for a Meeting House" (the forerunner of Sardis Baptist Chapel). His indenture, which also included a field nearby, ran for the duration of three named lives and cost him £1 17s 0d and six horse loads of coal a year. An inaccurate sketch plan accompanied the indenture.

Figure 147: Mowfield, formerly the White Lion Inn.

Originally Mowfield was a symmetrical, detached house of two storeys, under a stone-tiled roof. The centrally placed front door opened into a hall from which a straight staircase rose opposite the door. Much of the original good quality woodwork survives in doors, window casements, shutters and banisters. At some time the house was divided transversely into two dwellings, but has now been converted back into a single house. A small cellar, with an outside entrance at the back of the house, is a reminder of the period, in the nineteenth century until about 1860, when the house was licensed as the White Lion Inn. There are 'Brecon Hopper' windows on the east wall of the ground floor. Until recently there was a large fireplace with stone lintel in the room left of the front door. The original stone roof-tiles have been replaced by slates.

Dan-y-graig   SO 154191

Dan-y-graig is a small detached cottage built about 1800 beside Mardy Lane, the main road through Upper Llangynidr at that time. Recently the cottage has been carefully restored so that the character of the building and original features have been preserved. The symmetrical plan of the dwelling can be seen from Figure 148. The top two panes of the six-pane window casements are hinged to open. The old oak front door opens directly into the main living room, originally divided into two rooms by a lath and plaster partition.

Both rooms had a fireplace. There was a ceiling hatch to allow furniture, which was too large for the narrow stone stairs by the fireplace, to be moved to the first floor. The upstairs room was also originally partitioned to form two bedrooms, which were lighted by the gable windows. In the late nineteenth century a kitchen was built at the back and a recent extension has replaced the pigsty and 'ty bach' behind the cottage. During alterations an old channel passing through the wall of the front room to the pigsty was uncovered. Was this to allow the pigs to be fed directly with scraps from the table or connected with an early type of sink arrangement?

Figure 148: Dan-y-graig, viewed from Mardy Lane.

The Boathouse, Cwm Crawnon   SO 145199

An intriguing house has been formed by the conversion of a terrace of three identical small cottages into a single dwelling. The terrace was built about 1800, possibly to provide homes for workmen on the Brecon and Abergavenny Canal. The original layout can be deduced from the photograph (see Figure 149), and inside the three stairs still survive. There was probably an inn here from early in the nineteenth century called at first The Boatmen's Arms and later The Boatman's Arms. The parish vestry book records that in the 1840s there was a Boatmen's Arms Benefit Society which had invested £50 in the parish. The stewards of the 'club' were paid interest at a rate of 5% per annum, £2 10s 0d due on February 1st each year. From the 1851 census returns we find that the inn was restricted to one dwelling; a charwoman and a washerwoman occupied the other houses in the terrace. Without forensic assistance we cannot be sure whether a large iron vat found on the premises was used by William Lloyd, the innkeeper, to brew beer, or Margaret Evans, the washerwoman, for doing her laundry. From 1860 to the end of the nineteenth century the innkeeper and his family occupied the whole terrace. The Boatman's Arms closed down early in the twentieth century and the property was extensively renovated in the 1970s. Subsequent owners have carefully preserved the old bar.

Figure 149: The Boathouse about 1890 when it was The Boatman's Arms. Elizabeth Watkins, nee Jones (Great-grandmother of Linda Games) is seated outside. Her daughter, Mary-Ann, was married to the landlord, Charles Price.

Ffrwd   SO 157190

Figure 150: Ffrwd farmhouse from the northwest. The Thomas family from High Meadow farmed here for over 50 years from 1918.

This solidly constructed, symmetrical two-storey farmhouse was built about 1860-70, using dressed blocks of contrasting buff and purple sandstone, similar to that used for Waterloo House at about the same date. On the front there are handsome purple stone lintels above the front door and the twelve-pane sash windows. There is a slated roof with chimney stack at each gable. The front door opens onto a narrow hallway, from which a straight flight of stairs leads to a first floor landing. Much of the good quality woodwork is original. Jehoshaphat Powell farmed there from 1851-71. Possibly the farmhouse was rebuilt during his period of tenancy or perhaps after he had moved to Pentwyn. Ffrwd was recorded as 'unoccupied' in the 1881 census return. The barn next to the farmhouse is older, but east of the house there is a detached range of late nineteenth century farm buildings, including byre, hay barn and stable.

Glasgwm-isaf   SO 099162

Figure 151: Glasgwm-isaf from the south-west. This was the home of Will Evans, organist and choirmaster at Dyffryn Crawnon Chapel.

Glasgwm-isaf farmhouse is situated in a remote spot near the head of the Dyffryn Crawnon, facing south across the valley. Like Ffrwd, which it resembles in many ways, it was built about 1870 to replace an older dwelling. Glasgwm-isaf is also compact and symmetrical, built of dressed sandstone blocks (mainly purple). There is a slated roof with fairly wide eaves and chimney stacks at each gable. There are impressive stone lintels above the lower windows and the centrally placed front door. The sixteen-pane sash windows on the ground floor are more decorative than those upstairs, though all retain their shutters. Doors and windows, and their furniture, are of high quality and contemporary with the house.

Nearby, a range of mainly nineteenth century farm buildings, aligned down the slope, contains a small room with a fireplace which probably heated a boiler. Until its demolition about 1960, a parallel range of older buildings included the former farmhouse.

Figure 152: The Old Rectory. Built for the Rev William Davies about 1822 and the home of the Rectors of Llangynidr until 1972.

This fine Georgian house was built on church glebe, soon after 1821, as a rectory for Rev William Davies (Rector of Llangynidr 1821-61). From the front of the house there is a splendid view down the Usk valley to the Sugar Loaf and Black Mountains. The house is composed of two storeys plus attics, under an M-shaped, slated roof. A centrally placed front door opens into a spacious hall leading to elegant reception rooms on either side. These have their original moulded plaster ceilings and much contemporary woodwork, doors, windowcases and shutters. The drawing room has its original Georgian fireplace, but a Victorian window and fireplace have been installed in the dining room. An imposing staircase leads to the first floor where part of the landing has been converted into a small dressing room. The servants' stairway was removed, and the kitchen and servants' quarters were considerably altered after the house had been sold by the Church in Wales in 1972. It had ceased to be the rectory after the amalgamation of the parishes of Llangattock and Llangynidr. Soon afterwards the Rectory coach-house, which had been the village fire station during the Second World War, was converted into a separate dwelling. Later still the owners of the Old Coach House purchased the Church Room behind the Village Hall, which had been built from the Rectory stables in 1926.

Figure 153: Pwll Court viewed from the entrance drive on the east.

The Georgian two-storied house built for Thomas and Ann Prosser in 1770, originally called Pwll, is now the farmhouse of Pwll Court Farm. It has a simple slated gable roof with brick chimney stacks at each end. The front, south facing, was symmetrical, with two sash windows on either side of the front door and two similar windows on each side of the date-stone, marked 'T & AP 1770', at first floor level. The symmetry has been lost by the addition of an off-centre porch, blocking of windows and other alterations. The rooms are spacious and retain many original features, such as the window shutters. When Thomas Prosser died in 1822, he left the farm to his eldest son Llewellyn. By 1840 the farm was in the ownership of James Prosser Snead, magistrate and Deputy Lieutenant of Brecknockshire, who had married Edmontina, daughter of Sackville Gwynne of Glanbran Park, Carmarthenshire. He enlarged the property to form a gentleman's residence, adding the section which now forms the main part of Pwll Court. The extension was on a grand scale; the front of the two storey house with attics, at ninety degrees to the old house, presents an imposing facade when the house is approached along the driveway leading from Dyffryn Crawnon Road. A row of gable windows lighting the attic rooms is an attractive feature. Inside, the plan of the front part of the house is rather similar to that of the Old Rectory, with a large entrance hall and reception rooms on either side. An impressive staircase leads from the hall to the rooms on the first floor. One of the reception rooms of the old Georgian house was converted into a library. Since c.1968, the house has been divided into two dwellings. During the ownership of James Snead the farming operations were moved to new buildings, known as Court Farm, about half a kilometre to the south of Pwll Court.

Figure 154: Worcester Cottage. The Duke of Beaufort's Fishing Lodge. Mrs Mary Parry (seated) is seen here, in mourning for her husband William, the river-keeper, who died in 1900.

Situated in a commanding position overlooking the River Usk, the compact, stone house which forms the core of the present dwelling was built about 1870 as a fishing lodge for the 9th Duke of Beaufort. A description, from the sale catalogue of 1915, is given below (see Figure 155).

The Duke took tea in the parlour when he came on fishing expeditions. Under the Duke's parlour was a dairy, with a stone stairway from the kitchen and direct access to the garden. A wash-house at the back had water piped from the canal, which also flushed a WC by the cow house and pig's cot. All drinking water had to be carried up the 'rugged path'* from a spring beside the river. The fishing lodge replaced a smaller cottage on the same site on Cyffredin Common. On the Beaufort Estate Survey of 1760 this cottage is shown, with a small garden on the north side, in the tenancy of John Williams. Both the old cottage and the fishing lodge which succeeded it were occupied from 1840 to 1919 by the Parry family. Thomas Parry, the tenant from 1840 to 1885, was variously recorded in the census returns as woodkeeper, woodward, gamekeeper or fisherman. His son and grandson, both called William Parry, succeeded him as water bailiffs. In the census returns the house was called Cyffredin Cottage (1851), Duke's Cottage (1871) and Fishing Box (1881).

THE COTTAGE

(which is built of stone, with slate roof) contains : Parlour, Kitchen, Back Kitchen, and Offices on *Ground Floor* ; and Three Bed Rooms on *First Floor*.

THE BUILDINGS

comprise : Coachhouse and Stable (stone and tile) ; Wash-house (brick and slate) ; Cow House and Open Shed (stone, timber and tiled).

Figure 155: Description of the house from the 1915 sale catalogue.

When the fishing lodge was sold by the Beaufort Estate, in 1915, it was purchased by T G Cartwright, a Newport business man and reputedly somewhat of a recluse. Following the existing architectural pattern, he enlarged the house in 1919, and converted it into a gentleman's residence, set off by a beautiful garden. After the house was bought by Mrs S G Gibbs and her son Dr J M Gibbs in 1932, further alterations and additions were carried out by the local building firm of Watkins and Bevan.

* This was the name used by Mary and Hilda Davies, who lived with their grandmother at Worcester Cottage c.1908-1919 and had the task of collecting drinking water.

Figure 156: Worcester Cottage from the bank of the River Usk, about 1934.

References

Jones, S R and Smith, J T, "The houses of Breconshire in *Brycheiniog IX-XIII and XVI*. Part 4 (*Brycheiniog XII*) deals with the houses of the Crickhowell district, including Llangynidr.

Smith, P, *Houses of the Welsh Countryside*

NLW, Badminton 3, Beaufort Estate Survey (1587)

NLW, Badminton 7, Beaufort Estate Survey (1760)

We are very grateful to Will Hughes, Conservation Officer of the Brecon Beacons National Park, for his generous help with this study of our old buildings. During the past three years he has accompanied us on visits to over 70 houses in the community and his keen eye and extensive knowledge have been invaluable in the interpretation of their architecture. We are also deeply indebted to the householders; without their help and hospitality the study would not have been possible.

Figure 157: Post Office at Byways, about 1900. Note the slot in the window-shutter, allowing letters to be posted after closing time.

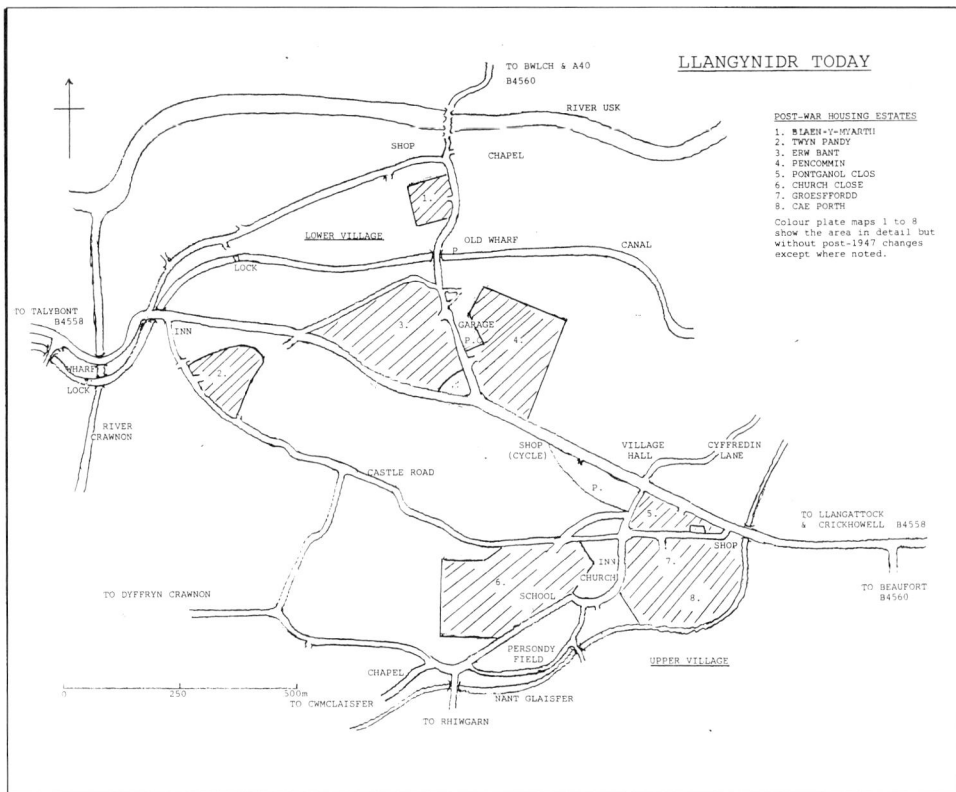

Figure 158: Sketch map of Llangynidr in AD 2000, showing the post-war housing estates.

Note: Colour plate maps

Please note the following points in using these maps:

For the pre-sixteenth century data (pale green) the dating of routes and sites is uncertain. The routes indicated are based on ground features such as deep-cut lanes, hedgerows and fords. They are possible or likely, not proven. Studies of aerial photographs have so far been unhelpful.

The features shown in dark green are based on the 1587 Badminton plans or other contemporary data. Many lanes shown in the plans coincide with today's: a few do not. Where lengths of lane are not included in the Badminton surveys, probable links are shown.

Not all the houses mentioned in the text are included on the maps by name, but are indicated by a coloured area embracing a black dot or shape. By following the postmen's itineraries, in which all nineteenth century (and many earlier) dwellings are mentioned, the reader can locate sites by interpolation. Where little or no trace of a site remains it is indicated by an area of colour with no black dot or shape.

Chapter 16

Twentieth Century Llangynidr

In the first fifty years of the twentieth century the village was little altered from its nineteenth century pattern - the major expansion, with six housing estates, was yet to come. Fifty years on, there are still a number of people living today who remember those years after the Second World War, which makes it a rewarding period to examine in detail. John Dinsdale, formerly of 'Little Aitee' on Cwmcrawnon Road, has extracted much valuable information from the decennial census returns from 1841 to 1891 and this, combined with Dorothea Watkins' recorded interviews with elderly residents, made twenty years ago, provides over 100 years of source material.

One good way of exploring the village of 1947 is through the eyes (and the soles of the feet) of the Postmen who delivered its mail. The role of the Post Office and its employees in linking a community is often overlooked. As far back as 1864 the Post Office claimed to deliver to 94% of homes daily except Sunday. By the end of the nineteenth century the rural postman was expected to deliver to every dwelling, however remote, on a daily basis. Many upland dwellings in occupation in the nineteenth century were empty by the post-war period, because of rural depopulation. The following sections will use the regular postman's rounds in 1947 (shown on the maps as blue when not on lanes) and their much more arduous routes of 1870 (in green) to identify the dwellings and the occupants over this 100 year period.

Using the 1841-91 census has presented some difficulty in our researches as few of the smaller dwellings in the village centres were identified by name - about 30 in Upper Llangynidr, 37 in Coed yr Ynys, as well as several in Cyffredin, and Cwmcrawnon, are un-named. It is not certain that the census enumerators followed a consistent sequence of visits and householders may have died or moved on between decades so continuity of occupancy fails to help match names to locations. Fortunately, most farms and larger houses were named - though, as will be made clear in the text, quite a number were known by different names at different times - not to mention variations in spelling between early maps, tithe maps and successive ordnance surveys.

Today, practically every dwelling extant from fifty years ago has a name. The balance of Welsh and English names reflects Llangynidr's closeness to the more anglicised Monmouthshire as well as the influence of the 'Welsh Not' in nineteenth century Welsh schools - when children were forbidden to speak Welsh at work or in play (see page 171). The majority of farms and the older houses retain Welsh names - High Meadow Farm is a rare exception. In the village, well established local families who built houses used Welsh: Garth or Ffrwd for example, but all the eighteenth century cottages bear English names - Ash, Ivy, Elder, Hawthorn for example, as well as Bridgend (three in all) and all the Inns. Occasionally a name change arose, as when Welsh-speaking Mrs Preston came to live here she renamed Windy Ridge to a Welsh equivalent, Can-y-gwynt (*Song of the Wind*).

Few people had both the literacy and the need to write letters until well into the nineteenth century. Early surviving letters tend to be from clergy or landed gentry such as Thynne Gwynne of Buckland. In a letter dated 6th Oct 1787 from 'Langynider', the Reverend David Phillips writes about the purchase of two local curacies at £5 10s and £10 10s per annum respectively. The letter was carried privately to Hereford and from there cost 5 pence by the newly introduced mailcoach which took two days to get to London. A decade later, a letter from 'Langunider', dated 17th January 1798, was sent to the Lord Bishop of St David's at his London address - unfortunately the sender's name had been torn off. A letter to a Bishop qualified for free postage nationally, but the local carrier charged 1 penny for taking it to Brecon where it caught the London Mail Coach via Bwlch and Abergavenny, arriving in London on 22nd January.

Crickhowell Post Office opened about 1798 but deliveries to the immediate area within the town only started in 1838. The Post Office in Llangynidr opened on 6th October 1850 with the postmark 'Llangunnidr'. The first postmistress was the wife of Benjamin Williams, Parish Clerk and Registrar; the Post Office was originally in Mardy Lane 'between Bridgend and the Old Workhouse'. By 1871 she had been succeeded by her daughter Eliza Louise who married a mason, William Watkins, and they lived at the cottage now called Byways. She is shown in front of Byways as Postmistress on a postcard of about 1900 (see Figure 157). The Watkins family continued to run the Post Office in Byways until 1958 except for a short period around 1918-19 when it was at Waterloo House run by the Prothero sisters who were strict Wesleyans. A story has it that they had to relinquish the role when they refused to pay a War Gratuity to a local ex-serviceman whom they considered unworthy!

Curtis Watkins was the last of the Byways Postmasters, moving to a new bungalow, 'Cae Bach' opposite Persondy field, in 1958. He was succeeded by his widow, local historian Dorothea. In 1971, after 100 years, the Watkins link was broken when Dorothea retired and Mrs Pat James took over at Penlan, Coed yr Ynys. Since 1975, Mrs Pat Williams has run the office from a site next to the garage on Forge Road.

Mail was brought from Crickhowell, at first on foot, the postman delivering letters en route and in the immediate vicinity of the Post Office. Mail for the outlying farms was displayed in the Post Office window. At one time the Postman was Mr Townsend who did shoe repairs in the village before returning at the end of the day with outgoing letters. Later, John Prosser used a pony and mail cart and delivered locally to every dwelling on alternate days. Other local people who delivered the letters around and after the turn of the century included Mrs Miriam Powell, who did the Crawnon round about 1900, William Pritchard and Norman Jenkins, who, after the 1939-45 war, was agent to the Brecon and Radnor MP, Tudor Watkins. The telegraph service reached the village in 1911.

Around 1947, letters were delivered by four postmen: Don Wallace brought the morning mail from Crickhowell in the sidecar of his motorbike. After sorting, he took the Lower Village and Cyffredin round before returning to Crickhowell with the outgoing letters. The other rounds were Cwm Claisfer and Penlan covered by Charles Laughton of Wesley House, a Boer War veteran who, in those less politically-correct days, always talked about the 'fuzziewuzzies'; Dyffryn Crawnon round by Arthur Cox of No3 Canal Cottages (now Bronelys) and the short Upper Village round of Albert Fifield of Persondy, who was also the Sexton. Llanddetty letters were delivered from Talybont Post Office using two postmen.

Postman's Rounds - Albert Fifield   Map 6

Leaving the Post Office (the building is today **Byways**, but it was previously the Post Office for about 100 years until 1958), part-time postman Albert Fifield would have called at the **Horse Shoe Inn** where the letters would have been addressed to landlord Williams and then he would have called at **Cynidr House**, built about 1900 on the site of two old cottages and in 1947 the home of the local taxi driver, Abraham Parry.

Following the lane, Fifield would have come to **Sycamore Cottages,** now a single dwelling, consisting of two stone cottages set at right angles, each with a stone spiral stair to the right of the fireplace. A Mr Hopkins lived here in 1947, making his living selling lime to farmers. From Sycamore cottages he would have passed the remains of **Yew Cottage** on the right before reaching **James Street,** a street which takes its name from a family of that name who lived here from 1841 to the mid 1880s - Joan James and her son David, a farmer and grocer. He would have called at **Elder Cottage** where Mrs 'Echo' Evans lived and then at **Belmont** on the south side of James Street, formerly a grocer's shop where Mrs Edwards lived in 1947. On the other side of the street **Rose Cottage** and **Laurel Cottage** were, according to Dorothea Watkins, built by a stonemason, William Watkins of Byways, in the 1850s. Both are unusual in that upstairs they had a 'flying freehold' with a bedroom from Rose Cottage extending over the living area of Laurel Cottage. At this time Henry Sheehy the cobbler was at Rose Cottage and the Briskhams lived in Laurel Cottage.

Earlier, in the nineteenth century, there were two further cottages in James Street and the footpath ran down to the Claisfer to allow access for water before the first piped water came to the village in 1902.

Hawthorn Cottages No1 and No2, dating from the nineteenth century, were occupied in 1947 by John Hodgkiss in No1 and Rod Watkins in No2. Hodgkiss, an electrical engineer, provided a vital service charging radio batteries so that villagers could hear the BBC, before mains electricity came to the village.

Then Fifield might have called at **Mardy Cottage,** which was built about 1800, to deliver to Dan Meredith. We know that earlier, in 1891, Ann Powell, a widow, had lived here and by the early 1900s Mrs Appleby, who provided a trap for hire, had moved in. Some time after Dan Meredith lived here, the house was restored and enlarged by William and Gilbert Games, in the 1970s.

Brookside Cottages Nos 1 and 2 face Mardy Cottages and are on the edge of Persondy Field, site of the medieval village. Calling here in August 1947, the postman might have paused to deliver some words of consolation to the widow of Alec Meredith. Alec, a quarryman at Trefil Quarry, had been tragically killed a month earlier after an explosive charge jammed. He left his wife to bring up three daughters and a son alone. Alec was one of several brothers and sisters who had moved to Llangynidr from Trefil in 1919. Widow Meredith's neighbour at Brookside was a Mr Pellowe.

Brookside Cottages date from the 1790s. The owner, Dr Philip Wake, is descended from the Brewers who came from Gloucestershire to farm locally about 1830. One farmed in Dyffryn Crawnon and his son John became Canal Agent. The field near Crawnon Wharf became known as Cae Sion Brewer (John Brewer's field). The deep pool just across Mardy Lane in the Claisfer is known as Brewer's Pool.

Bridgend would have been the next call for postman Fifield in 1947. Bridgend is one of three homes of that name in Llangynidr - one just above the Canal in lower village, one by the bridge over the Claisfer where the Rhiwgarn Lane meets Mardy Lane and this one at the foot of Ffrwd lane. The cellar of this eighteenth century cottage could well have served as an alehouse for travellers, but in 1947 tragedy had also struck here, with George Watkins grieving over the loss of his daughter to polio.

Going up Mardy Lane the postman would have called at **Holly Cottage,** which dates from about 1800 and has a spiral stone staircase, and to the right of this a stone lintel over the hearth. Mrs Maggie Williams, the village midwife, was living here in 1947, although she was to die in a fire at the cottage some years later.

Laurel Cottage in Mardy Lane was William Morgan's home from soon after 1900 right up to 1970. The house dates from 1740 and still contains fireplace stairs on the left and a brick arched oven but it was extensively remodelled in the early 1800s. Across the road, set in the wall, was one of the taps installed when the first piped water came to the village, while between Laurel Cottage and its neighbour is another alleyway to the Claisfer for water in earlier times.

Dan-y-graig might have been the next house on the postman's round. This cottage, a delightful miniature, lovingly restored by John Free, is described in more detail on page 209. It was earlier the home of Richmond, the cobbler, then until 1925 a sweet and paper shop, but in 1947, Sam and Frances Bevan were living there. Across the lane, the **Weaver's Cottage** now lay empty.

Figure 159: Bridgend House, 'Beaufort Square'.

Bridgend House might have been next. The house dates from the mid-nineteenth century and the 1851 census identifies a 'New House'. The iron railings round the tiny front garden bear the initials "J O" so they could have been the work of either of Llangynidr's two blacksmiths with those initials - John Owen the elder (who was 64 in 1851) or his son, John Owen, who was 39 and worked the forge behind Bridgend House (see page 138). The son had been involved in the Chartist movement and following the uprising in 1839 he was sentenced to six month's hard labour for manufacturing weapons. He had been actively involved in meetings to design pikes at the 'Lion beerhouse, Llangynidr' (this could have been the Red Lion or the White Lion in Coed yr Ynys) and with others of like mind planned to attack Brecon in November 1839. In the more peaceful summer of 1947, Fifield would no doubt have had letters for Norman Jenkins who lived here.

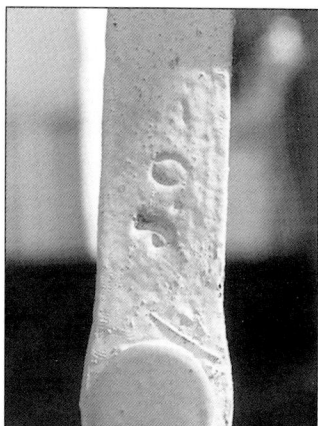

Figure 160: The intials J. O. (John Owen) on the railings at Bridgend House.

Figure 161: The fireplace of the village workhouse in the garden behind Bridgend House.

In the garden of Bridgend House are the remains of a forge and a cottage. At one time, the cottage was the village workhouse. Also there is a red corrugated iron shed, opening onto Mill Pitch or Rhiwgarn Lane, which, from 1898 to about 1970, was the paint and bicycle shop of Tom Thomas and, before him, his uncle John.

Nos 1 and 2 Mill Cottages were converted from the mill stables in the 1930s. Mail would have been delivered in 1947 to Mrs Sullivan at No1 and Mr Beerenbrock at No2, a German ex-prisoner of war who decided to stay on in Llangynidr and lives in the village to this day.

Llangynidr Mill is described in the section on mills (page 131), and in 1947 Mr Honeybun who had been the village 'Bobby' was living in the house converted from the old mill.

Just across the lane, the postman might have called at **Saladin House** which was built in the 1870s. In 1947, the unmarried brothers and sisters of the Thomas family were living here - Eleanor, Willie, Tom and Owen with Eleanor (Nelly) outliving all her brothers and living there until her death in 1993.

Further up the lane, **The Garth** dates from the 1850s. Its first occupant was John Watkins, a retired platelayer, perhaps from the Brinore Tramroad, but by 1947, Mrs Elizabeth Harris, widow of the Minister of Sardis Congregational Chapel, was living here.

Along the lane, below Saladin House, was **Rock House** and across the bridge the **Beaufort Arms,** which was run by Mrs Law in the late 1940s (see Inns, page 187).

Figure 162: Pentre Cottage, with Penpentre in the background.

Next call for the postman might have been **Ash Cottage** and **Pentre Cottage**. Both of these cottages have been carefully restored by George Moretta in the 1990s. They date from 1780-1800. Ash Cottage was occupied by a hard-drinking tailor, Twm Davies, who moved to Llangynidr from Brecon, and he was succeeded by Mrs Probert, who knitted stockings for a living, and then by her daughter 'Nanny' Baugh, caretaker of the old village hall.

Pentre Cottage, where the village school teacher, Miss Edith Smith, lived in the 1940s, has a hearth with an oven for which a fine stone door survives. The fireplace stairs are on the left. On the right, a doorway and steps lead down to a small store room - an unusual feature. The cottage has Brecon windows and down the path leading to the Claisfer is a fine well-preserved pigsty.

In 1947 the next call would perhaps have been on Mr David Morgan, a council employee who was living up Claisfer Lane at **Penpentre**. This is a fine eighteenth century yeoman's cottage with original roof and ceiling timbers, one of which has a cut-out to accommodate a grandfather clock. Next up the lane was **Rock Cottage**, occupied by the Wilson family in 1947, a mid-nineteenth century house about the same age as **Far End**, where Henry Small, the village milkman, lived after the war until the 1970s.

Coming back down the Claisfer Lane, past the Chapel, the postman might have called in the Chapel vestry, which, in 1947 was **The Bungalow**, home to Mr and Mrs Beddoe.

Penrheol would have been the next stop. This seventeenth century house was imposingly sited (as the name, from Pen yr Heol meaning *Head of the Road* suggests) to look down the sixteenth century road towards the church and in the fork of two equally ancient tracks to Cwm Claisfer and Cwm Crawnon. It is a typical regional house with upper cruck and scarf and joint collars, a late seventeenth century window in the loft above the byre and a largely intact eighteenth century staircase. For over 30 years at the end of the late nineteenth century it was an inn called the Mason's Arms (see Inns, page 187). By the 1940s it was divided into two dwellings with Mrs Tyler, the school cook, in one and Arthur Gillard, radio engineer, in the other. All these buildings relied for fresh water on the tap sited on the corner between Ash Cottage and Pentre Cottage.

Cartref across the Crawnon Road was, in 1947, the home of Dai 'Stormy' Morgan. It was a tiny cottage in 1841 and 1881, but was largely rebuilt around the turn of the century and for a time housed three families.

Crossing Beaufort Square, postman Fifield would have come to **Hope Cottage**, which dates from before 1841 but was extensively rebuilt in the 1900s. It was a shop in the 1930s and Mrs Francis lived here in 1947. Next door, **Ivy Cottage** is a solid late-Victorian house built on the site of a complex of cottages extending from the road to Mardy Lane. Tom George, a clog maker, lived there in the 1920s and Zillah Williams after the last war. Down the road Fifield would have strode past the former workshop of John Jenkins, late nineteenth century monumental mason, which faces Persondy Field. The present owner, Martin Preece, of **Stepaside**, proudly points out errors in carving which have been set into the interior walls.

Wesley House, next door down the road, is probably a mid-nineteenth century conversion of the mason's workshop which had been built onto the cottage behind. Upstairs the window sills and a passage wall have been constructed from pews from a nineteenth century chapel. Stone lintels, cupboards, fireplaces and ironwork all point to the same period. In 1947, Charles Laughton, the postman who did the Claisfer round, lived here.

Wesley Cottage is set back at right angles to the house, sharing a common wall. There was a dwelling on this site in 1760. Albert Fifield would have delivered the mail to his own home, **Persondy**, next door to the late seventeenth century tithe barn. In the nineteenth century Roger Probert, a shoemaker, lived here followed by John Harris, a gardener. In 1947, Fifield would no doubt have been glad to pause in his own kitchen for a cup of tea before reporting back to the Post Office.

Postman's rounds - Don Wallace   Maps 2 and 3

From the Post Office, Don Wallace would have taken the footpath across the fields, now occupied by the village school and houses of **Church Close** to **Glanyrafon**. Glanyrafon was, in the nineteenth century, known as Heoldwr Farm from the name of the old road skirting the Yail brook, which was shown as Heol Doore in 1587. By the eighteenth century, Heol Dwr was translated as *Watery Lane*, possibly leading to the modern name of Waterloo House for Heoldwr shop. The present house at Glanyrafon is Victorian or Edwardian and it was one of the more 'desirable residences' of the village. In the 1930s, when Captain Sparkes and his wife lived there, Mrs Jenny Morris recalls that,

> "... in Glanyrafon farmhouse they kept a domestic establishment with three servants living in and a cook and a parlour maid. He was a very punctual man, he had been known to drive to Crickhowell with his wife and then leave her to come back on the bus because she wasn't ready to come in the car at the exact time he'd arranged!"

After the war Mr Gilbertson lived at Glanyrafon and in 1947 he got the local electrical engineer, John Hodgkiss, to install a diesel generator for electric lighting - making Glanyrafon one of the first homes in the village to have such lighting.

Don Wallace would have gone back along Castle Road and called at **Brynheulog**, then the home of the Parry family. The adjacent cottage, **Turnpike Cottage**, was built in 1792 to house the toll-gate keeper. Of course, at that time, Castle Road was the main road carrying all traffic on Brecknock Way and from the new mountain road to the Usk bridge. The toll-gate is believed to have been sited about 30m down the road towards Brynheulog. In 1808, the toll-gate keeper was William Parry, and his descendant, Frank Parry, bought the cottage from the Beaufort Estate over 100 years later, in 1915. In the 1930s, Mrs Cox, grandmother of the present owner, Mr Bill Parry, ran it as a sweet shop.

The **Red Lion** was the postman's next call (see Inns, page 187), delivering letters to the 1947 publican, Mr Evans. Next, he called at **Pontganol**, which dates from the early 1800s. In 1834 William Parry, the toll-gate keeper had retired here. From c.1900-1920 it was the Police Station and PC Jones was here until the station was moved to the newly built **Springfield** in Coed-yr-ynys Road.

The postman's next call would have been over what is today the main road to the **Rectory** to call on the Rev Lewis. The history of the Rectory is described on page 213, but local recollections give an additional perspective. Here is Mrs Jenny Morris again:

> "Rev Sinnett was Rector for 45 years from 1867. He was Welsh and the church pulpit was erected in 1929 in memory of him. He employed a German lady as governess for his children, Jack and Mary."

Mrs Morris also remembered,

> "... the governess and the children walking through the fields with their dog. Rev Sinnett kept servants and had a carriage for transport. His grandson, the son of Jack Sinnett, become the officer commanding the Cwrtygollen camp outside Crickhowell in the 1960s."

Mary Sinnett, the Rector's daughter, married Captain Snead of **Pwll Court**. When the rectory was sold in 1972, the sale catalogue noted that a mint-condition 1806 penny had been found between the floorboards.

From the Rectory, Don Wallace would have next called at **Waterloo House**, which was probably built by the Hadleys of Llangynidr Mill about 1850. It was described as a grocery and general store and in 1855 an electoral leaflet from Brecon was addressed to 'Heoldwr Shop, near the Rectory'. In the 1880s Mr and Mrs Thomas Powell were running the business, but before 1891 they were followed by William Prothero, who had moved from Blaen-y-cwm with his wife and two daughters. They were staunch Wesleyans and became the mainstay of the Wesleyan Chapel in top village. After William's death, the two sisters ran the shop in a God-fearing way - children were examined in the Lord's Prayer before the sweets they had bought were handed over! Their nephew took over the shop when they retired. Wilfred Williams was there until the 1980s and today it is a bicycle business.

Crossing the road, the postman would have called at **Ynys Villa**, one of a small group of houses built between the wars. Then he would have called at **Can-y-gwynt** (formerly **Windy Ridge**) where a Mr Hale lived in 1947 and then to **Highfield**, the office of Watkins and Bevan, the building firm. Then he would have called at the **Old Village School**, now **Hen Ysgol** (see Education, page 169), which was converted into three houses around 1980. In 1947, the Headmaster was Mr Wellwood. He had two talented daughters - one had been a member of the famous Enigma code-breaking team in World War II and the other, Dorothea Watkins, wrote '*An introduction to the History of Llangynidr*' which was the inspiration for this book. We owe her a great debt of gratitude!

From the school Don Wallace would have gone along Cwmcrawnon Road and then up to **Castle Farm**. Built in 1857, the farm was rarely occupied in the nineteenth century. Then he would come down the field to **Glasfryn**, which was built in the inter-war period and in 1947 was the property of Mr and Mrs J O Wood, the owners of a yeast delivery business. He would have called at **Pen-yr-ale**, which was built around 1800. We know that in 1841 Margaret Rosser lived there; early in the twentieth century it was a food shop and before the second world war it was Williams the Butchers. By 1947 it had been modified into two houses - with Council Clerk Mr Williams living in the front and Mr Maidment living in the back. After Pen-yr-ale the postman would have passed a small green, once popular as a gypsy camp, a relic of the sixteenth century Coed yr Ynys Common. From here a lane runs south to join Castle Road, while another goes west, skirting **Twyn Pandy**. Walking along this lane, Don Wallace would have come to **Pentwyn Farm**.

Retracing his steps, he would then have come to the **Coach and Horses**. This pub was converted from a pre-1760 cottage once occupied by a John Prosser. In 1946 Emrys and Mary Morgan would have received the mail at the Coach and Horses and then the postman would have gone down the hill and crossed the Crawnon to call at **Lock Cottage,** which was built about 1806 by the Canal Company adjacent to the mill existing there at the time. The Baptist Chapel secretary and canal lock-keeper, Mr Morgan, lived there after the 1939-45 war.

Wallace would then have crossed back to the houses on the east bank of the Crawnon. Today there are just two houses here, **Cwm Crawnon House** and **Cwm Crawnon Cottage** but, in 1841, seven houses were occupied by families, including a miller, Don Parry (see Mills, page 129), a washerwoman, Margaret Evans and a canal labourer, John Powell. By 1891, there were only two occupied dwellings and in 1947, Don Wallace would have delivered to Cwm Crawnon House, to Mr and Mrs Smith and to Mr Bird, a chauffeur, at the cottage. He might then have taken the footpath down the Crawnon towards the Usk to call at **Ty'rywen**. There is good structural evidence - hearth, stairs and window aperture - that suggests the house was here in the sixteenth century, and the 1587 plan shows a dwelling on this spot. In 1947 he would have called on Farmer Richards, a specialist in animal castration, then he would have gone up the bank to **Pendarren**, as the name suggests, which dates from the early nineteenth century and in 1947 was the home of Mr Price, a retired farm bailiff.

Coming up the lane towards the canal, the postman would have called at what is today **The Boathouse** but was then an inn - the Boatman's Arms (see page 210). Mr Farr lived here when postman Wallace called in 1947. He also delivered mail to **Boat Cottage** next door, where Annie Bowen, who was the housekeeper at Oaklands, lived at that time.

Turning east along Coed-yr-ynys Road, the postman would have called at **Lower Lock Cottage**, just below the canal lock, which was being farmed by Frank Bufton in 1947. The original house here pre-dates the canal, although the name is post-1800. The present house dates from the late eighteenth century and it contains some attractive features from that period, including a wash house, front door and fine iron veranda. Further down the road, he would have come to **The Grove**. This cottage was one of the first to be built on Coed yr Ynys Common in the seventeenth century. The house has features dating from about 1720 and a fine pigsty nearby. Before the second world war a Bill Morgan was living here - and he was reported to be the fourteenth generation of the Williams family of Pant-teg to live in the village - but in 1947 the letters would have been delivered to Mr and Mrs Lewis Powell.

Then Don Wallace might have turned down the lane to the banks of the Usk to deliver to the house that is today called **Yew Tree Cottage**. We know there was a house here in 1760, but there is practically no evidence of the original building in the house today. In 1947 it was being farmed by William Pugh, but he moved the following year to Brightwell.

East of Yew Tree Cottage, on the southern bank of the Usk, three cottages were shown on the plan of 1587. This is the spot where the original Usk Bridge crossed the river to **Pen-y-bont**, a sixteenth century house standing on the north bank, but the three cottages had long since disappeared when Don Wallace trudged by in 1947.

Pen-y-bont, although not on his round in 1947, is worth mentioning here. This house still has its original fireplace with stairs on the left, and roof timbers. Home to Belgian refugees during the war, it later became derelict until its restoration around 1970. The Postman would have gone up Orchard Lane to **Pontgarreg** at the top of the lane, just below the canal bank. The present house here is twentieth century but there was an eighteenth century house in the present garden. William Perkins lived here in 1947. He worked on the canal and his wife kept a sweet shop in the house.

To the west of Coed yr Ynys, Wallace might have glanced across to the ruins of **Coed-yr-ynys Farm**. He would know the stories about the ruins being haunted, perhaps by a member of the Roberts family who worked this farm until the 1850s.

Coming back down the lane from Pontgarreg, the postman might have delivered to **1 and 2 Orchard Lane**. These are two late-eighteenth century farm labourers cottages and in 1947 a Mr Prosser, a roadman, lived in No1 and Edna Baugh lived in No2. Swinging right into Coed-yr-ynys Road, he would then have called at the new **Coed-yr-ynys Farmhouse**, built about 1861 by David Roberts - farmer, builder and carpenter, who had previously farmed the old Coed-yr-ynys Farm to the west of Orchard Lane, and then at **Usk View** and **Usk Cottage**. The Baptist Minister, Rev Tansill, was at Usk View in 1947, no doubt preparing for the wedding of his son Myrddin in September of that year, while next door lived Harriet and Matilda Jones who were sweet shop keepers.

Walnut Tree Stores was a grocers, run by Mr and Mrs Caine in 1947. Earlier it had been a drapers until a fire in 1928 destroyed the business. **Sonoma,** opposite, was one of John Hodgkiss' experimental bungalows, built in 1930. It was a drapers run by Mr and Mrs Haysom until 1980 when it became the hair salon that it is today. Next door, Don Wallace might have called at the two houses at **Springfield**, which had been built about 1910 by local builders, Watkins and Bevan. In 1947 one part was the Police Station, where Sgt Jones was to be found, and his next door neighbour was a roadman, Mr Morgan. Next along the road was **Lilac Cottage**, where yet another roadman, Mr Williams, lived. The house here dates from before 1760. It was certainly at various times a shop and may also have been an ale-house called 'The Castle' in 1841.

Crossing Forge Road, the postman probably called at **Usk Villa,** now renamed **Penlan,** which has housed several Baptist Ministers. In 1947 Messrs Wilson and Evans are recorded as living here. Going down the lane behind Usk Villa, he would have come to **Penishacoed**, which is a neat square house dating from about 1810, although there has been a dwelling on the site from 1587. The house changed hands in 1947 - a Mrs Lillwall was there from 1920 to 1947 when her son, Mr Griffiths the builder, moved in. Coming back up the lane past the Baptist Chapel he might have called on another roadman, Mr Morgan at **Mowfield** (see page 208), and then at **Rose Cottage** where a Mrs Davies would have received the mail.

On the other side of the road, **Oaklands**, which is today a Residential Home for the Elderly, was the **Three Salmons Inn** in the nineteenth century (see Inns, page 190). As the Jones family business flourished, they converted Oaklands into a fine house, employing workmen from the village and from Brynmawr. In 1947 a descendant of the Jones family, widow Mrs Llewelyn and her son Howard, a local solicitor, would have accepted their mail from postman Wallace.

Figure 163: Buckland Mill with undershot mill wheel in action. Tor y Foel is seen in the background. Coloured lithograph by A F Rolfe, 1844.

Figure 164: The tollgate on the Usk Bridge, as it might have looked about 1800. Drawn by Gwyn Briwnant Jones (2000).

Figure 165: A field of oats near Llwynyfedwen in 1968.

*Figure 166: Heol Rhiwgarn. The old lane leading from 'The Square' in Upper
Llangynidr to Llangynidr Mountain.*

Figure 167: Alley to River Claisfer near Ffrwd bridge for villagers to collect water.

Figure 168: Culvert under the canal for the Cwmcrawnon Mill leat.

Figure 169: Village tap near Laurel cottage in Mardy Lane.

Figure 170: Well on the bank of the River Usk upstream of Llangynidr Bridge.

Figure 171: The Smithy of Wyndham Davies, the last Llangynidr blacksmith, has been re-assembled in Brecknock Museum.

Figure 172: The New Village Hall, opened in 1995.

Figure 173: The 1993 production of the Opera group was 'Nabucco', directed and produced by Joan Hughes (centre).

Figure 174: 'Red Riding Hood' was the village pantomime in 2000.

Figure 175: Gala Day. Every year on August Bank Holiday a village carnival/fete takes place on the playing field. Colourful floats are a highlight of the event.

Figure 176: 'Swallows and Amazons', 1991

Figure 177: The ruins of Widow John's cottage, Cwm Claisfer. In the background (left) can be seen the Common wall of 1587.

Figure 178: The Croglofft of Rosser Prosser beside the old road (Heol ddu) at the head of Cwm Claisfer.

LLANDDETY

GRAIGLAS HOUSE

TUMP LANE

FORT

WENALL'T UCHAF

SETTLEMENT

B4558

WENALL'T ISAF

1

PANT-Y-WENALL'T

LLANDDETTY HALL

BUCKLAND MILL

CHURCH

3

RECTORY

GLAWCOED

LOCKS

2

DAN-Y-GRAIG

OLD WORKHOUSE

TOR Y FOEL 551m.

S

PEN-Y-BEILI

BRINORE
TRAMROAD

BWLCH-Y-WAUN

P

PENTIR RHIW STATION

CWM CRAWNON

GWERN-Y-GAFR

NORTH ▲	SITE	BUILDING	ROUTES
UP TO 1500			
C16			
TO Ca.1770			
1770 – 1860			
PRE 1947			

BRYN MELYN

TO-
PEN RHIW-CALCH
AND ROCK INN

ROADS ───── MINOR/ABANDONED ─ ─ ─ ─
OFF-ROAD POSTMEN'S PATHS 1870 ──────
          "   "   1947 ──────
FOOTPATHS IN USE TODAY 2000 ──────
LEATS ▮▮▮▮▮▮ BURIED/LINE OF ▶▶▶▶▶▶▶

STANDING STONES ●   ARTEFACT FINDS 9
STONE STILES   S   VILLAGE TAPS   ●
C21 CAR PARKING: LIMITED P SEVERAL P
N.B. ALL MAP INFORMATION PRE-1947 BAR
TODAY'S FOOTPATHS AND PARKING SITES.

0   ½   1Km

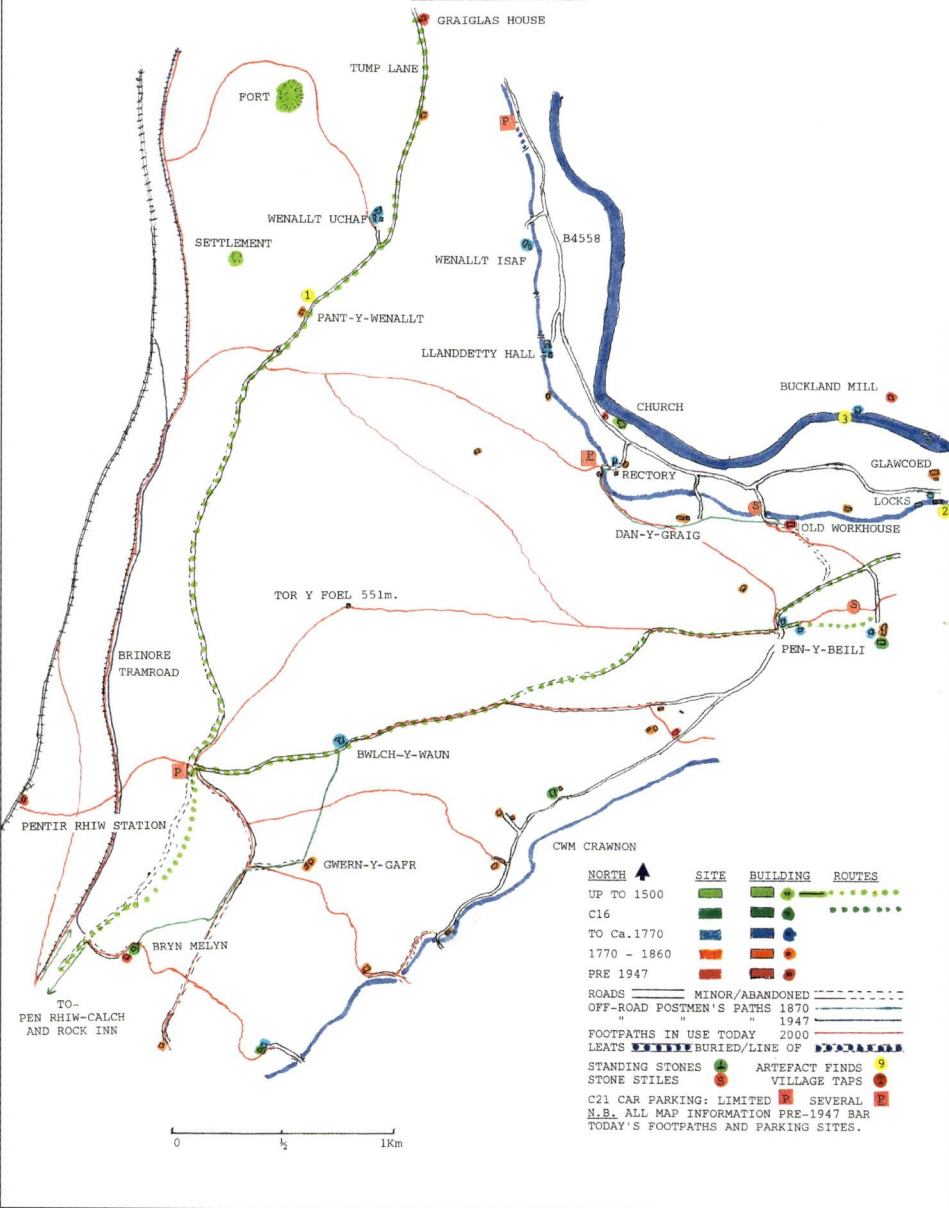

Figure 179: Postman's Round of Llanddetty (Map1).

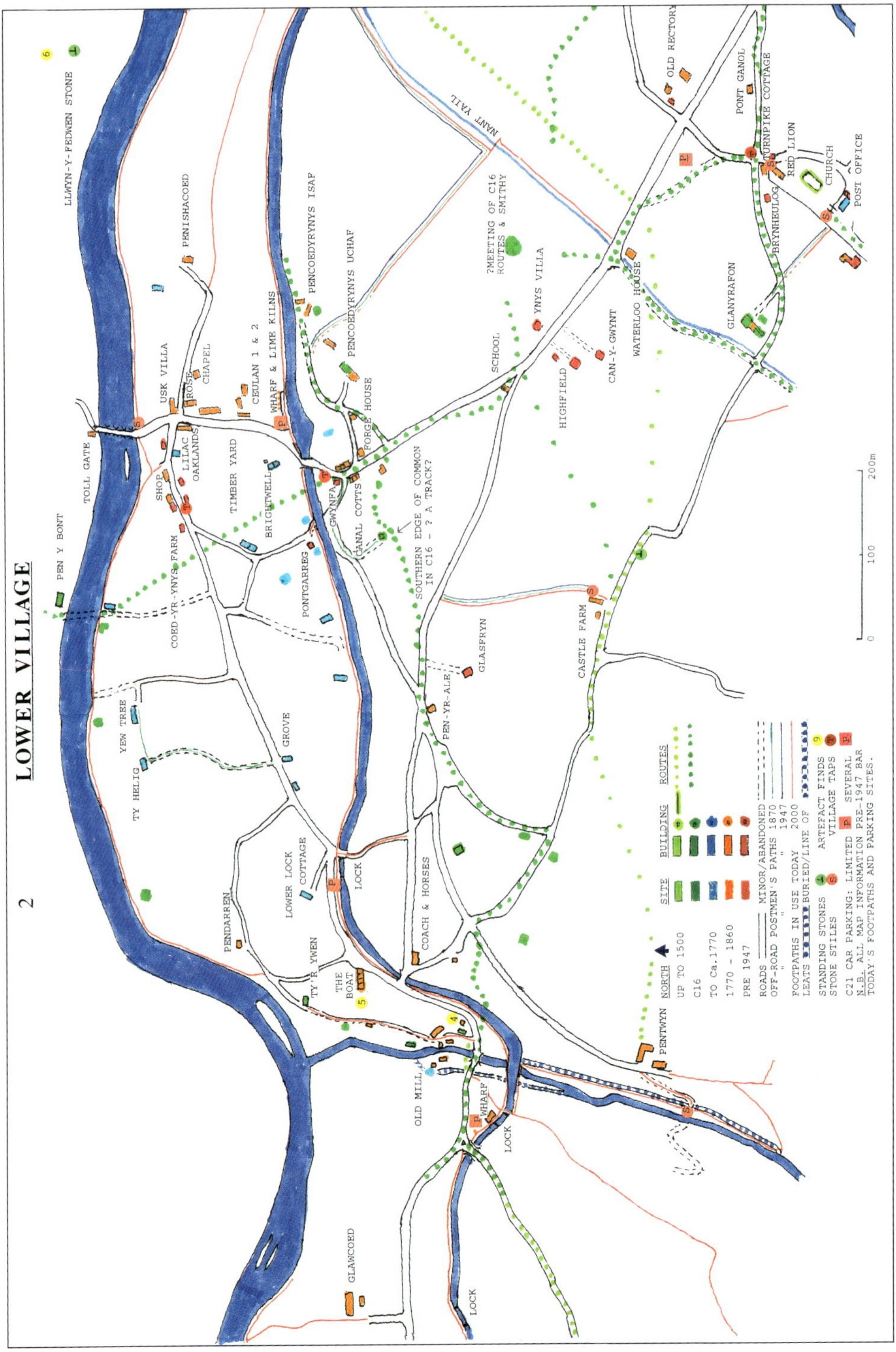

Figure 180: Postman's round of Lower Llangynidr (Map 2).

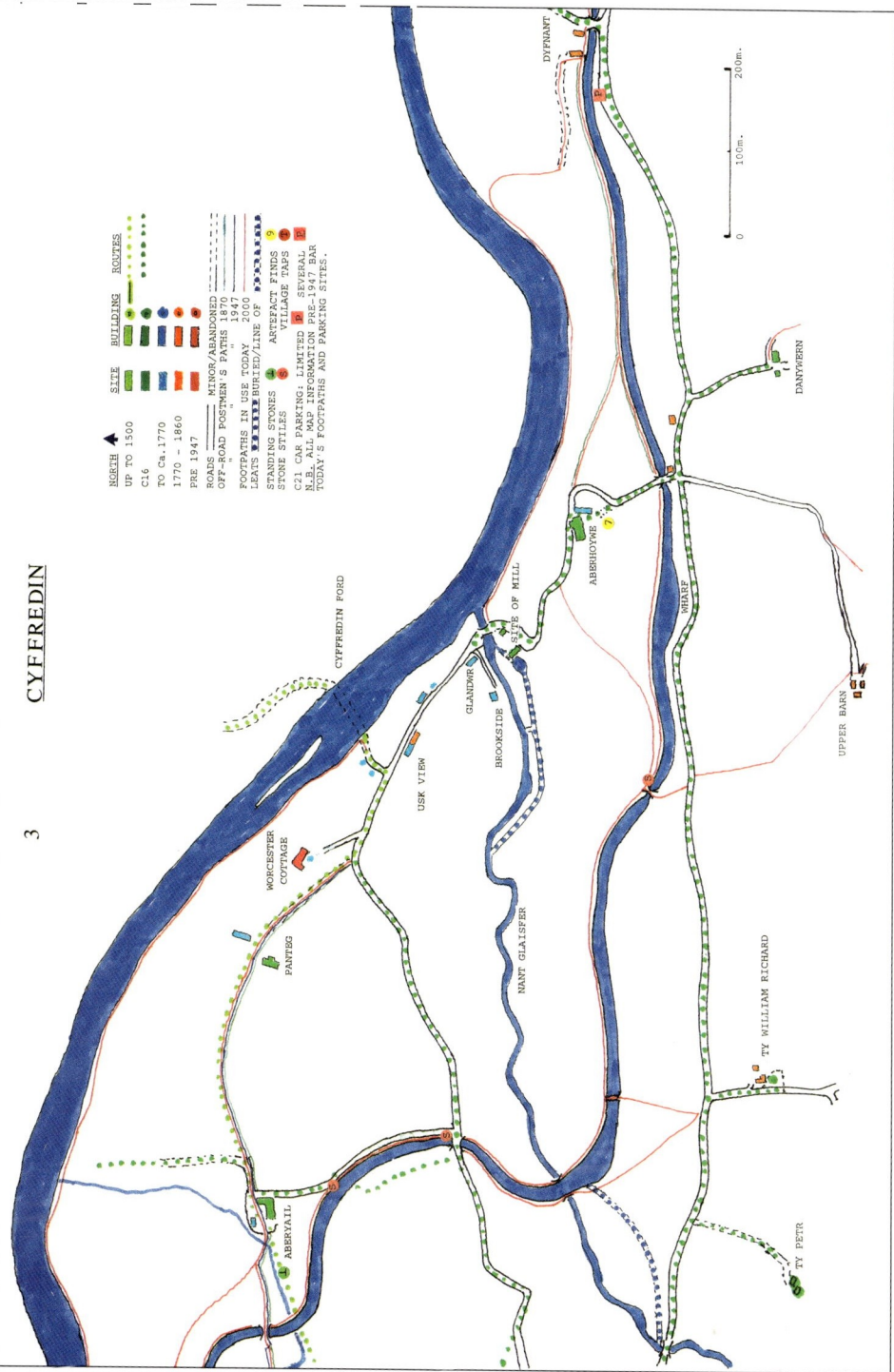

Figure 181: Postman's Round of Cyffredin (Map 3).

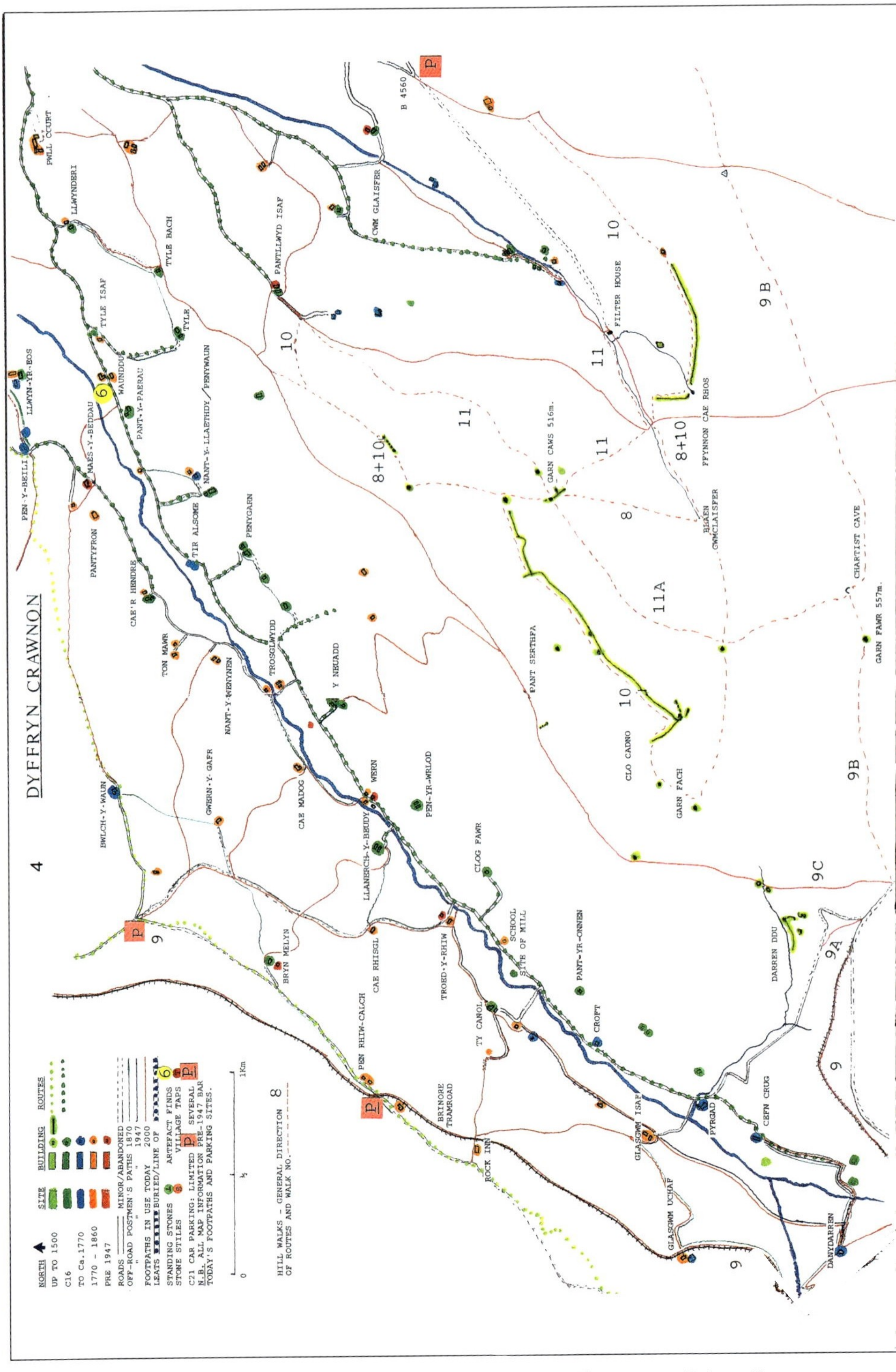

Figure 182: Postman's Round of Dyffryn Crawnon (Map 4).

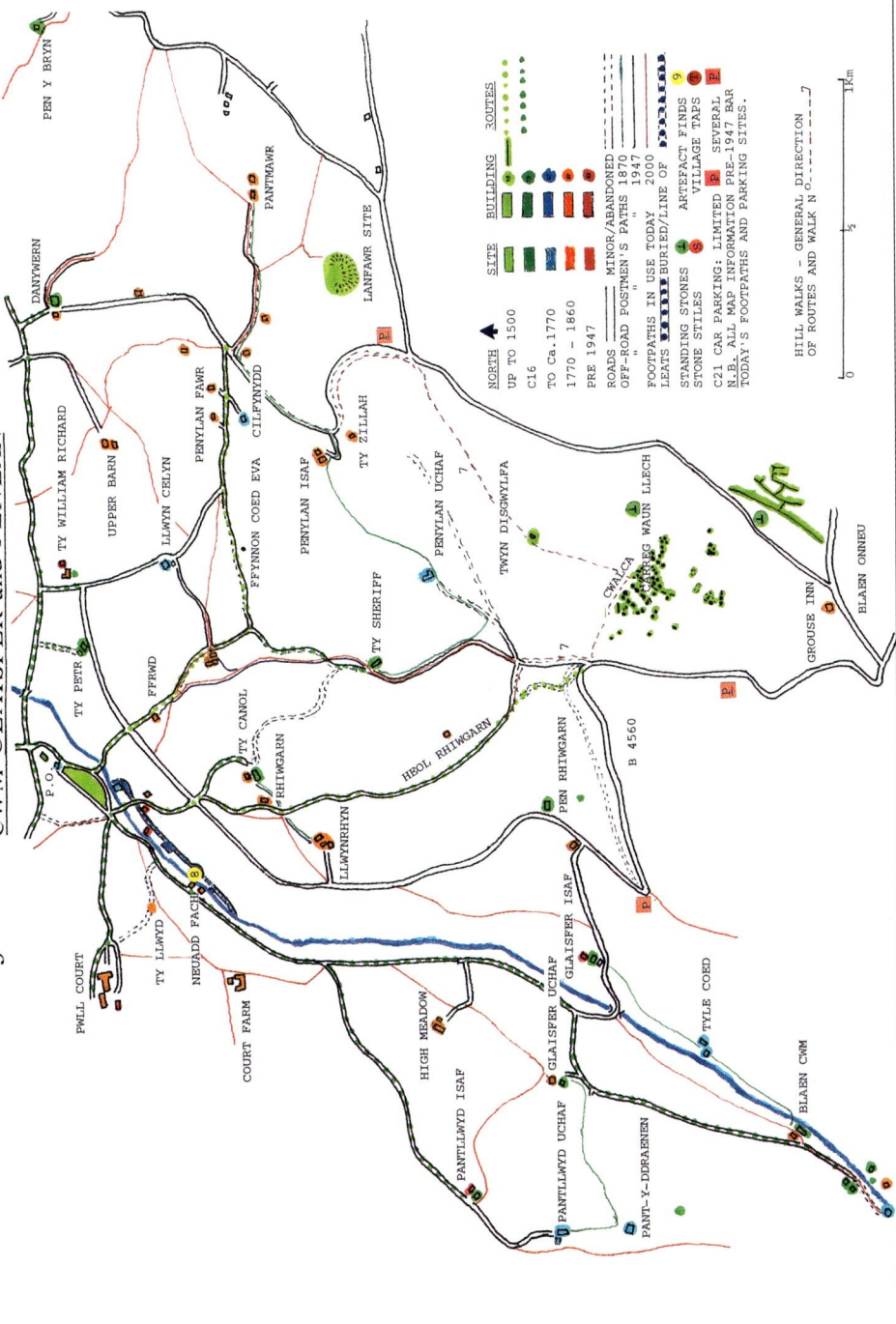

5 CWM CLAISFER and PENLAN

Figure 183: Postman's Round of Cwm Claisfer (Map 5).

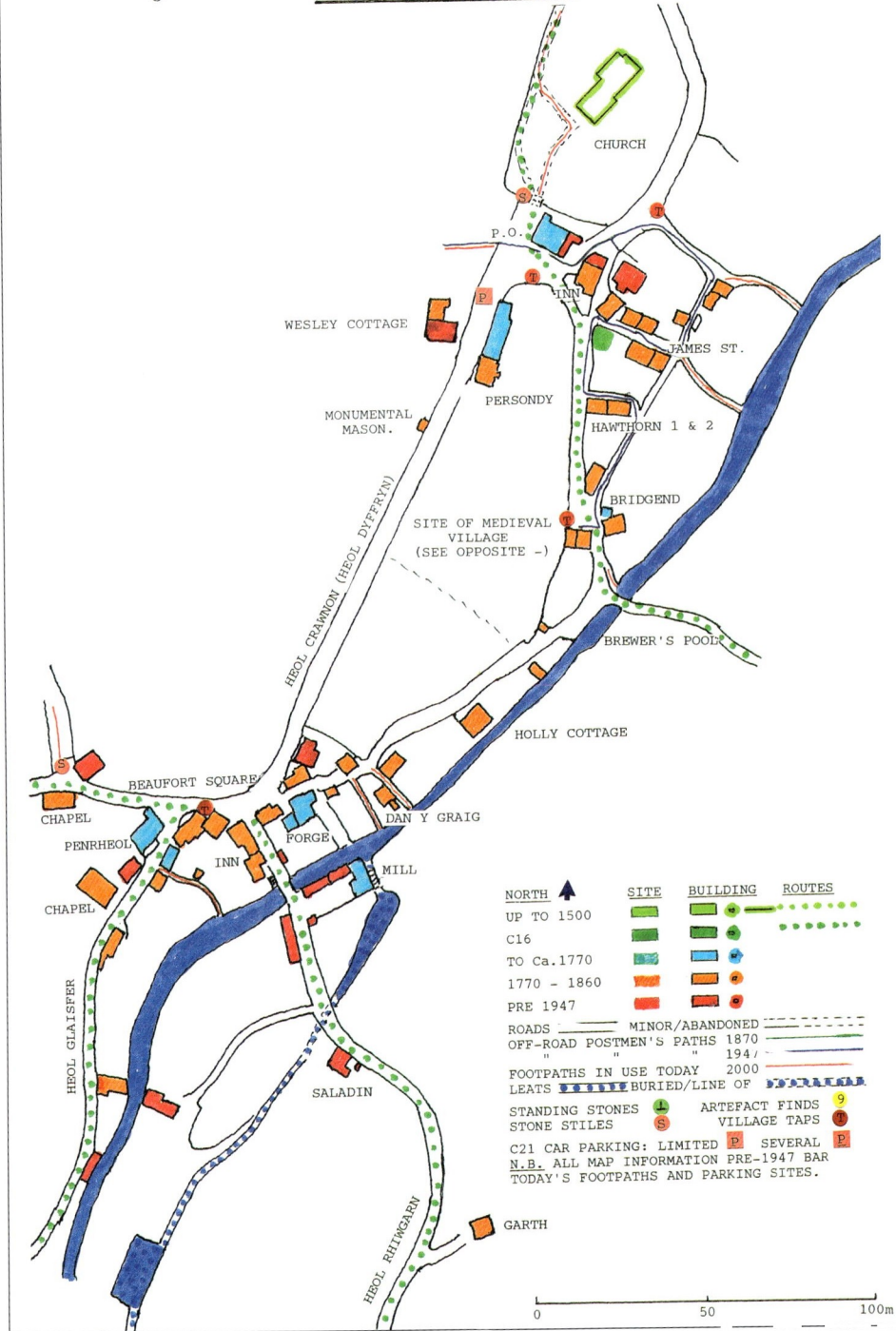

CHURCH

P.O.

WESLEY COTTAGE

INN

JAMES ST.

PERSONDY

MONUMENTAL
MASON.

HAWTHORN 1 & 2

BRIDGEND

SITE OF MEDIEVAL
VILLAGE
(SEE OPPOSITE -)

BREWER'S POOL

HOLLY COTTAGE

HEOL CRAWNON (HEOL DYFFRYN)

BEAUFORT SQUARE

CHAPEL

DAN Y GRAIG

PENRHEOL

FORGE

INN

MILL

CHAPEL

HEOL GLAISFER

SALADIN

HEOL RHIWGARN

GARTH

NORTH ▲	SITE	BUILDING	ROUTES
UP TO 1500			
C16			
TO Ca.1770			
1770 - 1860			
PRE 1947			

ROADS ———— MINOR/ABANDONED ------
OFF-ROAD POSTMEN'S PATHS 1870 ————
     "   "   " 194/ ————
FOOTPATHS IN USE TODAY 2000 ————
LEATS ▮▮▮▮▮▮ BURIED/LINE OF ▶▶◀▲▲◀◀◀

STANDING STONES ●   ARTEFACT FINDS ⑨
STONE STILES ⓢ   VILLAGE TAPS ⓣ
C21 CAR PARKING: LIMITED P SEVERAL P
N.B. ALL MAP INFORMATION PRE-1947 BAR
TODAY'S FOOTPATHS AND PARKING SITES.

0   50   100m

Figure 184: Postman's Round of Upper Llangynidr (Map 6).

7 PERSONDY FIELD SURVEYS   SUMMER 1997.

	HIGH	HOLLOWS OR LOW
TOPOGRAPHY		
RESISTIVITY		
MAGNETIC		

PLATFORMS

NOTES
Resistivity is high for stony loose-packed soils. low for wet, tight-packed soils.

Magnetic readings are high in the presence of ferrous materials which occur in hearths, slag etc. and very high with iron or steel objects.

HEOL
DYFFRYN

MARDY
LANE

0   10   20m.

RESTRICTIONS ON THE SURVEY

Not surveyed (shrubs etc)

Two power poles and transformer:
Underground earthing wires from the polesinterfered with magnetic measurements in the area cross-hatched. Resistivity was unaffected.

Figure 185: Plan of Persondy Field showing the results of recent investigations (Map 7).

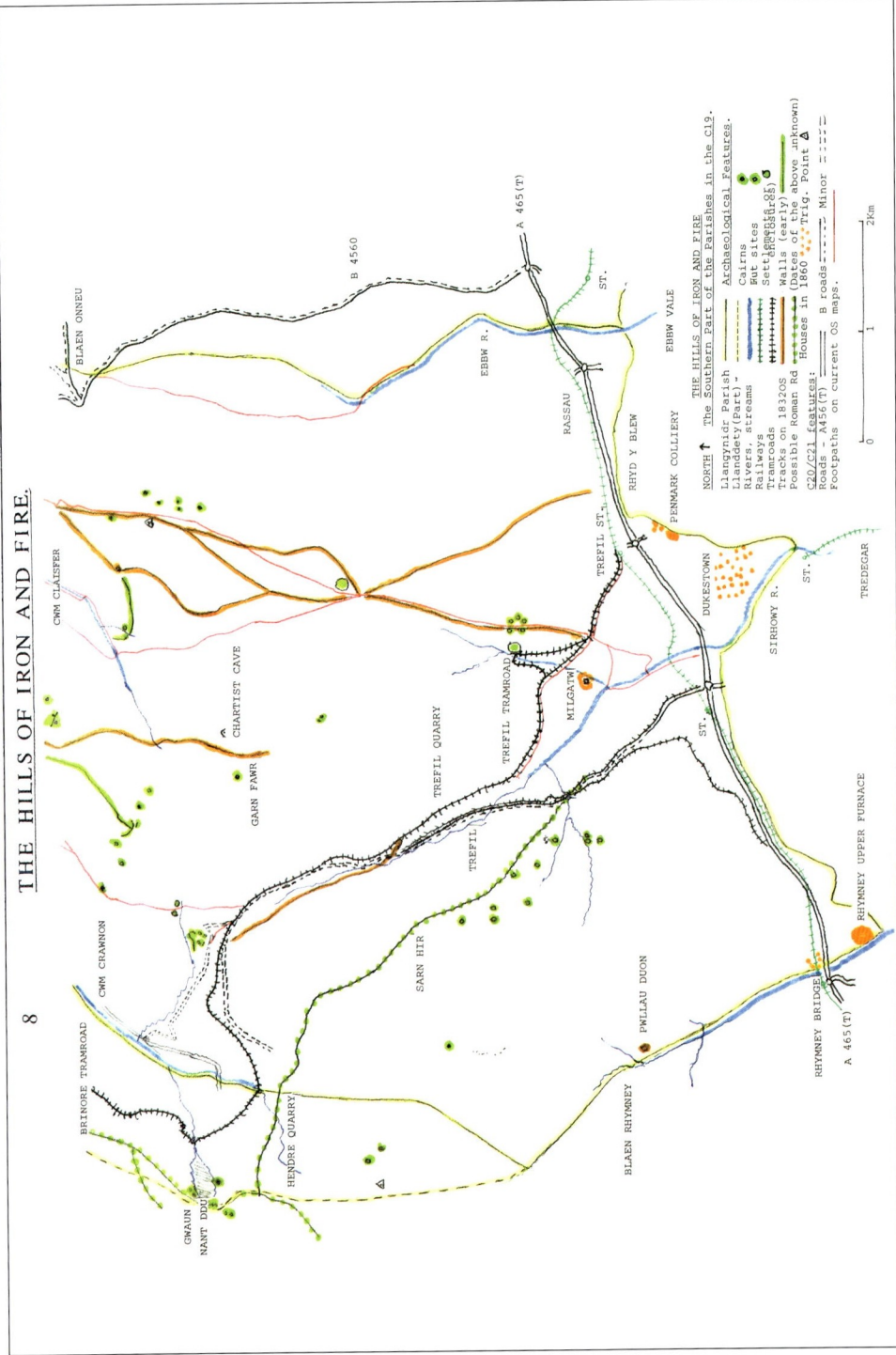

Figure 186: The southern part of the parish in the nineteenth century (Map 8).

Figure 187: The Machine House (now Braeside) about 1920. The small building (left) was the office for the Oaklands Timberyard weighbridge.

Up Forge Road he would have called at **Braeside,** opposite the Timber Yard, which has a history of association with the canal - it was both home and office for a succession of canal inspectors. The appropriately-named Mr Goodship was one such inspector, who was at the house in 1947, and round the corner were a couple of other cottages built by the canal company 200 years ago. Dewi Parry, a timber yard worker, was at one of them, called **Ceulan No2** in 1947 and next door in **Ceulan No1** or **Kiln Cottage** was Mr Edwards, a quarryman. Coming up the hill towards the canal, the postman might have called at the two dwellings comprising **Brightwell.** There was a building here in 1760, before the coming of the canal, but by 1947, a Mr Kite, back from service in the Army was living in **No1** and Bill Games, a wood-turner, was living in **No2.**

Figure 188: The two dwellings at Brightwell about 1920, known as Bridewell in the eighteenth century and until about 1850.

Crossing over the canal, Wallace would surely have had mail to deliver at **Gwynfa** on the right. This attractive nineteenth century house was the home of Edward Bevan, a carpenter who moved from Bwlch at the turn of the century. About 1908 he had gone into partnership with Wilfred Watkins to form builders Watkins and

Bevan. The large grey corrugated shed that can still be seen behind the house was the carpenter's workshop, with stables underneath. Next up the road from Gwynfa were the **Canal Cottages** - five in all. In 1947 two of the five were across the road, where two roadmen lived - a Mr Pullen in one and a Mr Padmore in another. These two cottages were demolished not long after, but the other three are still standing - and in 1947 they were occupied by, respectively, a Mr Price, a Mr Parry, who was a mechanic, and Mr Arthur Cox, another Llangynidr postman, who did the Crawnon round, which was subsequently taken on by Mr Vernon Hill-Male, who today lives in Cwm Crawnon House. Further up Forge Road was another bungalow, **Brynawel**, built by John Hodgkiss around 1930. Mr Jim Pugh was living here in 1947.

Figure 189: Old cottages opposite Gwynfa about 1948. The little girl in the beret is Margaret Thomas (Gwynfa).

Of course, the houses of **Erw Bant** were not there in 1947 - the land was a field, but there were three buildings in the field in 1851, which were occupied by huxters, paupers and widows. How times have changed for Erw Bant! **Bridgend** dates from the early 1800s and **Forge House** from the middle 1800s and Don Wallace would have delivered mail to them. He would then have turned down the lane to **Pencoedyrynys.** Perhaps he would have stopped at **The Smithy** (see Smithies, page 136), which has since been converted into a house, but with the essential structure of the workshop being retained in the kitchen. Then he would have headed for **Pencoedyrynys-uchaf** and **Pencoedyrynys-isaf**. After delivering letters to Gordon Edwards and David Powell in 1947, the postman would have taken the path across the fields to the canal bridge near **Aberyail Farm** which is described in detail on page 200. In 1947 the mail would have been delivered to John Watkins. Then he would have taken the ancient path to **Pant-teg,** where he would perhaps have had mail for either the Lloyd or Williams families - both of whom were farming here in 1947. The house was rebuilt c.1870 but the fine barn and other buildings are probably eighteenth century. Heading still further east, Wallace would have come to **Worcester Cottage**, which is described in detail on page 215. Then he would perhaps have called at **Usk View Cottages**, where the Powells and Bryn Price were living in 1947. Across the road is **Cyffredin Cottage**, which was built before 1760 and was extended and improved in the 1920s. When he visited it in 1947 to deliver to a Mr Prothero, Don Wallace would have known the house by its name at that time of **Glanyrafon**. He would then have gone on to give letters to Tom Edwards at **Glandwr** which had previously been for many years the home of Badgett's the tailors. He would have also called on Gordon Price, a fisherman, at **Brook House**, a dwelling some 70m back up the Claisfer stream, and then he would have called at **Aberhoywe Farm**. This fine building is described in detail on page 197. He also would have stopped at the **King's Arms** (see Inns, page 187) and then called at **Aberhoywe Cottage** where Mr Istance would have received his letters. The postman would perhaps be glad now to be heading back towards the village. **Tyr William Richard** would be his last call before reporting back to Mabel Watkins at the Post Office by the Church. There was a farmhouse here in 1587. In 1947 the farmer was Mr Gretton, who delivered milk locally, and his would be the last letters in Don Wallace's mail bag. Back at the Post Office, there would be time for a break before he started his round of the village letterboxes collecting the letters. Then, after emptying the Post Office box, he would depart for Crickhowell with the outgoing mail from the village to the world.

At the end of the 1870 round there was a long walk for the postman to **Dyfnant** and then back along the road to **Dan-y-wern**, a substantial sixteenth/seventeenth century farm destroyed by fire nearly a century ago.

Figure 190: The ruins of Dan-y-wern.

Postman's rounds - Charles Laughton

Map 4

While his colleague Don Wallace was delivering the mail to the residents of Lower Llangynidr, it was the job of Charles Laughton to do the same starting in the upper village and calling on the farms and cottages of the upper Claisfer valley. Leaving the Post Office near the Church, he would go past his own home, **Wesley House,** heading for Claisfer Lane. Just beyond Far End, at an S bend in the lane, a track used to go across the fields to **Ty Llwyd** and **Pwll Court**. Laughton would surely have called at **Neuadd-fach**, being farmed in 1947 by Frank Stokes, where the present house is mid-nineteenth century. The modern barn conversion here, now known as **Ty-cerrig**, despite its attractive use of timber and stone, has no features which can be linked to the earlier building which was known to be here in 1832.

Figure 191: Thomas Thomas of High Meadow, 1851.

High Meadow Farm is about one kilometre further up Claisfer Lane, where Farmer Millichap might have chatted for a while with the postman in 1947. The original longhouse structure of High Meadow has been remodelled over the years. We know that there has been a Thomas connection with this house for more than 200 years. David Thomas, born in Llangynidr in 1796, farmed here for much of the first half of the nineteenth century. His son, Thomas, born in 1827 was photographed at the Great Exhibition at Crystal Palace in 1851 and his great grandson Jeffrey was born in High Meadow in 1908. But while one branch of the family stayed put in Llangynidr, another branch has an American connection - John Thomas, the grandson of Jacob Thomas born in 1803 and first cousin to David Thomas, emigrated from Cardiff in 1852 on a salt boat and his descendant, Mark Thomas, is a Major in the US Airforce today.

A ten minute walk across the fields would have brought Charles Laughton to **Glaisfer-uchaf** where he called on County Councillor Charles Farr in 1947. His daughter, Olive, lives in Cwm Crawnon House to this day. Sadly, however, Glaisfer-uchaf which was a seventeenth century longhouse, was destroyed by fire in the 1970s. All that remains is a set of six bee-boles set in a SE-facing wall. Then the postman would have made the steep climb up to **Pantllwyd-isaf**, a sixteenth century farm just below the mountain wall. Across the farmyard is a fine example of a 'hammel' - built in the mid-nineteenth century and the only one in this area. A hammel is an open-fronted cattle shelter with an enclosed yard.

250

In the summer of 1947 he would have paused to chat with Griff Price. Griff and his family had come to the Claisfer valley during World War II when farms on the army ranges near Sennybridge had been cleared. They had survived the severe winter of 1947 when hill farmers like them had been cut off for days after a succession of blizzards. Temperatures remained below freezing for practically the whole of February 1947. Many sheep were lost because, although they could survive several days under snow, the deep drifts lasted from 20th January until the last, and most severe, blizzard came on 4th March. However, this terrible winter was followed by a fine summer and Griff Price would no doubt have told Charles Laughton that drifts of snow on lee slopes and in deep sink-holes on the hill above had not thawed fully until June of that year.

Then the postman would have gone straight down to **Glaisfer-isaf** across the valley. Seventy or so years earlier, a postman's round would have been much longer here, visiting high farms and cottages such as **Pantllwyd-uchaf, Pantyddraenen, Blaen-y-cwm** and **Tyle-coed**, but by 1947 these had all become vacant and started to become derelict. For example, the last known occupant of Pantllwyd-uchaf, a Thomas Price, eked out an existence for himself, his wife and six children at the end of the nineteenth century. When he died we are told that he was laid out in his coffin on the Welsh dresser - there being no other place to put it! Sadly, the cries of buzzards are no longer echoed by the laughter of children at play in the cottage gardens, the woods and the fields.

Glaisfer-isaf is a typical longhouse, dating from 1600 or so. In the nineteenth century a new house was built and the old house became farm buildings - although these have since been thoughtfully restored as a home, keeping many important early features. The Watkins family farmed Glaisfer-isaf through many decades in the nineteenth century but by the time of World War I the Davies family moved here from Scethrog. Postman Laughton would have delivered mail to the Davies family in 1947, though they were soon to be succeeded by the Mantle family, who own Glaisfer-isaf to this day. Then he would have climbed up to **Tyr Gwenllian** (also known as **Penrhiw-garn** and **Hillgate**), which lies on the bend of the mountain road. There was a house here as early as 1587 when John Herbert was the tenant, but it has been almost completely rebuilt since then. Johnny Edwards was living in the house in 1947.

Charles Laughton would have gone down the mountain road for a mile or so until he turned right up to **Llwyn-yr-ynn**. The beautifully-built farm buildings here date from 1839, but the house has been extended and modernised over the years. By 1881 Edward Reynallt was the farmer here and his son Octavius was still living in the house when postman Laughton called. From here, he would have taken the footpath across the field to the next farm, **Rhiwgarn**, which lies on the lane of that name going up onto Llangynidr Mountain. About 1890 Jehoshaphat Powell had moved from Pentwyn to farm at Rhiwgarn and his son Jack had taken over from him in 1912. No doubt Laughton would have carried a good sized bundle of letters to Jack Powell in 1947 because Jack was, at that time, chairman of the Farmers Union and he would have been busy with correspondence supporting the many farmers who had suffered great stock losses in the winter blizzards earlier that year.

Ty-canol, across the next field, was originally a sixteenth century longhouse. It has been renovated over the years but retains some old features, including a cellar under the oldest part. Letters for George Kidley would have come here in 1947.

Down the hill from Ty-canol, Laughton would have strode on to **Ffrwd,** which lies on the sixteenth century route from Llangynidr Church to the mountain. More details on Ffrwd are given on page 211. Here he would have delivered letters to the Thomas family and then he would strike up the steep footpath to **Ty Sheriff**. This interesting house is also described in more detail on page 206, but in 1947 the mail to Ty Sheriff would have been addressed to Mr Sidoli, of the well-known ice-cream family.

On the Lan Fawr hillside above Ty Sheriff there would once have been many more homes. Go back 150 years and there were eight occupied dwellings up here. The postman in 1870 would have called at five, but by 1947 all were uninhabited, leaving perhaps the ghosts of former residents to flit about the ruins of **Pen-y-lan, Penylan-uchaf, Penylan-isaf, Penylan-fawr, Ty Zillah, Pant-mawr,** and **Cilfynydd**. Rural depopulation was a reality here!

The postman would now have been heading for **Llwyncelyn**. This house has features which date it to about 1680 and there is also a substantial Victorian addition parallel with the old house, where the old kitchen has a fine Victorian elm bacon rack. We know that David Bevan was farming here from before 1930, because Dorothea Watkins tells us that

> "...about 1930, David Bevan who farmed Llwyncelyn, was ill with pneumonia. A sheep was killed and the lungs tied against the soles of his feet to draw out the inflammation and they remained there until they were putrid. Dr Townley did not object. More than one sheep was killed to keep up the supply of lungs."

No matter how smelly, the cure seems to have worked because about 17 years later, in 1947, David Bevan was well enough to receive the last delivery of letters from Don Laughton's post bag!

Postman's Rounds - Arthur Cox   Map 5

While his colleagues Don Wallace, Charles Laughton and Albert Fifield were shouldering responsibilities for the delivery of the mail to the residents of Lower Llangynidr and Cyffredin, Cwm Claisfer and Penlan and Upper Village respectively, it fell to Arthur Cox to manage the Dyffryn Crawnon round. Mervyn Watkins' recollection of Arthur Cox is worth recording:

"He was a village character. At the end of his life, he lived on the corner of Pen-yr-Ale Lane, opposite Gwynfa. He worked at the timber yard and was head ostler. Later, he became the village chimney sweep and in the late 1940s he became postman in the Dyffryn, travelling by bicycle and on foot. He could not read, but the letters were sorted into the correct order for him before he left the Post Office, and at each house he asked to be told where to go next. Delivering post in the Dyffryn gave him excellent scope for his great skill, which was poaching!"

Leaving the Post Office, with his letters sequenced by Postmistress Watkins, Cox would pedal up through the upper village to his first call at **Pwll Court**, an elegant country house described in more detail on page 213. We know that the house was acquired in 1887 by Morgan Powell Jones who ran the Oaklands timber yard and that, before the first world war, the house had been acquired by Captain Plenty and the adjacent farm lands were let to Captain Sparrow of Ashford, near Talybont-on-Usk. According to Mr Gordon Price, whose father became bailiff to Captain Sparrow, the Captain employed three wagoners, a pig man and a herdsman. He also tells us that,

"During the coal strike in the 1920s, Captain Sparrow employed, as casual labour, striking miners who had been in the same regiment as himself in the 1914-18 war. They slept during the week in the granary and walked home to Tredegar at week-ends carrying presents of potatoes, swedes etc. Every Christmas, every regular employee had a quarter of lamb given to them and a hamper was given as well to those men who had children at home."

Unfortunately, the financial affairs of Captain Sparrow were not as robust as his employees would have hoped. They collapsed in the late 1920s, putting all of them out of work. By 1947, Mr Buchan, the owner of Glanusk sawmills, was living at Pwll Court, and the farm was run by Jacob Williams. Gordon Price, later employed as a canal lengthman, was living in **Pwll Court Cottage**.

Continuing along Crawnon Road, Arthur Cox would perhaps call next at **Llwynderi**. This house has a sixteenth century window in the south end but little else survives from its early history. Mr Thomas was farming here in 1947, to be succeeded by Mr Vaughan, who moved here from Waun-ddu two years later. Cox would have headed on up the road, calling next at **Waun-ddu** where the house dates from the early nineteenth century, but the barn over the road is earlier. Mr and Mrs Vaughan were living at Waun-ddu in 1947 while the caravan in the field next door housed Mr and Mrs Maggs. Mrs Maggs taught in Llangynidr School. In 1909 roadmen looking for stone disturbed a burial site in the meadow below Waun-ddu. A late Middle Bronze Age urn with cremation remains dating from between 700 and 400 BC was discovered, but was broken during excavation. The urn was reconstructed and is currently in Brecknock Museum (see Figure 3). Next on the round would have been **Pantypaerau**. The original house is seventeenth century, with an early window on the west side and moulded beams, but much of the remainder of the house is Victorian. The Williams family had owned Pantypaerau for more than 100 years up to 1947.

Figure 192: Pantypaerau from the west. There was a farmhouse here in 1587 (see Figure 31).

His next call would have taken him high up on the southern side of the valley to **Pen-y-waun**, where 'Comrade' Williams was living, Other older houses such as **Nantyllaethdy** and **Tir Howell Sais** (see further details on page 203) were not occupied in 1947, so the postman would have returned to the road. He would not have called, either, at **Tir Alsome**. The house here has 1657 marked on a door lintel and John Bullock Lloyd owned it in 1760 but today, after much alteration, there is nothing to confirm the age of the dwelling. In 1947 the house was unoccupied, although happily it is a home again today. However, after going left up a very steep lane, Cox would have met with Bryn Powell, who was farming at **Pen-y-garn** in 1947. Bryn lives in the upper village to this day. Pen-y-garn was William Phillips' home in 1587. In 1760 it was designated **Tyr yr Arlwydd** and it was farmed for much of the nineteenth century by Rachel and then Phillip Price. Today it has been carefully restored to retain a number of features of the original house and of the barn across the yard.

The postman would have pedalled on, passing the road that drops down to the Crawnon river on the right. **Trosglwyd**, the house which is a short way down the road, was empty in 1947, so he would continue on to **Y Neuadd**. This important group of buildings is described in detail on page 205. Another kilometre on brought the postman to **Wern**. This little group of three dwellings, together with the chapel which dates from 1842, was the focal point of the Dyffryn community until well into the twentieth century. It had strong community links with Trefil and Tredegar as well as with Llangynidr - there were always miners or quarrymen in one or two of the homes and their wives frequently took

254

dairy produce over the mountain to sell in Tredegar market. In 1947 Bryn Probert was living at **Lower Wern Cottage**. His father, Meredith Probert, had come to the Dyffryn from Longtown on the other side of the Black Mountains in 1891. He married a Trefil girl and worked in the Trefil quarries. Every day he walked 5km up the old track past Clog-fawr to Twyn y Llyn and back with a rise of 300m each way! Meanwhile, his wife ran a small shop selling sweets and cigarettes, a business later carried on by the Skidmores, who had retired there from the Horse Shoe Inn.

Across the road, opposite the Chapel, is the smallest dwelling, **Yew Tree Cottage,** which is indeed overshadowed by an enormous yew. This is one of the only two croglofft dwellings recorded in the parish - they are common in West Wales. The postman would have delivered to the Phillips family here in 1947. **Wern House** or **Y Wern** dates back to at least the early eighteenth century. Cyril Thomas was farming here in 1947 and before him, Y Wern was farmed by Edwin Jones, who slaughtered all the local pigs here, sending local children off up the hillside for dry bracken to burn the hairs off the carcass. Pedalling on along the valley, Cox would have called at **Clog-fawr**. There was a farmhouse on this site in 1587 and in 1760. Meredith Probert was here in the 1920s. Mr Hurlow would have received the mail in 1947. Arthur Cox would leave his bike at the foot of Troed-y-rhiw lane to be picked up on his return.

Figure 193: The ruins of Croft, Dyffryn Crawnon.

The next delivery would have been at **Dyffryn Crawnon School** and then he would have passed by **Croft**, home of widow Elizabeth Perrot in 1851 but unoccupied in 1947, and come to **Pyrgad**. The present farmhouse was built on the site of an earlier building, probably in the late nineteenth century - the byre has the date 1881 on a beam. Tommy James Probert received the mail here in 1947. Forty years later, Probert intrigued Dorothea Watkins with this tale:

"Pyrgad means 'small battle'. He told us he had met a man who alleged he had an old manuscript which told how Pyrgad had been a Roman outpost. It had been attacked by people from up on the hill, whereupon a message had been sent to the Roman garrison at Y Gaer (the Roman site west of Brecon) asking for help. Roman troops came to quell the fighting but were attacked down the valley by the 'hill-men' and the battle raged for 53 weeks. This occurred at Maesybeddau (*Field of the Graves*). No Roman ever came into the valley for 68 years afterwards"

Cefn-crug might have been the next call, where Cliff Price would have accepted the mail in 1947. The house dates from the seventeenth century and, according to the Rev Jenkyn Edwards, was the home of Phillip Phillips from 1840 to 1880, who composed a Welsh verse to the waterfall of Crawnon.

> Ffynnon loew fel y grisal
> Rheda attom yn ddiatal
> I'n purhai, glanhai, a'n cynnal
> Tra par i'n dyfroedd pur

The final house, right at the top of Cwm Crawnon, was **Danydarren**, which lies across the infant Crawnon and up a long track. The house of the Gunter family in the seventeenth century, it is so far up the valley that to call there could add 40 minutes to the postman's round. Suspecting that his mail was being held back so that visits would only have to be made infrequently, one resident before the last war decided to order the Western Mail daily by post! The route from Danydarren to **Glasgwm-isaf** ran along a field path little used for much of the year and so perhaps postman Cox would have been able to check a snare from yesterday and reset it for tomorrow. A skilled poacher, he rarely returned home empty handed. Glasgwm-isaf is a beautifully-built Victorian home, with some fine wooden panelling. Mr Will Evans, organist at the Dyffryn Chapel, was farming here in 1947 (see page 212).

Then it would have been on to **Gelli-bant** via an old cart track. Here the building is extensive, but relatively modern. Mr Pritchard was farming here in 1947, having just taken over from Tommy James Probert when he moved to Pyrgad. The remains of **Llwyncelyn**, an eighteenth century farm, lie below the path that the postman would have taken to **Ty-canol**. This is a substantial farm, probably late sixteenth century, with an eighteenth century wing added as separate dwelling. It may even have accommodated three families at one time as there are the remains of at least three spiral staircases. In 1947 the mail for Ty-canol would have been for Mr Jones.

Troed-y-rhiw is at the end of a field path from Ty-canol, and Ray Price lived there in 1947. The present farmhouse appears Victorian, though it may incorporate an earlier building. Then the route would have been down the lane to pick up his bike and take the Crawnon road to **Llanerchybeudy**. Here the present building is made up from a barn and a modified longhouse of the early seventeenth century, joined by a more recent kitchen. Meredith Probert came here from Pyrgad about 1945. Next down the valley, Cox might call on Mr Evans at **Caemadog**, which is an L-shaped building rebuilt from the shell of an older dwelling; it was reached by a ford at Wern, recently replaced by a footbridge. Now the postman would continue along the north bank of the Crawnon to the road towards Penybeili and then would turn up a steep lane to the left to the eighteenth century cottage of **Ton-mawr**. John Bevan came to Ton-mawr in the 1920s and married for the third time at the ripe old age of 77! About 1940, Bryn Probert came here from Pen-y-waun and years later, Dorothea Watkins recorded this of the difficulties of farming at Ton-mawr in 1946-47:

> "In 1946, the summer weather was very poor and harvesting almost impossible. Mr Probert defied tradition and earned disapproval by hauling hay on a Sunday. Early in 1947, the winter was particularly severe and he was very thankful to have that hay to feed his stock. For 12-14 weeks, it was only possible to reach Llangynidr village by walking through the fields, as the lanes had filled with snow and were impassable. All food and paraffin (for oil lamps and stoves) had to be carried. Tracks dug out one day refilled with snow overnight and the water supply had to be broken free of ice every morning. On 4th June 1947 he brought down from the mountain near Carn Caws, above Pant Llwyd, a lump of snow which had been at the bottom of a sink hole since the winter."

Cae'rhendre was a farm rented from Colonel Davies, whose father owned **Bwlch-y-waun**, high up on the side of Tor y Foel, and who was Master of the Talybont Hunt. Fred Probert was farming here in 1947 when Arthur Cox stopped with the mail. Cae'rhendre is described in more detail on page 202. Next along the lane is **Maesybeddau Farm**. The postman would have delivered to the Thomas family here in 1947. The origin of the name is unknown - Tommy James Probert's conjecture is unconvincingly romantic - but wouldn't it be marvellous if we could prove it, one way or another? Then postman Cox would have gone on to **Penybailey** and **Penybeili**. The latter is an early seventeenth century dwelling with a fine exterior door and hollow chamfered mullions. It was extended about 100 years later to provide an extra ground floor room and a granary. Penybailey was described as eighteenth century. When Arthur Cox came by in 1947 he would have delivered mail to John Richards, animal doctor and, according to Tom Thomas, 'charmer'. From here, Cox would have returned to the lane to cycle round to **Llwynyreos**, which has been the home of the Reynallt family since the eighteenth century. Having made his last delivery, Cox's route would have taken him down the lane to Upper Crawnon Wharf and then back along Castle Road. Time to skin that rabbit now!

In 1870, the round would have been covered on foot or possibly horseback, and would have included steep climbs to **Tyle-bach**, **Tyle** and **Caerhisgl**.

Postman's Rounds - Jack Morgan & Jack Wozencraft Map 1

In 1947, the residents of Llanddetty and the western slopes of Dyffryn Crawnon received their mail from Talybont Post Office and there were two postmen covering this area. Full-timer John 'Jack' Morgan cycled along the B4558 from Talybont via Ashford to Glawcoed and back while part-timer Jack Wozencraft, an ex-First World War Sergeant Major, did the upland round on horseback. The photograph below shows Jack in

September 1941 near Craiglas House on Tump Lane with his daughter-in-law, Molly, on her honeymoon. In this part of the chapter, we'll first travel with Jack Morgan on his round and then we will join Jack Wozencraft on the upland circuit.

Figure 194: Jack Wozencraft, the Llanddetty postman, seen here with his daughter-in-law Mollie in 1947.

After passing Ashford Tunnel on his bike, Jack Morgan's first call would have been to **Lower Wenallt** where Mr Williams lived. This house is seventeenth century or earlier and is recorded as a type B longhouse with a hall conversion with post and panel partition and an ornate open roof with a cruck. Mr Morris at **Llanddetty Hall Farm** and Mr Davies at **Llanddetty Hall** would have been next. The Hall has a fascinating history - it was built by Jenkin Jones in about 1650, taking over the rectory glebe and church for his own use. Later, Wyndham Lewis MP lived at the Hall until his death in 1840; his widow married Benjamin Disraeli, Tory Prime Minister, soon after. Later still, Edmund Gwynne, Chief Constable of Breconshire, lived here until his death in 1906.

Llanddetty Cottage would have been empty in 1947, when Jack Morgan cycled by, because the former occupant, keen fisherman William Law, had died in May the year before. **The Rectory** also did not detain postman Morgan. This sixteenth century house was demolished in the early 1930s, some of the stone and timber being used in the restoration of Llanddetty Church at that time. Today, the site of the rectory is just a bump by the lane which goes over the old iron bridge over the canal. Morgan would probably have called on Captain Sparrow at **The Workhouse** in 1947. This building, now called **Glawcoed Cottage,** was constructed on the southern bank of the Canal about 1840 - and today is a pleasant home with gardens sweeping down to the canal.

At the eastern end of Morgan's round was **Glawcoed**. In 1947, Jim Pugh was farming here. The original farm may have been seventeenth century but, because of major alterations in Victorian times, little structural evidence of the house's early history survives - but it was named on the 1792 canal survey by Thomas Dadford. Jack Morgan would have completed his morning duties about 11am and then in the afternoon he would collect mail from the various post boxes in the Talybont area, then empty the box at the Post Office and take all the mail across the Usk Valley to Llansantffraed to meet the bus from Brecon at about 5.30pm, which took the mail to Abergavenny.

Meanwhile, Jack Wozencraft would have collected his horse from **Maesmawr Farm** and, with his black Labrador for company, he would have set off up Tump Lane to **Craiglas House** which was, in 1947, the home of Vivien Lewis, Lord Brecon, and then on to call on Mrs Powell at **Twmp Cottage**. Next stop would have been at **Upper Wenallt** where John Morgan was farming. This Type B longhouse with post and panel partition, ornate doorhead and cruck roof has a long history, linking the Morgans with the Gunters of Gilestone and the Lewises of Pyrgad. Next, up Tump Lane he would have called on farmer Albert Roberts at **Pantywenallt**. This farm lies about 0.5km south-east of a "settlement" of uncertain age. A socketed axe was found by the farmhouse. Further on, over the shoulder of Tor y Foel, a ride of a further 2.5km would have brought Wozencraft to **Bwlch-y-waun** where Colonel Davies, the master of the Talybont Hunt, was farming in 1947. A further 1km ride and the postman would have come to **Brynmelyn**, a sixteenth century longhouse, which at 400m is one of the highest and most exposed farms in the area. Given this height, it is illustrative to learn from Dorothea Watkins' interview with Dilys Parry in the early 1980s that:

> "Mrs Parry and her family walked to the Baptist Chapel every Sunday morning and back home for dinner. Then down to the Chapel for Sunday School in the afternoon and then back once again to the Baptist Chapel in the village in the evening. Her mother often rode the pony for this travelling and the children would hang on to the pony's tail."

The three return trips between Brynmelyn and the Baptist Chapel would total 20km distance and 800m of climbing - roughly the equivalent of a walk from Brecon to the top of Pen y Fan every Sunday. Could we imagine a 10 year-old in the year 2000 doing this?

Figure 195: Pant-y-rhiw Halt on the Brecon to Merthyr line provided access to the railway system for people at the top of the Dyffryn Crawnon.

No doubt, on his visits to Brynmelyn in the summer of 1947, Postman Wozencraft would have been told of Cyril Thomas's adventure in the great blizzard of the night of 4th March. Apparently Cyril, travelling by train from Merthyr on a day of such extreme snowfall that at least two trains were stuck in snowdrifts, one of them for 40 hours, struck out to climb home to Brynmelyn from Pant-y-rhiw Station in an easterly blizzard, which would have made conditions extremely arduous. Dorothea Watkins takes up the story ...

> "Fortunately, his father set out to look for him with a spade, found him and managed to get him home, half walking and half carrying him. His clothes had to be cut from him and he was soaked in a hot bath and dosed with whisky."

Cyril, who was a fit young man of 29, was none the worse for this adventure. Perhaps the rigours of life at Brynmelyn and the exercise of walking to all those services at the Baptist Chapel had saved his life on that March night!

No doubt after finishing his cup of tea and a chat at Brynmelyn, Jack would set off on his horse down the narrow footpath to the Brinore Tramroad and down to **Danywenallt** (today a study centre, below the dam of the Talybont Reservoir) and on to the rest of his round. Sadly, Jack Wozencraft died some weeks later in 1947. He was succeeded as postman by "Ike" Phillips, who lived near the Travellers Rest Inn in Talybont.

We are grateful to the following for information about the postmen and their rounds: Ursula Innes, Carolyn Jacob, Ron Jones and Molly Wozencraft.

Chapter 17

Walks in and around Llangynidr

Hill walking around Llangynidr

The walks suggested are just a few of those possible in the region and are readily adapted to suit individual requirements.

Hill walking necessitates strong footwear plus warm and waterproof clothing. Upland weather conditions can change rapidly with sharp drops in temperature. A knowledge of map and compass is helpful on higher moorlands and essential in conditions of poor weather and visibility. At such times swallow holes and rough ground can be hazardous, when paths so clearly marked on OS maps become difficult to follow. However, with a few simple precautions, local hills provide some of the best walking in Wales.

Geology and Topography

Landscape reflects underlying rock strata. Llangynidr lies on Old Red Sandstone which creates a gentler topography with rich red soil. Above this rock lies Carboniferous Limestone, which forms the high southern ridges and scarps particularly visible near Llangattock. Honeycombed with cave-systems, this thick strata is capped by a thin layer of hard Millstone Grit which gives the high moorlands their thin soil and raw character. This became 'Farewell Rock' for colliers because all coal lay above it. Limestone and Grit formed the South Wales coal-basin which contained rich seams of coal, iron-stone and fireclay, making possible the eighteenth and nineteenth century iron and coal industries. The north-south tilt of these rocks forces damp south-west winds and clouds upwards, causing them to precipitate rainfall far heavier than that experienced at Llangynidr but a few miles north.

Walking hints

Footpaths are shown in red on the six maps of the village environs. The lanes normally have very little traffic so, by avoiding the B4560 and B4558, walking in the area can be very pleasant. Many field footpaths have stiles - not always easy for small children and dogs. Stone stiles are a feature of the area and are shown on the maps by an 'S'. Wheel-chair-users and pram-pushers will find most lanes easy, but the canal towpath can be rough except for a specially surfaced and graded stretch from Lower Lock towards Llanddetty. Open access to the towpath other than by stile can be gained at Lower Lock, Forge Road and Dyfnant. The riverside paths are rough and can be flooded when the river is high.

The reader will find it helpful to use National Park maps in conjunction with this book: all but the extreme west end of the Crawnon is covered by the 1:25000 Outdoor Leisure 13, Brecon Beacons Eastern Area map, south sheet. Outdoor Leisure 12, Brecon Beacons West and Central Areas map, completes the coverage.

Visitors, having read about the area in this book, will choose their own itineraries round the village, using the footpaths and lanes shown. However, we describe thirteen walks to upland sites which offer fine panoramic views and a wide variety of historic archaeological sites are pointed out. They are all covered by the maps in this book with the exception of Walks 4 and 13 but the hillwalker is strongly advised to carry the National Park map covering the intended route on all upland walks.

Walk 1: Blaen Crawnon   Map 4

The walk embraces part of the postman's round of the Dyffryn Crawnon and can include the Forest Nature Reserve at Blaen Crawnon.

From the Village Hall to upper village and Dyffryn Crawnon road to the furthest point at Cefn-crug, or, from upper village, the footpath from Chapel on Claisfer Lane over the fields to the open mountain, going south-west to meet the metalled road and the line of the Brinore Tramroad. Descend to Danydarren and the forest nature reserve if wished.

Return routes: Brinore to Pen Rhiw Calch, lane to Bryn Melyn and choice of footpaths to the valley, or the valley footpath from Danydarren via Glasgwm-isaf to Troed-y-rhiw, crossing the Crawnon by footbridge, then by lane past Wern back to the village. For a shorter walk (half day), the moderately graded footpath and lane from the upland path down to Neuadd provides a convenient link.

Walk 2: Llanddetty Church and Waun-ddu   Maps 1 and 4

After visiting Llandetty Church, this route involves a moderate climb and steep descent on paths across fields.

From Crawnon Wharf car park follow the towpath to the lane right to Llanddetty Church. After visiting the church retrace to the canal, cross and bear left on footpath going south-east, climbing steadily, passing above remains of Dan-y-graig and on to Penybailey. Follow road round to Maesybeddau, footpath skirts left below the farm buildings and steeply down the fields to the footbridge over the Crawnon. Join the road just west of Waun-ddu and continue for 500m to the footpath going north-east towards Pentwyn Farm. Just short of the farm a path descends sharp left to the head of the leat serving the canal and runs beside the leat to the wharf.

Walk 3: Blaen-y-cwm   Maps 4 and 5

This walk includes early house sites at Cwm Claisfer.

Figure 196: The ruins of Blaen-y-cwm, a sixteenth century farmhouse at the head of Cwm Claisfer.

From Beaufort Square, take the lane to Rhiwgarn and the footpath over fields, B4560 and fields to Glaisfer-isaf, across Claisfer Bridge and footpath up fields to Blaen-y-cwm and the old Filter House. Follow the rough path up the right bank of the Claisfer (Path 11 on map 4) for 500m to a footpath bearing north-east and then north above plantations to Pant-llwyd. Note the bee boles on the wall right of the entrance to the farm. Then by lane or choice of marked footpaths to the upper village.

Walk 4: Buckland Hill   National Park map, Leisure 13

This walk offers fine views of Llangynidr from the north. The return route passes close to standing stones.

From the village, walk to Usk Bridge and up the B4560 to the first cross-roads. Turn left to Cil-wych House, noting just as the lane enters woods below Cil-wych, the second world war pillbox on the left. The lane zigzags round to Cil-wych. The footpath leads west and north to the summit at a height of 316m. The view of Llangynidr and the valleys complements the fine view from Twyn Disgwylfa across the valley. The path continues across the hill and down a lane towards Bwlch. On the left, on the hillside which slopes down to the Farmer's Arms Inn, can be discerned the line of an old road which was one of the various ways to climb the steep north bank before the modern road cutting was made. Coming down onto the

A40, cross it and follow the pavement left to the foot of the cutting - it is possible to identify the old road where it leaves the present line of the road opposite. This was just one of two or more variations - by taking the footpath to the right, climbing steeply to an open common area, it is possible to make out at least two other tracks which preceded the present road. There is a choice of routes back to Llangynidr:

Coming out onto the A40, just past the New Inn going south is the old road, the line of which continues across the A40, 400m down, to Llygadwy. Parallel to this narrow overgrown hedged lane is another line of road with a standing stone (S3) half way down. The footpath continues down to the A40 and is one way back to Llangynidr by continuing on to Llwyfen.

Alternatively, just after starting down the old road, a path/lane bears left between a field and a house on the right. In the centre of the field is the Bwlch Stone. This lane is the top part of the Roman road which skirted the north side of the Ewyn valley. The lane crosses the A40 (the Roman road bears left (see Walk 13)), but follow the footpath due south-east across the fields to the A40, turn right to Llwyfen and left round the lane to Llwynyfedwen; the footpath crosses the fields to the B4560 near the Usk Bridge. Note on the left the magnificent Llwynyfedwen stone (S9).

Walk 5: Tor y Foel   Map 1

This walk involves a steep climb, over tracks which are rough in places, but offers superb views of the mountains.

From Crawnon Wharf car park take the field footpath to Penybeili. Continue due west up the ridge path, noting how deeply sunk this ancient track is. After 500m the original trackway bears left, contouring around towards Bwlch-y-waun, the middle section erased by ploughing and fenced off. Follow the footpath continuing west up the ridge (about 600m along, a footpath bears right to contour round the mountain to the cattle grid above Pantywenallt). A steepish climb up the ridge continues to the summit at 551m. There are magnificent views from here towards Plynlimon north-west, Radnor Forest north-east, Black Mountains east, into Gloucestershire and the Valleys, and west across to Pen y Fan. The summit has a small circular ditch - its age and significance are unknown.

Descend south-west to a small parking area, then east to Bwlch-y-waun and along the bridle way which joins the lane above Maesybeddau. Follow the lane back past Penybailey to the B4558 and the Wharf. An alternative is to take the footpath south-east from the parking area, which then bears east and south-east to Nant y Wenynen and the valley road.

At an early stage the walk follows the canal towpath. There are attractive glimpses of woodland scenery and fine views of the Black Mountains from the Hill Fort.

Figure 197: Lan Fawr Hill Fort, a hill fort of uncertain age, above Pant-mawr on the northern slope of Llangynidr Mountain. There are traces of an older field system nearby.

Follow Cyffredin Lane from the Village Hall to the canal towpath, to Aberhoywe Bridge, over the B4558 to Dan-y-wern, a footpath south and east through woods and fields to Pant-mawr. 250m beyond Pant-mawr a footpath climbs south-east to a stile in the field fence. The Lan Fawr site lies west of the stile. Return the same way to the Pant-mawr footpath but turn left to the lane from Llwyncelyn. Continue down the lane and across the field paths to Ffrwd and Upper Village or go due north from the top of Llwyncelyn lane down the fields to Upper Barn and the canal towpath some 300m west of Aberhoywe Bridge.

Walk 7: Pant-mawr and Twyn Disgwylfa   Maps 3 and 4

A circular hill-walk climbing to and descending from Twyn Disgwylfa (SO 166182) which affords wide-reaching views over Usk Valley and Black Mountains (see the Prologue).

Village Hall to Ty Zillah

From the Village Hall walk north along Cyffredin Lane to join the canal towpath south towards bridge 125. Notice the widening of the canal in the vicinity of the wharf above Aberhoywe. Cross bridge 125 and the B4558. 50m east along the road is a stile on a steep bank on the right. Follow the footpath leading upwards to Pen-y-bryn, Neuadd-fawr and Llwyn-onn Farm (SO 180189). From here the path climbs south-west through attractive woodland to Pant-mawr then west and south-west to the site of Ty Zillah (*Zillah's House*) at SO 165183.

Canal Wharf: Any widening of canal banks usually indicates an unloading/loading point, in this case for local village purposes.

Pen-y-bryn: A seventeenth century house with many interesting features and whose hall retains an original high seat built into its panelling.

Ty Zillah: This ruined cottage and enclosure was occupied in the early nineteenth century by one Zillah, a lady who dispensed home-brewed ale to thirsty travellers making to or from the moorland and coalfield above.

Ty Zillah to Disgwylfa

From Ty Zillah a track turns sharply east and then south to join the road from Ffawyddog to Blaen Onneu, from where there is an easy ascent onto the summit of Twyn Disgwylfa (SO 166182)

Twyn Disgwylfa and area: A ditch of uncertain purpose and age is cut along the northern edge of this scarp. Immediately south are several prehistoric stone cairns and the Carreg Waun Llech Standing Stone (see Figure 11). South and east of the Cwalca limestone outcrop are possibly-contemporary stone embankments and hut-sites plus 40 stone cairns/heaps in close proximity. These are suggested as field clearance and/or burial sites. All the evidence points to this having been an important Bronze Age settlement area.

Return Routes from Twyn Disgwylfa

Two routes are possible:

From the B4560 Beaufort-Llangynidr road bend south-west of Disgwylfa, north to Ty Sheriff and Ffrwd, or

By retracing the outward route north-east and then due west down the lane past Penylan-fawr and the marked footpath past Beiliau and Ffrwd to the village, or past Llwyncelyn to the main road.

From Llangynidr to the ridge between the Crawnon and Claisfer valleys, returning either via the B4560 road or Ty Sheriff footpath. Largely moorland country above 350m altitude where paths are not always distinct. Strong footwear, OS Map and compass are necessary. The walk takes in several interesting prehistoric and later features and provides excellent views.

From Llangynidr to the southern Claisfer ridge

From the Village Hall car park either follow Cyffredin Lane to the canal or walk to the Coach and Horses Inn and join the towpath towards Brecon. At the first lock cross the canal, follow the feeder-leat to the weir and ascend a lane approaching it steeply from the left. At the head of the bank turn right and follow footpath south-west to metalled road at SO 142192. Turn left for 150m before turning right at Llwynderi farm. Pass through farm up to Tyle-bach and onto the hill keeping the field-wall line on your left. Where the wall ends continue on this same bearing south-west towards outcrops at SO 133173, passing the Stone Row and cairns.

Stone Row: A north-east to south-west row of seven stones, the largest fallen, align on a small stone some 40m north-east.

Cairns: OS-marked as 'cairns', the two structures may be ring-cairns containing burials, or perhaps small enclosures of unknown purpose. The three prehistoric monuments appear to form an equilateral triangle. Other structures of indeterminate age are sited in rock outcrop and scree 0.4km south-west. This ridge between Claisfer and Crawnon is rich in features of possible prehistoric date.

From Stone Row to Carn Caws

From the Stone Row continue almost due south to Carn Caws and associated cairn .

Carn Caws (*Cheese Cairn*): probably takes its name from the Welsh use of 'caws', (*cheese*) for limestone (which can resemble dried-up cheese). This large upland cairn may have been partially constructed with this stone - removed by later lime-burners. Notice adjacent walls and enclosures on east and west flanks. Another large cairn lies 0.2km north. For fuller information see the section on the Bronze Age, page 4.

From Carn Caws to Blaen Cwmclaisfer

A gradual descent due south leads towards Blaen Cwmclaisfer (SO 130160), passing limestone outcrops, small quarries and various stone-banked enclosures of uncertain date. For more information on this interesting area see page 3 onwards. The Claisfer spring rises at SO 129160 near a thorn tree.

From Blaen Cwmclaisfer to 'Filter House'

A rough path follows the northern stream bank to a pumping station (marked 'Filter House' on OS map) at SO 138164. Alternatively, it is possible to contour on an upper track to above the pump house and then descend steeply.

'Filter House' to Llangynidr

Follow the path north of the stream ignoring the footbridge across the pump house dam (the track on the opposite bank is not a public right-of-way) to the hairpin bend on the B4560, from which either of two routes to Llangynidr may be followed, either down the road to the village or via the hill and Ty Sheriff.

The upland sections of this walk may be attempted in a reverse direction from the hairpin bend, where cars can be left. However, heading south-west the path veers south at a gate, climbing upwards to follow the forestry edge before roughly contouring the hill towards Blaen Cwmclaisfer.

Walk 9: Pen Rhiw Calch and southern   Maps 4 and 8
Crawnon Scarp (and the Chartist Cave)

A walk providing superb views and much interest, entailing a steady climb onto the ridge between Collwn and Crawnon Valleys. From here there is an ancient (Roman?) road to Pen Rhiw Calch (Head of limestone track) after which the Brinore Tramroad (AD 1815) is followed around the head of the Crawnon to a metalled road. Return may be either via moorland and the southern Crawnon scarp, (possible visit to the Chartist Cave) or along the Crawnon Valley directly to the village.

Llangynidr to Penybailey

From the Village Hall car park, either follow the towpath towards Brecon (west) and cross the second lock to the footpath climbing across fields to Llwynyreos and Penybailey, or take the road joining the B4558 beyond Crawnon bridge.

Penybailey to Bwlch-y-waun

Take the road to Maesybeddau and bear right along the bridleway to Bwlch-y-waun. Continue past Bwlch-y-waun to the ridge with fine view over Glyn Collwn and Talybont Reservoir into the Beacons. Turn south along the road (believed Roman in origin) to Pen Rhiw Calch (stone seat and ruined building).

Glyn Collwn: The valley was flooded in 1927 to provide water for Newport. From Torpantau at its head (the highest UK railway tunnel) runs the rail-bed of the 1863 'Brecknock & Merthyr' line, known colloquially as 'Breakneck & Murder' because of runaway coal-trains. This is now a footpath and cycle-route.

Roman Road: The Penydarren (Merthyr Tydfil) - Dolygaer - Talybont - Y Gaer (Brecon) road is believed to be represented by the green lane which runs north of Cwm Callan from Dolygaer to Pen Rhiw Calch, after which point it becomes a metalled road to Talybont-on-Usk. However, the route descending east from the ridge via Bwlch-y-waun and contouring round Tor y Foel could have provided a more direct route to Pen-y-gaer fort (near Bwlch) and Gobannium (Abergavenny). Both may be Roman, at least in usage.

Pen Rhiw Calch: (*Head of limestone track*). The Brinore Tramroad from Trefil to Talybont crosses the ridge at this point. Horse-drawn trams had wheels immobilised in iron shoes and skidded down the steep descent, often causing the L-shaped track-plates to break. Three inns, one the celebrated 'Rock', are recorded here serving both ancient ridge (Roman?) road and tramroad. The Brinore Tramroad may be followed almost for its entirety from Trefil to Talybont-on-Usk canal wharf. 'Brinore' is the correct name, not 'Bryn Oer' (*Cold Hill*), from which it mutated.

Pen Rhiw Calch to Ystrad Quarries and road

From Pen Rhiw Calch follow the Brinore Tramroad south (now covered by forestry road for about 500m). This is pleasant and easy but can be wet in places.

Brinore Tramroad: Constructed in 1815 by Dixon and Overton for Ben Hall (father of 'Big Ben' Hall, after whom the bell was named). The 1793 Canal Act's 'Eight Mile Clause' permitted iron and coal owners to build tramroads up to this length. Hall's tramroad from Trefil quarries to Talybont was eight miles long but, linked with that from Trefil to Rhymney Works, became both longer and illegal. Hall was obliged to hand over the eight miles to Dixon and Overton. Industrial traffic ceased in 1864 but until the early twentieth century Trefil coffins and mourners were carried along it to Talybont Chapel graveyard.

At SO 003162 tramroad-doubling and ruins mark the site of Glasgwm-uchaf (also known as Maesybeddau) farm and beer house. The tramroad continues around Dyffryn Crawnon head, where there is an unusual outcrop of tufa, a degraded limestone, at SO 091155, near a stream draining from Gwaun Nant Ddu bog. It then crosses the Crawnon river via a wooden footbridge and eventually joins the Ystrad and Hendre Quarry road at SO 108153.

Lake-Site and associated prehistoric discoveries: Extensive peat-sampling has proved a post-glacial lake existed at Gwaun Nant Ddu (around SO 087153). Pollen and other analysis provided extensive evidence of plant life and human settlement around it. Clearly indicated were the effects of the Hekla 3 (Iceland) volcanic eruption of 1120 BC, which through climate change and soil erosion virtually ended prehistoric upland settlement. Flint tools have been found nearby.

Maesybeddau (*Field of graves*): Before afforestation 14 long mounds were visible in the field above Glasgwm-uchaf. Being just below a Roman road, these were claimed as Welsh or Roman burials. However, they were probably nineteenth century rabbit-farming warrens providing skins for the hat-trade.

Dyffryn Crawnon: This is a fine example of a U-shaped glaciated valley with the Forest Nature Reserve at its head. Evidence that 'Crawnon' is a corruption of 'Garw Nant' arises from early nineteenth century Henry Thomas Payne's use of 'Blaen Cwm Garw Nant' when describing its upper reaches, while a few years later his friend, Theophilus Jones, was calling the same location 'Blaenau Crawnon'.

Ystrad and Hendre Quarries: These quarries formerly supplied Ebbw Vale Steelworks. South-west of the quarry, on an ancient green (Roman?) road, is the Ystrad Ogham Stone (seventh century inscribed burial) and Buarth-y-caerau (*Castle fields*), an extensive area of hut-sites/enclosures of uncertain date.

An optional return-route leads down into Cwm Pyrgad, Dyffryn Crawnon and Llangynidr (**9A**).

Cwm Pyrgad: Literally *'Valley of the Pure-to-Arms'*, suggested as commemorating some tribal gathering. However, such names may be mutations of others meaning something quite different.

Optional visit to Chartist Cave   **9B**
On good days this is a pleasant upland walk but **should not** be attempted in poor weather.

Head east from the quarry road to Garn Fawr, a massive Bronze Age burial cairn at SO 123152. The Chartist Cave, well concealed, lies in limestone outcrops 250m east-north-east of the cairn.

Chartist Cave: Formerly 'Big Stable' because "hill animals sheltered here", it now has a legendary connection with the Chartist Uprising (more correctly an abortive British Revolution), of 1839. A plaque, ignoring contemporary evidence, perpetuates the myth that it provided a meeting-place and weapon storage. A grimmer reason for its name arises from the discovery of Chartist-period axe-severed human bones, possibly the remains of murdered informers.

Garn Fawr: A massive Bronze Age cairn with a hollowed-out centre. Most upland cairns were robbed by eighteenth and nineteenth century antiquarians, their hollow centres were formed when stone was thrown outwards during 'excavation'.

The higher, moorland, route continues from Cwm Pyrgad's head, initially following a clear trackway (passing enclosures marked 'settlements' on the OS map at SO 112156), heading generally north towards Garn Fach and Clo Cadno. Both are prehistoric Bronze Age sites, the latter providing an outstanding viewpoint. (There are also other tracks leading more directly to the latter.) Passing Clo Cadno the route crosses a pleasant shelf of land beneath limestone escarpments. A large bog, clearly visible south-west of Clo Cadno, should be avoided - the only dangerously soft ground in this area.

Enclosures (SO 112156): Stone-banked enclosures and hut-sites of possible prehistoric date. The siting, near a stream-ford and trackway, may be significant.

Clo Cadno: (*Foxes Lock*): - an enigmatic title. There is a fine limestone pavement plus, at the highest point, a denuded Bronze Age burial cairn of which only the kerb remains. (See Prehistory, page 1).

Garn Fach (*Little Cairn*): a Bronze Age burial site, lies south-west of Clo Cadno.

Enclosures: The area adjacent to Clo Cadno has proved rich in settlement sites, the several hut-sites, enclosures, and other features indicating intensive human activity. Field-system banks have also been noted between Darren Ddu and the quarry road.

From Clo Cadno to Y Neuadd track

Several interesting features of indeterminate date may be seen. At SO 118169 is a stone row while at SO 122169 is a small, upright and shaped stone. (A notch cut through the Bryn Melyn ridge at SO 106182, on which the stone might align, is visible from here). Hut circles have also been noted near Pant Serthfa. From Pant Serthfa a lower track leads down to Y Neuadd and Crawnon via a series of zigzags before joining the road to Llangynidr. An alternative route follows the higher track, which descends to Tyle-bach and Llwynderi to join the Crawnon road.

Walk 10: The Long Wall And Upper Claisfer   Map 4

An upland walk along the ridge dividing the Crawnon and Claisfer valleys, to Clo Cadno (around SO 116164), returning via Blaenclaisfer and southern Claisfer scarp to the B4560 hairpin bend. Fine views and many prehistoric and other objects of interest.

From Llangynidr to ridge:

Take the road past the Red Lion Public House and the church, then from Beaufort Square follow Claisfer Lane. After about 1km turn right at junction (SO 147185) to Pant-llwyd farm and open moorland, a steady climb. Head south-west to Pant Llwyd (passing the Stone Row and cairns - Walk 8), continuing south-west over higher ground to near a large Bronze Age burial cairn at SO 129170. From this point a long stone-banked wall may be seen running south-west in the direction of Clo Cadno (see Figure 2).

> **Long Wall:** A low stone bank approximately 2.5km long. At SO 128170, near a Bronze Age cairn, it appears to arise out of peat-cover. At its south-west end, (where there are other embankments), it swings sharply north before again disappearing beneath the ground. Of probable prehistoric date, it may have been a tribal or territorial boundary.

From end-of-wall to Clo Cadno

Follow the wall for 2.5km, noting large number of swallow holes traversed.

> **Swallow Holes:** reveal where underlying strata have collapsed, in this case a probable result of acid rain-water beating against the stone bank, which then percolated downwards along its length to dissolve underlying limestone.

Clo Cadno to Blaen Cwmclaisfer and the B4560 hairpin bend

The route turns due east for 1km to Blaen Cwmclaisfer. There are several enclosures and hut-sites of uncertain date, some of which may be associated with post-medieval lime-working. The path then follows the infant stream east-north-east to the junction of footpaths at SO 134162. From here contour around the stream's south bank to the foot of a bank and ditch running due south up the slope. An enclosure of some 50m square lies 300m east-north-east on the east bank of the stream emanating from the spring. A few yards east of the spring a 600m long curved wall runs east then east-north-east to within 150m of the corner of the forestry plantation at SO 143163. The wall crosses the line of the modern buried pipeline roughly half way along and it fades out in the vicinity of the escarpment where one of the tracks shown on the 1832 OS map climbs the slope towards Tredegar (Map 8). 40m further on is a 2m square traveller's shelter or shepherd's bothy, with hearth still intact, snuggled into the rocky slope. The age of all these features above Cwm Claisfer is unknown. The appearance of the wall, which is shown as a dashed line on the 1832 OS map, suggests that it is likely to be much more than 200 years old.

The footpath skirts the south-east edge of the forestry plantation and then descends north-north-east to the B4560 hairpin bend. Note the remains of a lime kiln half way along. Towards the end of the plantation edge the ground is covered with ashes left from lime-burning activities in the nineteenth century. Half way down the slope, on a platform on the hillside, are the remains of two early buildings, one about 2m square, again with hearth and doorway, the other some 5m square.

Walk 11: Cwm Claisfer & Carn Caws   Map 4

An upland, circular walk which crosses the Claisfer Valley west of Llangynidr and ascends its northern ridge. Rolling moorland country, rich in prehistoric and other interests. Fine viewpoints into the Beacons and Black Mountains.

From Village to Claisfer Pumping Station

From Village Hall to Upper Village, passing Red Lion Inn. Take Heol Rhiwgarn from Beaufort Square to the B4560 Beaufort-Llangynidr road, as in Walk 3. Either turn right, ascending 1.5km to the first turning right (SO 153175), or avoid some road-walking by crossing the stile and joining the footpath at SO 151183. Both routes lead to the valley bottom beyond Glaisfer-isaf farm, where, immediately after crossing the stream, is a path to Blaen-y-cwm and 'Filter House' - in fact a pumping station.

Filter House to Carn Caws

From the 'Filter House' it is possible to climb the steep hillside south-west or, alternatively, continue along the stream for about 0.5km to ascend less steeply. The route - no path - climbs gradually towards Carn Caws (SO 128168), passing limestone outcrops with evidence of quarrying and lime-burning, and a small Bronze Age burial cairn at SO 132168. Another large cairn lies 0.6km west near which, at SO 127170, is the eastern end of a probably prehistoric stone-bank/wall (the 'Long Wall'), which crosses an area marked with swallow-holes (see Walk 10).

Carn Caws is a Bronze Age burial site in association with enclosures of unknown significance (see Walk 8 and Prehistory chapter).

Lime burning: Many limestone outcrops were worked in pre- and post-industrial periods to provide lime, used both to sweeten soil and lime-wash buildings. Kilns were fired with coal carried by horse or mule from the coalfield, some 4-5km south. The resulting caustic 'quick lime' was 'slaked' by rainfall. Greener and sweeter grass near kilns attracts sheep which manure and improve it.

Swallow Holes: Circular funnel-shaped depressions of various sizes which mark where underlying limestone strata has collapsed. Originally believed of antiquity, it is now realised these represent a continuing process. It is possible that some may mark where a surface cairn (Bronze Age burial?), or other heavy structure, trapped and concentrated rainwater, which then dissolved the limestone beneath. The stones at the bottom of several may be the remains of such monuments.

Optional continuation to 'Chartist Cave' (11A)

From Carn Caws it is possible to continue 1.75km south-south-west to the 'Chartist Cave' at SO 127153 - see Walk 9 for details. This is a good moorland walk crossing the upper Claisfer Valley and its spring, passing several hut-sites and enclosures of indeterminate date.

Claisfer Valley and springs: In the early twentieth century a 3-mile long tunnel, beautifully engineered and constructed, was cut from Beaufort, north of Ebbw Vale, directly towards the Claisfer spring with the intention of providing water for Ebbw Vale works and town. For some unknown reason (bad ground?), it was abandoned just short of its destination. This (locked) tunnel is still in excellent condition and, by virtue of its cutting through underground systems, is used by cavers exploring the extensive cave-systems lying beneath this area.

From Carn Caws to Pant-llwyd and Llangynidr

North-east of Carn Caws the walk, on indistinct paths, crosses a limestone outcrop before descending to Pant-llwyd. From here a direct return is down the track to Claisfer Lane. Alternatively there is a descending footpath through Glaisfer-uchaf and High Meadow to Claisfer Lane.

Walk 12: Talybont and 'Tump Fort' via the canal and a section of the Brinore Tramroad

Map - Outdoor Leisure 13

A circular walk, steep in places, encompassing interesting sections of the canal and its Brinore Tramroad link, plus a prehistoric fort and Roman road.

To Lock Flight

From the Village Hall car park walk to the Coach and Horses Inn near the canal lock. Join the canal towpath north past Crawnon Leat, lock flight and aqueduct towards Llanddetty and Talybont-on-Usk.

Crawnon Leat: A major water source entered the canal via a leat from the Crawnon river just below the lock flights. A short path alongside leads up to the river.

Canal & locks: The Brecon - Newport Canal, engineered by Thomas Dadford Junior, was navigable to this point by 1798 and to Brecon two years later. So well was its route surveyed that this was the first series of locks in the 14 mile stretch from Pontymoile near Pontypool. Designed to transport iron, coal and lime from the coalfield, it was not linked with the sea until 1812. All transportation developments were to maximise horse-power. One animal could carry 3 cwt on its back, pull half a ton or more in a cart, pull two tons or more on a tramroad or twenty tons in a canal barge. Early steam locomotives were regarded as replacement iron horses.

Lock Flight: Locks caused delays and high-water usage. Thus canals were widened for several boats to wait. 'Holding ponds' were provided to minimise water use, and public houses tended to be near, e.g. the Coach and Horses and The Boatman's Arms (now a private house).

Aqueduct: The canal is carried on a short aqueduct across the Crawnon river.

To Llanddetty and Talybont

From the lock-flight the towpath passes several canal bridges, Llanddetty Church and Hall and Brinore Wharf on its way to Talybont.

Llanddetty Hall: A fine seventeenth century house once owned by Colonel Jenkin Jones and in the early nineteenth century variously by Dixon and Overton, engineers and operators of the Brinore Tramroad.

Llanddetty Church: A hall-type church containing a ninth century pillar stone bearing the inscription "Guadan the Priest made this cross for his friends Ninid and Gurhi". The priest's door (south) has a bullet hole, seemingly caused by Colonel Jenkin Jones. A staunch puritan, he had supported King Charles' execution, as well as keeping sheep in the church. Learning of the restoration he fled, firing his pistol at the church as he went. Last century a pistol bullet was found embedded in the chancel wall opposite the priest's door. See Henderson, J, *History of Llanddetty Church*.

Brinore Wharf: A short distance south of Talybont the Brinore Tramroad ended at limekilns and wharf. Limestone from Trefil and coal from Rhymney were burned here, the resulting quick lime slaked with canal water. By using his own tramroad and only a short canal length (for which he had to pay tolls) Ironmaster Benjamin Hall hoped to lower costs and thus gain most of the Breconshire and Radnorshire's coal and lime trade.

From Talybont to Tump Fort.

Near the White Hart public house, cross the canal and follow the footpath, climbing south-west along the Brinore Tramroad. The route follows the forestry edge for approximately 1.25km to SO 108217, where a track ascends steeply left (east) though forestry onto open hillside 0.5km north of Tump. It then heads south to Upper Wenallt, passing below 'Tump Fort' and 'Settlement'.

Tump Fort: (on private land). A small twin-banked (Iron Age?) fort, its weaker south side provided with a third bank and ditch, lies at SO 112214. Although damaged by forestry the defences of stone and earth are still in good condition. Other banks of uncertain purpose lie 200m south-east.

Settlement: (on private land). A small enclosure, much damaged by modern farming, is possibly contemporary with Tump Fort. Without proper excavation such sites cannot be accurately dated and both these could be earlier than the Iron Age date usually ascribed.

From Upper Wenallt to Canal and Llangynidr

Join the metalled Roman Road (?) south to Pantywenallt, continuing to the cattle grid at SO 114205. A path now descends east to cross the hillside above Llanddetty Hall (good views) to the canal. Alternatively a path ascends from the north-east corner of the forestry to Penybailey (SO 134194) from where there is a choice of return routes.

Walk 13: The Roman Road   Map - Outdoor Leisure 13

A circular walk starting from and ending at Tretower Castle and Court. This follows the Roman Road though Pen-y-gaer Roman fort to Bwlch, returning via lanes and footpaths to Maesllechau and Felindre.

Roman road: Although its actual line is uncertain, the position of Tretower Castle and the three Gaer farms suggest it passed close by, approximating to the present footpath and lane. Early castles were usually within bowshot of an existing road; Tretower being sited where two roads now meet suggests that both existed previously. However, the Pen-y-gaer - Tretower Roman route might be indicated by the existing Cwmdu -Tretower road, thus avoiding flood-prone ground.

Tretower to Upper Gaer

From Tretower Court follow the lane left (west) past the Castle to a field gate, continuing across the field and the river to a further right-hand gate. The path runs to Lower Gaer, Middle Gaer and Upper Gaer Farms. Two Roman centurial stones, believed from Pen-y-gaer fort, are incorporated into village houses.

Tretower Castle: The first castle was built circa AD 1090 by Roger Picard, one of Bernard de Neufmarche's followers, at the possible junction of two ancient (Roman?) routes. Existing outer keep walls are mid twelfth century, partially demolished to provide protection while a thirteenth century round tower was built within. Unusually, these were retained after completion. The earlier structure has the finest Norman kitchen in Wales.

Tretower Court: Originally a fourteenth century manor house built when the castle was abandoned, which was progressively added-to thereafter. Tretower castle and court reveal clearly how medieval domestic architecture, and the search for comfort, evolved. Strong, rather than 'fortified', its existing apparently-defensive features are largely decorative. There are fine timber roof-trusses, wind-braces and interior panelling. Legend has local bowmen being mustered for French wars, particularly Agincourt, in its courtyard. Henry Vaughan, the seventeenth century poet ('The Silurist') buried at Llansantffraed, spent part of his childhood here.

Lower Gaer Farm: Now much altered, this was the eighteenth century home of a farmer who introduced the Agrarian Revolution to this area by growing turnips for winter stock-feed. Previously all other than breeding stock were killed at Michaelmas. Some lane surfacing and culverts may date from this prosperous period.

Middle Gaer Farm: The original farmhouse is now a barn alongside the road. A finely-built early fifteenth century building, until recently it possessed painted wall decorations, now largely destroyed. The original window ironwork was made on a charcoal forge, therefore high carbon and very rust-resistant.

Upper Gaer Farm: Of the same period as Middle Gaer, but details are hidden under cement plaster. A projecting upper fireplace may be seen. In the north wall is a small carved figure of uncertain date, seemingly incorporated when the house was built. This may have had some connection with nearby Pen-y-gaer Roman fort.

Middle Gaer to Bwlch

Turn right (north) at Upper Gaer farm to Maesllechau, passing though Pen-y-gaer Roman Fort (lane approximates to its N-S Via Decumana). At the junction turn left (west) and follow the lane. After 0.5km take the right fork along the lane to Ty-mawr Farm. Climb the gradual ascent towards Bwlch, turning right immediately before A40 road to cross a field and children's playground into a small estate.

Pen-y-gaer fort: (SO 168219) A small fort controlling the Roman Road. Mostly ploughed-out by eighteenth century turnip farming but its rectangular enclosure remains visible, a transverse lane approximating to its N-S road. The lane running east to Felindre has been suggested as Roman in origin and may be the original route to Tretower.

Bwlch: (*Notch*) Prehistoric, Roman and later routes passed this way. In a field south of the settlement is a postulated standing stone. Llygadwy at the A40 & B4560 junction has the remains of a finely-built fifteenth century house, similar to the Gaer farms. An ancient track and vertical (prehistoric?) stone are nearby. The upper lane leading east from the settlement towards Felindre provides superb views. At Tremynfa (SO 160224) car-parking enables fine walks towards Mynydd Llangorse, an area with wide-reaching views and rich in prehistoric remains.

Bwlch to Tre-graig and Maesllechau

Follow the lane climbing right (east) from the estate to Tre-graig. Turn right (east) opposite a house and descend a marked footpath to Maesllechau. An alternative footpath leads directly on (north-east) from Tre Graig, crossing fields to Felindre junction (SO 176232).

Maesllechau: It has been suggested that the lower area, immediately above Pen-y-gaer fort, was the site of a Roman bathhouse. Interestingly, a stone-lined underground water conduit discovered at Tre-graig appeared to run in this direction.

Maesllechau to Lower Mill and Tretower

From the junction near Lower Mill (SO 175228) an unsurfaced lane leads right (south) to rejoin your outward route 0.25km east of Lower Gaer Farm. In a field immediately east of the junction a raised area has been suggested as a Roman 'agger', i.e. road platform.

Lower Mill and Felindre: Felindre (*Mill House*) takes its name from a mill once existing there, its leat and mill pond remaining visible. The lane east of the modern road, which runs north towards Castell Dinas, may approximate to a Roman or earlier route. Coed y Gaer fort, of Bronze/Iron Age, is at SO 176240.

List of subscribers

Michael Scott Archer
Phyllis Scott Archer
John Badgett
Colin Baker
Graham, Moyra and Elaine Ball
Hywel Ball
Mr and Mrs V G Bartlett
James Bowen
Dr and Mrs Bowman
Steve and Sue Candy
M T Cashell
Charles and Joan Clarke
Igor and Tricia Cusack
Margaret Davies,
Rob, Jean, Greg and Holly Dunning
Mrs S P Evans
David Filsell,
Mr and Mrs C French
John Games
Sarah Gammage
John and Elizabeth Gibbs
Dr and Mrs Gowler
Ian Harmond
R and M Hockey
Colin and Nora Jenkins
Ann and Den Jessopp
Adele Jones
Peter Jones

Crickhowell Local History Society
Gliffaes Hotel
Llangynidr WEA
Powell Design
Stephan's Cellar
The Cheese Press

Mrs C J King
Ian and June Lawson
Lynda Lloyd
Janet Lourens
Harry Porter
Jon Porter
Mike and Chris Porter
Robin Porter
Rory Porter
Thomas Porter
Tim Porter
Miss G L Powell
Mrs C M Rhydderch-Preece
M Rhydderch-Roberts
Ron and Rita Roberts
RR Saundby
Antonia Spowers
David Taylor
Mark and Diane Thomas
Nancy, Jeff and Margaret Thomas
Philip Wake
Heather Waring
Anthony Watkins
Michael Watkins
Lorraine Wibberley
Mike and Apphia Willett
Pat and Brendan Williams

Index

—C—

Llwyncelyn, 67, 74, 95, 141, 158, 187, 252, 256, 265
Llwynderi, 67, 253, 267, 271
Llwyn-onn Farm, 266
Llwynyfedwen, 100
Llwynyfedwen stone, 264
Llwynyreos, 68, 120, 257, 268
Llwyn-yr-ynn, 44, 120, 251
Llygadwy, 32, 264, 278
Llyn Cwm Llwch, 5
Llyn Fawr Hoard, 6
Llyn y Fan Fach, 5
Llywelyn ab Iorwerth, 40
Llywelyn ap Gruffudd, 40
Llywelyn, Zelophead, 102
Lock Cottage, 101, 228
London, 91, 152, 220
London and North Western Railway Company, 88
Long Wall, 29, **272**, 273
Longtown, 255
Lord Berkeley, 44
Lord of the Manor, 35
Lower Gaer Farm, 26, 276, **277**, 278
Lower Llangynidr, 169
Lower Lock Cottage, 229
Lower Mill, 278
Lower Pencommin, 89
Lower Village, 221
Lower Wenallt, 258
Lower Wern Cottage, 255
Lucas, Rev William, 167
Lucy, William, 153

—M—

Machine House, 102, 103
Maddock, Thomas David, 55
Madocks, Thomas, 77
Maesderwen, 12
Maesderwen House, 26
Maesllechau, 276, 277, 278
Maesmawr Farm, 259
Maesybeddau, 256, 257, 264, 269, 270
Maggs, Mr and Mrs, 253
Magistrates, 145, 146, 147, 190, 214
Maidment, Mr, 228
Mail Coach, 220
Manchester wagon, 93
Manorial Court, 188
Marcher Lordships, 145
Marches, 40
Mardy, 220
Mardy Cottages, 222

Mardy Lane, 70, 79, 136, 141, 147, 158, 209, 222, 225
Marquis of Worcester, 60, 154
Mason's Arms, 136, 149, 192, 225
Masons, 101, 142, 163, 220, 221, 226
Mechanics Arms, 140
Melin yr Arlwydd, 132
Memorial College, Brecon, 160
Meredeth
    Meredeth ap, 57
    Nest verch John, 56
    Watkin (1527), 66
Meredith
    Alec, 222
    Dan, 222
    David, 52
    Thomas (1672), 188
    Walter, 59
Meredith ap Higgin, 59
Merthyr Tydfil, 76, 91, 139, 162, 260, 269
Merthyr Uprising, 149
Mesolithic, 2, **3**, 8, 24, 29
Middle Bronze Age, 253
Middle Gaer Farm, 25, 276, **277**
Miles, Walter, 140
Milford Haven, 91
Milgatw, 139
Mill Cottages, 224
Mill House, 130
Mill Pitch, 224
Miller, Lewis, 57
Millers, 69, 101, 127, 131, 132, 135, 228
Millichap, Mr, Farmer, 250
Mills, **129–35**
    Buckland, 130, 134
    Clog-fawr, 132
    Corn, 129
    Cwmcrawnon, 134
    Cyffredin, 45, 100, 132
    Felin-genol, 60, 133
    Fulling, 129
    Llangynidr, 89, 131, 224
    Suit of Mill, 55, 129, 133
Milnes & Company, 91
Miners, 99, 100, 101, 139, 253, 254
Moderator Boat Co, 87
Moderator Wharf, 87
Mole-catcher, 101
Monmouth, 76, 112
Monmouthshire, 76, 81, 87, 112
Monmouthshire Canal, 81, 82
Monmouthshire Railway and Canal Company, 88
Morgan
    Ann and Gwenllian, 101

—T—